Deepening Trauma Practice

Deepening Trauma Practice

A Gestalt approach to ecology and ethics

Miriam Taylor

Mc
Graw
Hill

Open University Press

Open University Press
McGraw Hill
8th Floor, 338 Euston Road
London
England
NW1 3BH

email: enquiries@openup.co.uk
world wide web: www.openup.co.uk

First edition published 2021

A catalogue record of this book is available from the British Library

ISBN-13: 9780335249770
ISBN-10: 0335249779
eISBN: 9780335249787

Library of Congress Cataloging-in-Publication Data
CIP data applied for

Typeset by Transforma Pvt. Ltd., Chennai, India

Praise Page

Miriam Taylor offers us a multi-lensed study of trauma and trauma practice. We are invited to consider relationship, ecology, ethics, compassion and care, intersectionality, somatic experience and neuroscience. This builds to a thought-provoking and scholarly study illustrated with stories, real-life examples and invitations to practices. This is a book of many parts which builds to a whole and comprehensive understanding of trauma practice.

Kim S Golding, CBE, Clinical Psychologist and Author, UK

This book is a very welcome and valuable addition to the plethora of books about trauma. Taylor emphases the huge importance of a contextual, ecological and ethical perspective in understanding the significance of traumatic events. Particular emphasis is placed on the relational aspect of working with trauma: how the therapist is "with" the client and how the client learns to "live with" the trauma. Taylor draws on her own experience and case studies to illustrate how to work with the complex tension of staying with the experience whilst simultaneously creating conditions for change.

Dr Di Hodgson, Director of Gestalt Psychotherapy at the Metanoia institute, UK and trainer, supervisor and psychotherapist, UK

Miriam Taylor, eminent Gestalt therapy trainer and widely-known leader in the humanistic psychotherapies, has written a courageous book for courageous therapists. She brings us right into the complex lifeworlds of our traumatized neighbours, and teaches us to inhabit our personal trauma so that we can accompany the Other. This book will become a treasured companion in the search for a radically ethical practice.

Dr Donna Orange, Simon Silverman Phenomenology Center, Duquesne University, USA

With a critical eye for specific techniques to treat trauma, in this book Miriam Taylor takes a non-pathologizing approach to the subject, considering trauma as an innate attempt at survival, an existential issue and a chance to deeply meet between human beings.

The result is a clinical model that gets to the heart of the therapist and puts them on the right track to treat their patients' trauma with depth and effectiveness. Trauma, a problem that in a post-pandemic world affects everyone, patients and therapists alike, becomes an opportunity to become better human beings, more able to connect with each other.

Margherita Spagnuolo Lobb, Psy.D., Istituto di Gestalt HCC, Italy

To my sister Jane, who first taught me to be interested in people

Contents

Acknowledgements   *xii*

Prologue   *xiv*

1   INTRODUCTION   1

    Uh-huh moments   1
    Towards an ecological turn in trauma   3
    Some definitions   6
    Thinking about neuroscience   7
    An inner chorus   10
    Chaos, confusion, and contradiction   11
    A field guide to the book   14

PART 1   SITUATING TRAUMA   **19**

Trickster story: Black and white thinking   19

2   THE CONTEXT OF TRAUMA   21

    The importance of context   21
    The SOS model: An ecological template   22
    The subsoil of trauma: Situational structures   26
    Dale   30
    Discussion   31
    The bedrock of trauma: Situational processes   33
    The role of denial   38
    Miriam Part 1: Roots   39
    Therapeutic reflections   40

3   SOMETHING IN THE AIR   42

    Systemic trauma   42
    Trauma-organized systems   43
    Duncan   45
    Discussion   47
    Luisa   48
    Discussion   50
    Hugh   52
    Discussion   53
    Alesha   54
    Discussion   56
    Concluding reflections   57

4	DO NO HARM	59
	Stella Part 1	59
	Discussion: The lived and the unlived body	60
	Stella Part 2	61
	Discussion: Framing suffering	62
	Stella Part 3	63
	Discussion: Labels and formulation	64
	Stella Part 4	67
	Discussion: Pills and other interventions	68
	Gender, power, and psychiatry	69
	Talking therapies in context	71

PART 2 THE SPACE BETWEEN   **75**

Trickster story: Subverting reality   75

5	IN THE FACE OF TRAUMA	77
	Stephanie	78
	Knowing and not-knowing	79
	Absence	81
	Luke holds up a mirror	84
	Bisi	86
	Implicit bias	88
	The ethics of being in relationship	90
	Absence becomes presence	91
	Note	92

6	ME VOICI	93
	The key question	93
	Fields of mutual influence	94
	Taking responsibility	96
	The mission	97
	Miriam Part 2: Seismic shifts or the making of a therapist	99
	Altruism	100
	Beyond self-care	104
	On being a wounded healer	108

7	WALKING THE LINE	112
	Co-transference and enduring relational themes	112
	Stephanie revisited	114
	The over-reach model	118
	Certainty	120
	Power	121
	Identification	123
	Ego	123
	The edges of relationality	124
	Limits of a relational approach	126
	Limits of capacity	127

PART 3 ECOLOGICAL PERSPECTIVES   **129**

Trickster story: Waking up   129

8   THE SHARED MINDFUL FIELD   131

   Hannah   132
   Shifts of consciousness   133
   Meeting difference   134
   Developing curiosity   136
   Tolerating uncertainty   137
   Reflections on presence   139
   Mindfulness and trauma   142
   David   144
   Therapeutic skill set   146
   A widening space   147

9   THE WELL-GROUNDED THERAPIST   148

   Situating the work   148
   Mapping new territory   150
   Snow: After the storm   153
   Discussion   155
   Rain: A conversation   157
   Sun: Grounding the self   159
   Storytelling   161
   Conversing   161
   Expressing   162
   Seeing and being seen   162
   Discussion   163
   Conclusion: Call and response   164
   Notes   165

10   VITAL CONNECTIONS   167

   Multilarities and complexity   168
   An ecological SOS   170
   Liz   173
   Reconnecting   174
   Interdependence: Reimagining relationships   176
   Vital presence   178
   Miriam Part 3: The buck stops here – a work in progress   178
   Trickster revisited   180
   Decolonization   181

Epilogue: 2020 vision   *184*

Appendix A   *188*

Appendix B   *192*

References   *195*

Index   *208*

Acknowledgements

Much of the credit for this book goes to other people. Countless others have stimulated my thinking through their questions and discussion; this has been fertile ground in which ideas have flourished. Their spirit of enquiry is embedded in this book.

Foremost are my colleagues on the Leadership Team of Relational Change whose inspiration, warmth, and encouragement have been vital to this project. They are: Martin Capps, Marie-Anne Chidiac, Sally Denham-Vaughan, Kate Glenholmes, Helena Kallner, and Lynda Osborne. I am immensely grateful also to Vienna Duff for her grounded wisdom and collaboration.

Both directly and indirectly, the following people have supported, guided, and advised me as this book began to emerge and became a reality: Ayhan Alman de la Osa; Carole Ashton; Rolf Aspestrand; Sue Baxter; Steffi Bednarek; Ann Boyd; Kate Briggs; Billy Desmond; Mark Fairfield; Nickei Falconer; Ed Fellows; Kay Ferriter; Jane Frances; Graham Gee; Sharon Gray; Ross Hoar; Sonja Hookway; Tony Jackson; Heather Anne Keyes; Camille MacDonald; Penny Madrell; Kath McCarthy; Marlene Moss Blumental; Donna Orange; Paddy O'Regan; Leanne O'Shea; Ashleigh Power; Jan Roubal; Angela Shaw; Emily Skye; Margherita Spagnuolo Lobb; Heather Styles; Jay Tropianskia; Greer White; Andrew Woodgate; Sue Wright; at nscience, Ravi Kumar and Helen Smith; and at the School of Lost Borders, Joseph Lazenka and Petra Lentz Snow.

Margaret Landale's compassion and insight have been hard to do justice to but remain a profound influence. I still learn most from my students, supervisees, and the people I have the privilege of working with; they call me to listen and suspend what I think I know.

Because I cannot separate parts of my life, I extend my gratitude for the friendship of others whose presence continues to sustain me: Judith Armstrong; Emily Ashton; Mairead Boyce; Malcolm Brain; Sue Brock-Hollinshead; Malcolm Busby; Sarah Buxton; Ruth Dowley; Hoonie Feltham; Cary Outis; Hugh Palmer; Val Parker; Jane Russ; Jan Seed; Linda Spiers; Sue Taylor; Jenny Yeong; members of the Cambridge TNH sangha; and Thich Nhat Hanh, my guiding light. Emma Coonan has, with grace, sensitivity, and wisdom, bridged both personal and professional worlds.

It is an enormous privilege to call every one of these my tribe and for their contributions to this book.

That the editorial team at McGraw-Hill Education put their faith in me again has been an honour, and they have been a pleasure to work with. Without them this would have been so much harder. I extend my gratitude also therefore to Hannah Kenner, Laura Pacey, Eleanor Christie, and Beth Summers. Thanks also to Dave Cummings for copyediting the script. Mark Howlett has ensured a professional finish with his design contributions.

For permission to include material from other sources, I acknowledge also the support of the *British Gestalt Journal*, *The Gestalt Review*, Hachette Books, *International Journal of Psycho-Analysis*, Sally Denham-Vaughan and Marie-Anne Chidiac, Malcolm Parlett, and the M.C. Escher Foundation.

Finally, my heartfelt gratitude to Ben, Rachael, Kat, Amelie, Ophelia, Erica, and Sylvia, who will always be my everything.

Prologue

We are five mature and experienced psychotherapists from different modalities who spend a day together as a peer group three or four times a year. On this occasion we start as always with a check-in on our current lives and situations. This takes some time, because support is needed and offered as accounts of family responsibility, loss, professional demands, and organizational challenges are shared. This spacious, connecting, accepting, and receptive process establishes the relational ground for the rest of the day. After lunch one of us presents some material she has prepared on intergenerational trauma, based on a literature survey and the contributions of some key thinkers. The ensuing discussion gives rise first to clinical reflections and then later to some personal stories. Early cross-generational memories of dislocation, loss, immigration, teenage pregnancy, and the horrors of the two world wars of our parents' and grandparents' generations emerge. The discussion turns spontaneously to the remembrance of place – connections to the land from which we had come, grounding our stories in a deeper and richer history. We speak of community rituals and the power of storytelling. We agree that our connection as a group is strong enough that the next time we meet we will create a ritual in which to tell our own stories of trauma. Experience and place are indivisible; place gives experience meaning.

1 Introduction

Uh-huh moments

There is an old story, presumably apocryphal, about therapists of diverse modalities who came together to explore whether there was anything they had in common. After a weekend of deliberation and discord, they came finally to agree on one thing, '*Uh-Huh*': 'I understand', 'I am with you'. Or maybe it has an inflection, '*Uh-Huh?*': 'I am interested', 'Please tell me more'. I imagine these delivered with a gracious tone and rhythm, a softening of gaze, a receptivity that reaches beyond the utterance. With such voicing something settles between you. But it only takes a small shift for an 'Uh-huh' to become abrupt, impatient, uncomprehending. *How* these utterances are delivered really matters. The *quality* of the contact we make is of great interest to Gestalt therapists like myself, who focus attention on process rather than content or story. The difference between these interventions depends on the self-awareness of the therapist, and their willingness to attend to the impact they have on others. It depends also on what each party brings to the encounter, on their worldview and values. However, even with the best will in the world, in the presence of intense suffering such that trauma brings, some small part of us will not want to understand, would rather not know more. This increases the likelihood of a more defensive form of 'Uh-Huh' being unwittingly conveyed. Effective trauma therapy can stand or fall with such microscopic changes.

There has been a proliferation of ideas about how to work with trauma, all of which have their place: EMDR, EFT, TRE, Havening, and more. Most of these are body-based practices with underpinnings of neuroscience. The problem with them, as Marlock and Weiss point out, is that

> … as many of these methods do not specifically and systematically address and integrate the psyche in their approaches, do not directly make psychological experience the focus of their therapeutic work, and do not highlight the client–therapist relationship, they cannot properly be classified as 'Body *Psycho*therapies'. (2015: 11, original emphasis)

A further key point about the moment-to-moment process of interaction is made by Carroll and Shaw:

> '*I know what I will do in advance*' is not really a human response, it is more robotic. It is treating human behaviour as if it were water in a bucket from a

stream rather than a moving, fluid, changing process called a river. (2013: 201, emphasis added)

When we offer something in a formulaic manner, we diminish our own humanity and that of the person we are with. Critically and subtly, this replicates the dynamics of relational trauma. My proposition is that trauma is not so much something 'to be fixed' as to be lived with; the question is how we find a way to do this. As a first ethic, it is this point that I wish to address in this book. Running somewhat counter to prevailing conditions in the wider field of mental health, there is a recognition that this work is often slow and painstaking, involving incredible commitment, tolerance, and rigour on the part of the therapist. Effective trauma therapy has to reach beyond the comfort and 'certainty' of a formula. Inherent in trauma is a feeling of helplessness – we can urgently feel the need to *do* something, and are plunged into uncertainty, self-doubt, and loss of ground. This is a fear-based response. The task we undertake is to find a way to *be* with the trauma in order to create the possibility of meeting it with clarity and grace.

Before we get too far ahead, let me back up a little. My own modality of Gestalt is not short on techniques, and yet is still sometimes misrepresented for its 'empty chair' method and a confrontational approach (see Taylor, 2104: 12–13). The truth is that there are many varieties of Gestalt therapist, some more experimental than others, and some working with more relational emphasis. I am less experimental than many; even as a trainee I apprehended that being in contact is experiment enough for some people. An experimental attitude opens the possibility of leaning towards growth, founded upon a belief in human goodwill and emergence into wholeness. This is in keeping with the spirit of the human potential movement from which Gestalt therapy sprang. (For some key concepts in Gestalt theory, see Appendix A.) Attending to aspects of personality that are unfamiliar, unsupported, disowned, or split off is a valuable counterfoil to the fixed and habitual responses that we see in people who have experienced trauma. The psyche, for want of a better word, is very much integral to this undertaking. One of the key splits we take seriously is that between body and mind, partly because contact becomes compromised following trauma, but also because contact is fundamentally embodied, as suggested above.

We cannot, of course, speak of contact without referring to relationship. Gestalt therapists understand that contact is at all times between one person and something else. Relationship is the configuration between one thing and another, the 'how' of their connection. Nothing can ever stand alone; even in a hypothetical vacuum we would still have a relationship to the vacuum. Our very existence depends on relationship, a fluid interaction between inner and outer, an exchange of energies. The experience of trauma breaches connection points between us; this imposes such uncertainty, such a rupture that the connections on which an ordered predictable life depends are cast aside. It is difficult to overstate the importance of this. At any one moment, we are engaged in a vast multiplicity of relationships. This creates a complex fabric of connections on which we depend, and which depend, in turn, on us. A co-arising interdependence is then the natural order of things to which we need to lay claim. And it is this fabric that is torn as a consequence of traumatic events.

Vital to our understanding of the role of relatedness in recovery from trauma are the ways in which these connected 'Uh-Huh' and other moments of meeting contribute incrementally to the process of change. Contributions from the Boston Change Process Study Group (2010) and Stern (2004), for example, underscore this point, and Westland (2015) later emphasized the non-verbal aspects of such interventions. Gestalt therapy again has a particular theory of change (see Appendix A) that emphasizes paradoxically staying with experience without trying to change it, which I modified in relation to trauma in my earlier book (Taylor, 2014: 35). Creating the conditions for change has been an abiding interest of mine, to which in the present volume I add my attempt to understand the conditions that give rise to trauma in the first place.

Towards an ecological turn in trauma

The relational turn in psychoanalysis began in the late twentieth century with a move away from free association and interpretation. A number of relational psychoanalysts have influenced my thinking, not least because of a parallel and largely complementary move in the Gestalt world towards a more relational focus. This in no way contradicts the theory of our founders but offers a refinement of it. As indicated earlier, concepts such as contact, the contact boundary, and self and environment all rest in essence on relationality (see Appendix A). Among prominent relational thinkers in Gestalt, spanning more than two decades, are Lynne Jacobs, Rich Hycner, Gary Yontef, Margherita Spagnuolo Lobb, Gianni Francesetti, Jan Roubal, Sally Denham-Vaughan, and Marie-Anne Chidiac, providing a rich and vibrant, often personal body of literature on the subject.

A fundamental premise of relational therapy is sometimes missed. A relational approach goes beyond the formation of a good working alliance, and further than consideration of transference dynamics. It questions instead, in an unbiased appraisal, 'How are we doing together? What part am I playing in the relationship and what dance do we make together?' (Spagnuolo Lobb, 2013). How we describe any relationship can be revealing for the ways in which we repeat habitual ways of thinking about ourselves and others, including the power relationship at play. How do we think about the people we work with in private or in supervision, for example? The relational turn is supported by developments in interpersonal neuroscience, to a large degree confirming what we have known intuitively for a long time. I will say more about this shortly (see also Appendix B).

A later development comes in the form of the 'ethical turn' (Goodman and Severson, 2016). This is not the ethics of accountability and standards of practice, but is instead deeply sensitive to the question of our '*inescapable implication in the suffering of others*' (2016: 6, emphasis added). This brings us straight to the heart of trauma, as we shall see. I will be arguing later that modern societies and the relationships that they depend on are organized around trauma. This, therefore, positions trauma as an existential issue, the need to survive and thrive enmeshed in it: 'How I represent the world to myself and respond to the world around me – the very construction of my existence – is at first an ethical question. It implicates me in the world' (2016: 7). Goodman and Severson are asking, I think, to what extent we might position ourselves in the world from a fundamental basis of safety or of fear. How people see themselves in relation to the world has, of course, long been within the purview of psychotherapy: 'I don't feel as though I fit in', 'I'm worried about what people will think of me' are as ever grist for the therapeutic mill. Notice how this changes when we add something different: 'I'm worried about what people will think of me when I cross-dress in public/talk about my abortion/tell them I have a criminal record'. In other words, what societal 'norms' shape this person's being-in-the-world, and do you, as their therapist, represent? Context is critical to how we shape our response, consciously or unconsciously. This change in emphasis begins to shift the work out of the therapy hour and beyond the walls of the consulting room into a wider frame.

We can also appreciate that the ground we stand on holds a history. The history of place, whether personal or collective, has significance for us, and there is a strong connection between the land and the people who have lived on it or used it. Archaeologists record the ancient relationships between people and place, and identify what are known as ritual or sacred landscapes. We build monuments, for example, at the sites of battles, the Great Fire of London, or of the martyrdom of notable leaders of the English Reformation in Oxford. We place flowers at the site of fatal accidents.

> *Place* has its own energy, its own memory, its own pain transference and healing capacities which are held over many generations. *Places* hold trauma just as people do. (Atkinson, [2002] 2018: 184, original emphasis)

The notion of traumatized landscape and the role of nature in well-being will be picked up later in the book.

Falling into the slipstream of this discussion is the emerging branch of ecotherapy (see Chapter 9 and, among others, Adams, 2020 and Totton, 2011). This speaks to a still wider set of possible relationships within the natural – or other-than-human – world, and its relevance to therapy. 'The world of the therapy room can no longer ignore the world outside the therapy room, which impinges directly or indirectly on therapist and client alike' (Evans, in Gonzi, 2020: 6). Heralded perhaps by Orange, a relational psychoanalyst and friend of Gestalt therapy, in her 2017 book *Climate Crisis, Psychoanalysis and Radical Ethics*, we find ourselves on the cusp of an 'ecological turn'. This term was coined, to the best of my knowledge, independently by me for this volume, and concurrently by Wright (in press); Chidiac and Denham-Vaughan similarly advocate for a shift towards an ecological perspective (2020). It would not surprise me to find that others are thinking along the same lines. I propose that the

[marginal handwritten note: * I call this shame.?]

concept of the ecological turn is uniquely helpful to our understanding of trauma because a more than systems orientation is called for. The experience of trauma is not confined to the individual or even to collective experience, but can be applied to the greater whole.

Circling back to Gestalt theory for a moment, an ecological mindset relates closely to the concept of 'field'. In everyday usage, we might speak of the 'field of medicine', or of a particular field of study. Field theory is one of the fundamental premises of Gestalt theory, which underpins our conceptualization of the relational frame (see Appendix A), and which is a broad enough concept to include all interdependent parts of experience and the world in which we live. However, despite almost thirty years of a move beyond individualism (Wheeler, 2000), Gestalt therapists often have difficulty looking beyond the separate and conjoined fields of therapist and the person they are working with. *It is a considerable challenge to consider ourselves as part of an ecological system* even though we might notionally subscribe to a field perspective; we live in times that are self-focused and, therefore, I suggest, disconnected, isolated, and split. We remain very much embedded in an individualist mindset.

> In practice, much of our focus in the Gestalt community does not operate outside of the dominant anthropocentric focus. There is a split between the breadth of our theory and how we choose to frame it. (Bednarek, 2018: 11–12)

This remains something of a puzzle, until we begin to frame this within a broad definition of trauma processes. The split Bednarek speaks of calls attention to some trauma, a pull between integration and fragmentation. One way of dealing with this is to shift from seeing our work as therapists as being about the people who we work with, to something far broader that gives it context. An ecological mindset brings something new to the table, because we cannot go searching for answers in the same places. While the notion of field concerns the properties of it, an ecological mindset draws us towards thinking about the relationships between those properties, the connections and disconnections that are part and parcel of the human condition. Our interpretation of what we mean by field becomes an organizing principle for the ways in which we approach our work, and determines the parameters of relationship.

To shift to an ecological perspective involves an extension of systems thinking. Ecological, in the sense that I mean it here, refers to the network of relationships in its entirety, interconnected and interdependent. 'Systems' may be smaller, embedded within the whole, with more determinate boundaries. Applied to trauma, we see the same patterns of adaptation on different scales. The study of fractal geometry is a branch of complexity theory which recognizes that characteristic patterns of organization can be found repeatedly at descending or ascending scales, 'so that their parts, at any scale, are similar in shape to the whole' (Capra and Luisi, 2014: 117). An ecological orientation can clarify the traumatic bonds between an individual and their environment, following the words of Ullman and Demaris: 'With a more accurate, holistic perspective, beyond individualism we naturally end up in a much wider field, a self-environment field the size of our entire Earth's biosphere' (2020: 218). An ecological perspective therefore allows us to reflect on both the conditions that create and maintain trauma and those that support its recovery.

Some definitions

There are a number of possible definitions of trauma that are helpful. For the purposes of this discussion, I am going to put to one side the categorizations commonly used by psychiatrists (so called 'PTSD') because I don't think they get close enough to the lived experience of trauma and lean towards box-ticking and dehumanizing (see also Chapter 4). The first to look at here is a classical definition used by therapists: 'Trauma is the experience of a situation in which your ability to cope using your existing strategies is overwhelmed'; we do not have the resources to deal with this, and feel overwhelmed. This implies dysregulation of the autonomic nervous system, commonly accepted as being symptomatic of trauma (see below, and for more neurobiological background, Appendix B). The second way of looking at trauma would be well appreciated by contemporary, neurobiologically inclined therapists: 'Trauma is the experience of a situation in which your ability to cope *on your own* using your existing strategies is overwhelmed'. This directs our attention to the key question of relationship. Levine (2010) gives a personal account of the difference a soothing relationship made to his recovery following an accident. Stolorow evocatively says something similar:

> When my traumatized states could not find a relational home, I became deadened, and my world became dulled. When such a home became once again present, I came alive, and the vividness of my world returned. (2007: 26)

Existential questions about what brings life and what deadens it come to the fore, and invite a consideration of the relationships that create trauma and support its recovery. There is something about the extremes that traumatic experiences take people to that forces us to question what we mean by relationship. I commented earlier about the importance of relationship to the process of change. In a similar vein, Badenoch describes trauma in this way: *'Any experience of fear or pain that doesn't have the support it needs to be digested and integrated into the flow of our developing brains'* (2018: 23, original emphasis). When we are unsupported in the task of assimilating or metabolizing a traumatic experience, we cannot move on and flourish. Notice, once again, the implicit embodiment of this.

I believe that a nuanced understanding of trauma has to include how we meet. My own rendition of a trauma definition, in Gestalt language, reads like this: 'Trauma is an experience that causes a catastrophic rupture at the contact boundary' (see Appendix A). There are many degrees of possible separation in such ruptures, from bodily and psychic intrusion to indifference. What I mean to convey is that, without support, the experience of trauma leads to a massive adaptation between the experience of 'self' and everything that is experienced as 'not self'. The very fabric of the world seems torn; it is profoundly isolating. 'After the trauma, the individual is left in a space that has lost its unity. The trauma takes place in *no place*, or nowhere, thus revoking the very notion of a place' (Ataria 2017: 165, original emphasis).

Typically, trauma responses can be seen as a constellation of dynamic processes and creative adjustments, some chaotic, some rigid, that limit or govern a person's way of being in the world. Broadly speaking, trauma takes one or more of the following forms: (a) trauma based on gender and sexuality, not exclusively but often perpetrated by men over women, and frequently expressed as some form of sexual violence; (b) trauma that is derived from a sense of difference, which can be adversarial, a sense of 'them and us', or 'Othering' including race; (c) trauma which derives from inequality, including disability, wealth, class, and education; (d) trauma that is inherent in the domination and exploitation by humans of the non-human world. Whichever way we cut it, relational traumas such as this inevitably involve a moral injury.

An ecological mindset raises other questions, which I will touch on briefly here for linguistic purposes:

> The word 'trauma' refers to something that is past; the current situation is of suffering, and a violation of human rights. Trauma constructs a different landscape, where we see neither martyr nor combatant, nor even ordinary people, but rather the intimate suffering of victims. (Fassin and Rechtman 2007: 198)

Who, then, is the self who is traumatized and who are we in relation to one another? What does using the word 'victim', or having a preference for 'survivor', say about someone? A similar debate centres around the choice of terms 'client', 'patient', or 'service user'. What separation makes this an instance of 'them and us'? It all depends on our culture and values. I have been inspired since reading Badenoch (2018: xix) to adopt the less loaded and more human words 'person' and 'people'. This levels the playing field between me and the people I meet in the course of my work, and is in keeping with the spirit of this book. This is more than a neat linguistic device; it has been my experience that this small change alters my perceptions of the people I work with and who I am in relation to them. Small interventions, as we shall see, can make a big difference. I therefore speak throughout this book of the people who come to see me, or the people I work with. Exceptions appear only in quotes from other writers or workshop participants.

Thinking about neuroscience

Without a doubt, research into neuroscience has opened a window onto the phenomenon we call trauma, creating a necessary shift in how we make sense of it. In my opinion, the most important consequence of this is that *we can begin to conceive of a therapeutic approach to trauma that does not, in and of itself, retraumatize.* The window of tolerance model proposes that any state outside of the 'window' is potentially retraumatizing (see Appendix B for an update on this model). Modern neuroscience has allowed us to understand that the effects of traumatic events have more in common than the types of event do. Even while saying this, the obvious uniquely individual constellation of symptoms and meanings must be borne in mind. We can, however, reasonably expect some variations of the following incomplete list of 'symptoms': difficulty regulating thoughts, feelings, and sensations; a feeling of not being in control; the feeling of not being safe; the inability to organize and put words to the experience. Relationships are invariably at stake, and the person's experience of relationship is crucial. The experience of trauma is not in the past, it is now, ongoing, unreformed. This calls into question whether there is such a thing as 'post trauma'.

The human brain is hardwired for connections, which our survival and growth depend upon. This is neatly captured by Cozolino:

- the brain is a social organ linked to other brains
- the brain is an organ of adaptation and change
- relationships are our primary environment
- the brain can *only be understood in relationship to other brains*
                              (in Carroll and Shaw 2013: 93, emphasis added)

Interpersonal neuroscientist Daniel Siegel seems to contradict the last point, in this interesting excerpt from my first book:

Siegel states this: 'we can ... imagine that the *social nature of our brains may have something to do with our minds in solitude*' (2007: 170, my italics). What this seems to suggest is that a process of neural reconnection takes place in solitude which helps to create the conditions for social connection. The need is to restore the wiring for contact ... we can postulate that this neuronal repair in solitude is also a function of the relational field. It is neither in the realm of the individualistic paradigm, nor that of the other, but both. (Taylor, 2014: 142)

This thinking suggests that we can restore brain *function* in solitude, but we can only make *connections* together.

In keeping with a move away from the individual pathology that neuroscience supposes, I take a relentlessly non-pathologizing approach to trauma in my work and this book. It makes no sense to me to treat what is an innate attempt at survival as a 'problem' or, worse still, as a 'disorder'. In the worst case, to do so recreates the conditions in which the traumatic event took place. Far more appropriate, in my experience, is to examine 'symptoms' compassionately for their purpose and meaning, without necessarily condoning certain behaviours they may give rise to. In particular, the need to regulate, as indicated by the window of tolerance model, proves to be a useful map for understanding the presence and maintenance of trauma-based phenomena.

Therefore, when referring to what are diagnostic conditions, I use the term 'so-called' or quotation marks throughout the text.

Readers of my first book may be surprised to find that in this volume I make little explicit reference to neuroscience. *It is no less important in shaping my thinking,* but it has receded from the foreground. A few key concepts are still very much part of the ground I rely on, and continue to teach. Some knowledge of neuroscience can be very settling, but I find nowadays that the facts matter less than an embodied, almost second-nature 'felt sense' of what is going on and the direction of the work. We need to digest the information until it simply becomes part of who we are. An overarching principle I offered then still applies at every moment in which I am working with someone: *'The therapist needs to be ... a steward of arousal'* (Taylor, 2014: 180, original emphasis). My stewardship of arousal comes not from cognitive knowing when someone is overloaded and needs a break: 'There may be an excess of cortisol which needs rebalancing', but from an implicit shared embodied knowing. Consistent with an emphasis on interpersonal neurobiology, McGilchrist suggests that the right hemisphere has an openness to the interconnectedness of things; it is 'interested in others as individuals and how we relate to them' (2009: 57).

It is through our nervous systems that we connect – the brain in the body. We quickly learn following a traumatic experience to disconnect from the signals that the body gives us. These are often signals that convey great somatic distress, held in those visceral organs under the influence of the vagus nerve. Many people believe that it is safer not to feel, at some considerable cost further down the line.

> An interest in our own bodily feelings has been neglected and often disrespected in our contemporary society. Often we have been taught, as part of a strategy to manage our behavior, to reject the feedback that our body is telling us. (Porges, 2017: 142)

Much of this book takes its tone from this implicit state of somatic regulation, illustrating and inviting a deepening of integration. (For further discussion of neurobiology, see Appendix B.)

Having said all this, I have also become increasingly cautious about the reductionism of a neurobiological mindset. The science is still very new and we don't know how far it can go in providing information we might find useful. It is illuminating, for example, to see starkly different fMRI images of brains responding to traumatic triggers (van der Kolk, 2014: 68, 71) – one showing lots of activity in the amygdala of the right hemisphere in particular, the other showing scant activity. However, we run the risk of over-interpreting this; all we can really tell is that two individuals reacted to the same stimulus in markedly different ways at the moment the scan was produced. We simply do not know what these images mean or how generalizable they might be. It would be foolhardy to try to draw conclusions about anyone's subjective experience based on these, or to use such images to predict a course of 'treatment'. Above all is my concern that we risk relying too heavily on neurobiology to the exclusion of listening deeply.

An inner chorus

In her book *Nourishing the Inner Life of Clinicians* (2016a), Orange speaks of being accompanied by an inner chorus of other writers who inspire and support her. My version of an inner therapy chorus comprises a handful of key quotes, each of which captures something important, and which I keep returning to. All have something to say about taking a therapeutic position in relation to trauma. Most find their way into discussions later in the book, but I introduce them together here.

The first comes from Pearlman and Saakvitne:

> Trauma therapy profoundly changes the therapist. We give up our familiar ways of being and beliefs about the world when we embark on this work with survivors of traumatic life events. These changes are both inspiring and disturbing, involving gains and losses. (1995: 279)

In training placements, many aspiring therapists are thrown unprepared into the world of trauma therapy, as I was. At the deep end, we face unexpected distress, chaos, and uncertainty, and can end up somewhat on the defensive. It is uncomfortable to admit that I learnt more from my mistakes than my successes, as is surely true for most of us. I still squirm at some of the things I have done and said, yet experience is no guarantee that we do better. But change we must, as we grow into the work, in ways we don't all sign up for.

The defences we employ are echoed in this quote from Laub and Auerhahn:

> We all hover at different distances between knowing and not knowing about trauma, caught between the compulsion to complete the process of knowing and the inability or fear of doing so. It is in the nature of trauma to elude our knowledge, because of both defence and deficit. The knowledge of trauma is fiercely defended against, for it can be a momentous, threatening, cognitive and affective task, involving an unjaundiced appraisal of events and our own injuries, failures, conflicts and losses. (1993: 288)

I see this as an ethical statement which locates the responsibility for change first in the therapist's examination of their own wounds and limitations. This relational ethic is a core theme in this book.

A more recent voice in my personal chorus adds to the relational dynamic. This voice is that of Parlett, whose concern is about the distance we create between us and others, affecting the humanity of those we meet:

> 'Identification with' is to be aligned with, or to join together; while 'alienation from' involves distancing from 'the other'. And with this distancing goes a small, subtle, and yet discernible reduction in the personhood of the other, or others ... All of us are part of this phenomenon of identifying and alienating. It takes an enormous shift in consciousness to transcend this dynamic, to step outside it, to recognise it, and to avoid being caught in it. (2015: 124)

We will consider later the extent to which 'alienation from' is also useful.

The spaces between us are also reflected in these words attributed to Holocaust survivor Viktor Frankl:

Between stimulus and response there is a space. In that space is our power to choose our response. In our response lies our growth and our freedom.

I have written before about the importance of creating some experiential distance from trauma in order to metabolize its effects. Developing the self-function of witnessing capacity is crucial in recovery (Taylor, 2014: 184) enlarging the field of choice from instinctive and reactive responses. In the pages to come we will also shine a light on the issue of power, in both creative and destructive manifestations.

Lastly, we come to Judith Lewis Herman, who writes:

Traumatic events ... breach the attachments of family, friendship, love and community ... Traumatic events destroy the victim's fundamental assumptions about the safety of the world, the positive value of the self, and the meaningful order of creation ... Traumatized people feel utterly abandoned, utterly alone, cast out of the human and divine systems of care and protection that sustain life. (1992: 51–52)

Reprinted by permission of Basic Books, an imprint of Hachette Book Group, Inc.

This eloquent description captures the relational and existential dimensions of traumatic experience, which provides a summary explanation for the difficulty and complexity of this work.

Chaos, confusion, and contradiction

For many reasons, trauma can be difficult to think about and harder to see. Trauma sometimes hides in plain sight; at other times it is like a faint echo carried on the breeze. It is dangerous when something is all around us and we don't notice it – trauma, MeToo, racism, and climate change all come to mind. 'You don't see something until you have the right metaphor to perceive it' (Shaw, in Bloom and Farragher, 2013: 23). I have noticed that trauma has the qualities of the Trickster; here, then, is my metaphor for trauma. This may not be the perfect metaphor but I have found it to be one that works, for it helps us not only see but to think more clearly. According to Sheldrake, it 'is well established in the sciences that metaphors can help generate new ways of thinking' (2020: 235).

The Trickster is an archetypal figure or presence that occurs in the folk tales of cultures across the world.

In picaresque tales, in carnivals and revels, in magic rites and healing, in man's [sic] religious fears and exaltations, this phantom of the trickster haunts the mythology of all ages, sometimes in quite unmistakable form, sometimes in strangely modulated guise. (Jung, 1972: para. 465)

Hyde suggests that the Trickster inserts himself (usually referred to in masculine form) into the intersections of the cultural web (2008: 205). While the Trickster motif contains aspects of a mischief-making anti-hero, this figure can easily be identified through contradictions and paradox, 'working by means of a lie that is really a truth, a deception that is in fact a revelation ... for trickster's lies provoke doubt' (Jung, 1972: para. 457). Since he has on occasion described himself as a soul in hell, the motif of subjective suffering would not seem to be lacking either. Examples are numerous: from the Greek god Hermes (Hyde, 2008) to the Green Man, Wile E. Coyote, Willy Wonka, Br'er Rabbit, Anansi the spider of African origin, and Loki from Scandinavia, the Trickster has an interesting and compelling history. The Trickster is a shape-shifter, a psychopomp, and shows up in parallel process regularly, thus shedding light on what is going on.

The Trickster represents a number of psychological processes which can illuminate the essence of trauma. One of the properties of the Trickster is to disorganize coherent experience by means of fragmentation, separation, and the creation of conflict. The Trickster often confuses identity and a sense of reality, and serves to deflect attention from his modus operandi. He has the ability to alter perceptions, to create splits, to use cunning to survive, to change consciousness, to confuse identities. His artfulness deceives and can lead us on a merry dance. Part of the confusion the Trickster creates is that we don't always know which is the true Trickster in a story; is it Road Runner or Wile E. Coyote? In stories of trauma, so often the 'victim' is turned quickly into the 'perpetrator'. Or, as in the M.C. Escher drawing here (Figure 1.1), we simply don't know which way is up. It may seem that the Trickster's main business is to create havoc, upturning the given order of things.

However, an appreciation of such a contextually emergent notion suggests an opening to change and transformation, as some trickster tales indicate. We can consider the disorganization of order as a necessary precursor to change in psychotherapy. '[The Trickster's] seemingly anti-social actions continue to keep our world lively and give it the flexibility to endure' (Hyde, 2008: 9). In some traditions, the Trickster tests the soul in order to prepare it for the next stage of its journey.

The Trickster inhabits a liminal space between states of consciousness, and as such changes boundaries. Boundaries are invariably problematic in trauma; the contact boundary which is so compromised (Hyde, 2008: 25) places the Trickster as go-between, a mediator between worlds. Hyde suggests that the Trickster invites us into

> ... threshold consciousness [which] is partly a matter of temperament and partly a matter of setting. Put on the threshold, trickster mind may awaken in almost anyone. Those who are given to the pleasures of liminality may actively seek out such settings ... but such settings will also leave their mark on those otherwise predisposed. (2008: 227)

Figure 1.1 M.C. Escher, *Infinity*

This aligns with Denham-Vaughan's conceptualization of the liminal space, which she describes as an emergent state responsive to context. It is 'one that emphasises individual emergence as indivisibly intertwined with and responsive to a specific situational context, including time and place, as well as person' (2010: 36).

Hyde understands the Trickster as a boundary crosser.

> Every group has its edge, its sense of in and out, and trickster is always there … We constantly distinguish – right and wrong, sacred and profane, clean and dirty, male and female, young and old, living and dead – and in every case trickster will cross the line and confuse the distinction. (2008: 7)

The Trickster entity suggests we dismiss that which we need to take seriously, to be blind to that which is right in front of us, to be deaf to what is calling loudest for attention, to sleep when we most need to be awake. Apparent contradictions, these pairings can be seem as binaries – or maybe, because the Trickster is at play they are not. Confusion and disarray, after all, are the Trickster's trademarks.

True to paradoxical form, I have also experienced the Trickster reveal itself by its absence, when a particular story eluded me. What I came to understand was in part that this particular story was not mine to tell, but more that its very absence made the extent and depth of the trauma I was circling around more vividly present to me. This affected me greatly; what was not there, what was unformulated experience when I got in touch with it, felt very unsettling. Sometimes, as a therapist, I have experienced the need to really take something on myself, in order to process it and give it back. When I listen deeply, the Trickster tells me what I need to hear, even if it's uncomfortable, even if it's personal. The Trickster motif will accompany us through the book, each part of which is prefaced with a Trickster story. However, there is a caveat to this. Trickster stories derive in the main from oral traditions. It is regrettable that the provenance of many of those that appear in print is not guaranteed and they may have been appropriated by those to whom they do not belong. The same may be true in this instance.

A field guide to the book

Starting from an ecological premise, this book attempts to weave together a number of complex themes. Some themes are obvious but we shed light also on others that are less visible, at times taking us to surprising places. The image of a mobius strip (Figure 1.2) guides us; it represents flow, connection, and an interplay of inner and outer which reflects some of the experience of trauma.

The book is intended to be a companion volume to my previous one. Some of the seeds of this present work lie in the old one, but were calling for expansion. This time, I present less of a road map and more of a way of thinking differently about ourselves, the people we work with, and the world around us. I invite you to approach it as a learning experience, which mixes didactic material, clinical examples, and experiential tasks as a workshop would. Despite asking some searching questions, you will find fewer answers here than you might wish for. This book is generally not prescriptive, but I strongly encourage you to follow the guidance in the 'Dropping in' points in each chapter. It is these that may deepen your practice, as the book's title suggests. My hope is that it will support some sort of change, and that you will in the process take from it something that is uniquely yours.

Figure 1.2 A mobius strip

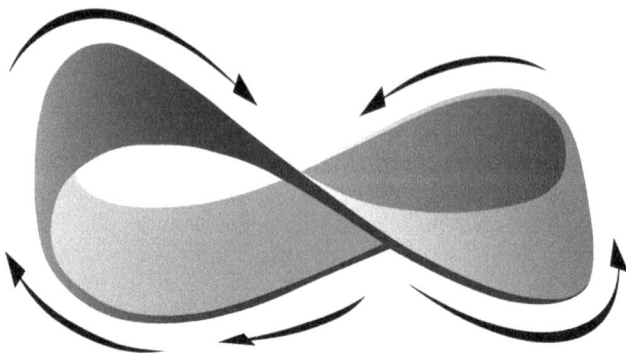

The scope of this book is extremely wide. I cannot claim to have any specialist knowledge of all the big themes it contains and for those who are better informed, my ignorance may rankle. What I hope you will glean from the material are some of the common threads of trauma as they manifest in early twenty-first century society. One of my biases – and we will examine this later – is that I write from a Euro-centric position. The lines I have chosen to draw out reflect my biases, and I have inevitably omitted other potential lines of enquiry. I am aware that this may cause a sense of exclusion for readers whose life space and interests create a preference for a different focus. It is regrettably an impossible task to try to be either comprehensive or knowledgeable about all possible parameters of this vast subject; while my intention is to be inclusive, I cannot be. If you wonder why I have gone this way and not that, perhaps you can take a breath and step back as you read. This is not personal to anyone, but a representation of bigger themes in which some cross-fertilization from one area to another may be possible. I don't intend to generalize or make assumptions and am aware also that at times my use of language may not be as culturally sensitive as I would wish. I have done my best, and invite your curiosity, which is far more important than my need to be 'right'.

I base my work as a trainer and supervisor on the premise that many of the therapists I see have a background of personal trauma; I do too. My decision to include my own story in three segments is considered and has been well-supported. I want to make clear that this is not 'about me', but is illustrative of a shared reality. Given that a major focus of this book is on the self of the therapist, it would simply be incongruous not to include it. Elsewhere, I have sought to keep 'story' to a minimum in order to focus more on the clinical process. Where stories have been told, they are fictitious, though process points are fairly faithful to what actually transpired. I weave many of the broad themes into them; that they came to me with some ease has taken me aback. They are so frequently there if we look for and take account of them. If at any point, in reading the stories or trying out a 'Dropping in' experiment you feel distressed, I urge you to slow down, and find the support of another person – a therapist even.

Deepening Trauma Practice is in three parts, each comprised of three chapters. While many of the arguments are not necessarily linear, there is a pattern. I start with some broad themes, following the mobius strip to a narrower focus on those moments of meeting – or mis-meeting. Finally, I broaden out once more.

Part 1, Situating Trauma, follows the fractal premise mentioned earlier, and explores how trauma is represented in some of the structures of society, changing and reshaping them. This implicates us as therapists at every turn. The idea of the contact boundary or meeting point encompasses the adaptations that we make to our ways of being in the world, so often in response to relational disturbances. Chapter 2 sets the scene with some theory and introduces the SOS model. This is an ecological lens through which we begin to contextualize trauma, as evidence of the relational dynamics we work with. I go on to reconceptualize the model to include the breakdown at the contact boundary that defines trauma (see above) and the black hole that lies within. This leads towards a discussion of how trauma organizes cultures and how culture may be expressed very personally in the body. Consideration of collective trauma, and events that have largely gone underground complete the picture, implicating us all. Trauma is a common ground on which we stand. This gives rise to some differentiation between situational structures (such as colonialism and class) and situational processes (such as disconnection and dehumanization). A major theme throughout the book concerns power and oppression, evidenced in particular by colonialism, and this is introduced here to give some shape to the whole text. Chapter 3, Something in the Air, picks up some of the themes already outlined, and considers how they may present in a clinical setting. A theoretical backdrop examines how systems organize themselves around trauma, and for some who get caught in their reach, may retraumatize. The chapter presents four case studies, illustrating how experience is embedded in the wider context. The themes covered put into context homosexuality, workplace bullying, institutional abuse, and the sexual exploitation of a minor, all embedded systemically within society and organizations. Closer to home, perhaps, in Chapter 4 an extended case study of a young woman's experience provides the vehicle for discussion and questioning of retraumatization within mental health services. Through the lens of gender, we see how dehumanization and the power dynamics introduced in Chapter 2 play out in different areas of mental health provision. Objectification of the female body is implicit. Of particular concern are the use of diagnosis and psychotropic medications, and I look for evidence of effective interventions. Some critical reflections about how psychotherapy reflects the majority social discourse surrounding 'expertise' and the legacy of a colonial mindset also affect us in our profession. Themes of privilege and oppression emerge for discussion.

The primary concern in Part 2 is about how we might find a way to meet. Shifting from a situational lens, the focus here is on the Other and Self elements of the SOS model. The first two chapters are an expansion of an article based on a plenary presentation I gave at a conference, and raise questions about facing the challenges of working with severe trauma. Chapter 5 in essence addresses our responsibility and the ethics of our response to the traumatized Other, and how we in turn become traumatized by them. Based in the thinking of philosopher Emmanuel Levinas, our encounter with the suffering of the Other is the primary focus. I delve into the realm of the unknown and the unspeakable, and question how we can find a way to face the suffering that is present and that stirs in us too. Faced with dissociated states in particular, therapists can feel as though they are reaching into a void, in which the 'meeting' point is hard to discern. The intersubjective space is formulated as a necessary search for appropriate distance, with an intention to 'meet'. Some of the style of this chapter is necessarily imprecise and evocative, conveying the provisional quality of the work. It reflects the unformulated and unformulatable nature of unprocessed trauma. Shaping our ability to meet are our implicit biases, and I consider this from an unjaundiced standpoint. Returning to

Levinas, the chapter concludes with a consideration of ethics and responsibility. Chapter 6 positions the therapist clearly as an active participant within the traumatized relational field. It is a development of some of the ideas in the key chapter of my earlier work, 'Chapter 11: The Well-Resourced Therapist'. Here I invite therapists to consider the many ways in which they are implicated in the trauma which they seek to relieve. How we bring wounds of our own to the therapeutic encounter, and what motivates us in this work are key considerations. This draws on the work of Cozolino (2004) and Marie Adams (2014), in which our personal history may be part of our motivation. A detailed exploration of the pros and cons of serving others is offered, alongside a critical discussion of the popular notion of 'self-care'. Unpacking what we might assume to be the necessary clinical attribute of empathy, I go on to look at five stages of developing compassion, drawing on the thinking of Germer. I begin to consider the relevance of vulnerability as a therapeutic attribute. In Chapter 7, attention turns to how the therapist brings their own trauma responses into the mix. This includes an exploration of what is traditionally understood as countertransference, and in Gestalt is known as co-transference or 'enduring relational themes' (Jacobs, 2017). A longer verbatim example offers a structure for an understanding of how therapists' reactions are often trauma-based. Sympathetic to the nuance of meaning and interpretation as we track them moment by moment, a new concept of 'over-reach' shows how difficult it is to calibrate our response. The text illustrates how the dynamics of power and oppression play out in the enactments of the consulting room and can retraumatize. Under the spotlight, too, are the limits of a relational approach and how we orient ourselves accordingly.

Moving towards a reimagined situation, Part 3 begins with a chapter about the shared mindful field. Here questions about the qualities of therapeutic presence come to the fore, and how this may helpfully influence the progress of therapy. With a revision of my earlier thinking, mindfulness is critically positioned within the therapy space, contributing to a shared understanding of what is possible or tolerable. Here we think also about meeting difference, with all the discomfort and potential for growth that can bring. This brings in a reapplication of the five-part model presented in Chapter 6. Bearing discomfort is further explored in the necessity to sit with uncertainty, especially challenging in the presence of deep pain. Picking up the theme of power, different qualities are discussed for their ability to block or enable the therapeutic process. Chapter 9, The Well-Grounded Therapist, is a revision of an article previously published, and co-written with my colleague Vienna Duff. Together we have run several residential retreats for therapists, with the intention of resourcing one another through reconnection with the land. Outlining the background to our thinking, the chapter includes an account of a walk I took on a beach, and a discussion Vienna and I had as we walked along a section of canal. The chapter considers trauma from other-than-human perspectives and touches on regeneration. We present a description of and some of the findings from the workshops we ran together. The chapter also addresses a key question about why the natural environment is so important in recovery from trauma. The book closes by drawing together some of the themes under an ecological umbrella, making links with complexity theory. A revision of the SOS model offers a more nuanced approach to thinking about the operation of power on the whole situation. The notion of interdependence is central, supported by lessons in deep listening learned from the nature of the wider field. We move towards an understanding of trauma as common ground, shared with the other-than-human world. In previous chapters, we took a deep dive into the deadening feel of the black hole of trauma, and a Gestalt perspective points in the direction of a more energetic engagement with the world. This leads to positioning the restoration of an embodied sense of vitality as a new way of being in the world. Some conclusions about the Trickster are presented, before ending with some implications for the way forward.

We are not quite finished: an Epilogue has been added with some contemporary reflections on writing as the world changes at an alarming pace, and is followed by two appendices, respectively offering an overview of Gestalt and neurobiological concepts.

Part 1

Situating Trauma

'A man rode through the farm, greeting us as he went by,' said the first friend. 'He was wearing a black cap, but my friend tells me it was a white cap and that I must be tired or blind or both.'

The second friend insisted that the man had been wearing a white cap. One of them must be mistaken, but it was not he.

'Both of you are right,' said Eshu.

'How can that be?'

'I am the man who paid the visit over which you now quarrel, and here is the cap that caused the dissension.' Eshu put his hand in his pocket and brought out the two-colored cap, saying, 'As you can see, one side is white and the other is black. You each saw one side and, therefore, are right about what you saw. Are you not the two friends who made vows of friendship? When you vowed to be friends always, to be faithful and true to each other, did you reckon with Eshu? Do you know that he who does not put Eshu first in all his doings has himself to blame if things misfire?'

– Lewis Hyde, 2008: 238

2 The context of trauma

The importance of context

Putting trauma into context is important for a number of reasons. These include aspects of field, phenomenology, and neurobiology. First, individually and collectively the experience of trauma is an experience of deep disconnect and disorientation. The disorganization of the experiential field that is a hallmark of trauma is often felt as extreme, as though points of reference and all previous experience are rent asunder in the process. It can be compared to having a map without the territory; in a sense ground is lost. In such circumstances, shock and confusion serve to increase a sense of disorientation. To reiterate that so eloquently put by Herman:

> Traumatic events ... breach the attachments of family, friendship, love and community ... Traumatic events destroy the victim's fundamental assumptions about the safety of the world, the positive value of the self, and the meaningful order of creation ... Traumatized people feel utterly abandoned, utterly alone, cast out of the human and divine systems of care and protection that sustain life. (1992: 51–52)

As suggested in the previous chapter, this quote captures the essence of the experience of trauma, that of disconnection, of which we will say more shortly. Difficult though it may be to do so, it is crucial to appreciate how such an individual becomes lost in time, place, safety, embodiment, narrative, and relationship.

Stolorow adds: 'Massive deconstruction of the absolutisms of everyday life exposes the inescapable contingency of existence on a universe that is random and unpredictable and in which no safety or continuity of being can be assured' (2007: 16). What was once ordinary and mundane becomes thick with new meanings by virtue of its dislocation. New associations become triggers to an internal state of terror. Without the conditions in which traumatic experiences can be formulated and processed, it's all out of context. 'Traumatic reactions spill over from the individual to the collective in parallel processes which maintain and reinforce the trauma' (Soth, 2006: 74). Viewed through the lens of the ecological context, the absolutisms of everyday life might include those concerned with race, gender, nationality, and education; in other words, the constructs that define and support our particular place and way of being in the world.

The second thread for understanding the experience of de-contextualization is that trauma feels individual when it is actually relational – trauma *always* happens in a context, in relation to something. 'What is essentially contextual – an engagement between the [person] and a particular environment – will be perceived as personal *when it is removed from its context*' (Kepner, 1995: 5, original emphasis). While self-reliance becomes our first line of defence, this may paradoxically further increase our vulnerability by distorting threads of the relational ground on which we would otherwise rely. In reality, this ancient ground is so much part of the fabric of our lives, woven into our DNA, that it forms the basis of many of our old assumptions about the way the world works. Aspects of it have become hidden, and I suggest that it is our business to make them more visible if we intend to work relationally. Like a bad smell in the air, what remains in the dark can continue to do its toxic work unabated.

Finally, without context, the event or experience of trauma becomes an all-consuming and recursive focus of attention, an exhausting and never-ending hypervigilance for the perceived threat and real attempts to restore a sense of safety via a settling of the nervous system. Perception then narrows and becomes over-focused on one element of a bigger picture to the exclusion of other important elements (Taylor, 2014: 52–53). When the sense of past danger is imprinted in the physiology of the individual, current markers of safety are often overlooked; this narrowing of focus is hardwired and reactive and not open to what appears to be situational evidence. Similarly, the sense of oneself as a victim may override any acknowledgment of one's survival capacity and personal strengths.

The SOS model: An ecological template

The SOS model (Figure 2.1), developed by Denham-Vaughan and Chidiac (2013), provides a wonderfully accessible formula for expanding our understanding of what it means to be relational. It can thus help us to situate trauma – or, indeed,

Figure 2.1 The SOS model

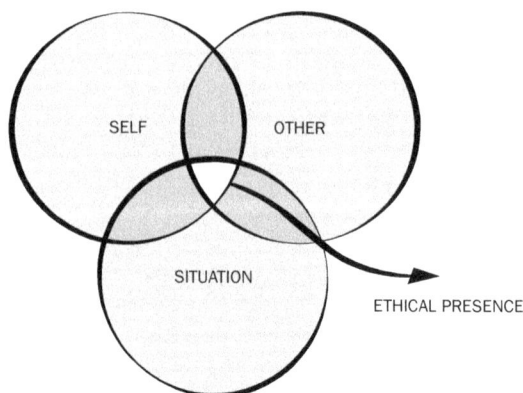

any other lived experience. The model refers to the intertwined dimensions of Self, Other, and Situation (SOS), as well as the interplay between the three, in the totality of their relationships. It is fully grounded in core Gestalt theory of self (see Appendix A for further background to the concepts in this section).

According to this model,

> [this] relational orientation means finding an optimal balance between three interrelated elements:
> - self; which can be seen as either the individual, group, community or organisation;
> - other; as the 'other' in the relationship at any given moment; and
> - situation or overall context/culture in which the issues are embedded. (Denham-Vaughan and Chidiac, 2013: 102)

The distinction between the elements of the SOS model can be helpful when applied to people who have experienced trauma. The disconnection described in the quote from Herman above can create a sense of not knowing where one ends and another begins. When experience is denied or invalidated, it is a positive move to be able to claim for oneself, 'This is what happened to me'. However, this separation may also limit our thinking about where trauma actually begins and ends. For the purposes of this chapter and the two that follow, the focus is on the total situation, which includes Self and Other; this is an ecological perspective. Wollants clarifies further:

> In a total-situation perspective we do not need a concept of 'Self' as an entity *within* a person. Such a self isolates me from my environment ... The term self, however, refers solely to the personal pole of the interactional person-world field. (2012: 112–113; see also Appendix A)

The SOS model was developed as a way of challenging the individualist approach to responding to distress. Many approaches to psychotherapy have traditionally paid heed to the 'Other' dimension, including the effects of family and upbringing, understanding the localized 'culture' that shapes an individual and their way of being in the world – while the significance of some of the social determinants influencing the family have been overlooked. For example, I often enquire about the Second World War experiences of the parents and grandparents of the people who come to see me. This begins to locate their distress in an intergenerational context. It is necessary to understand what our parents and grandparents did to survive (Kubesch, 2005: 73) because that is part of our own survival. The situation in this model includes the explicit, such as facts, structures, legislation, and customs, as well as the implicit, such as beliefs, values, shared memory, bias, and assumptions. Together these become ways of organizing society.

Bear in mind, if you will, that the elements of the SOS model are not separate, but are *dynamically interrelated*, with a *change in one part of the field implying change in another*, as Lewin proposed in his work on field theory

([1948] 1997: 24). We are in a ceaseless engagement with, and response to, the environment in which we find ourselves, and which shapes our experience. The SOS model arguably represents an idealized theoretical 'healthy field'. We may question whether such a field exists. In reality, the three components of the model may not be so evenly distributed. Noting that the concept of 'ethical presence' lies at the intersection of the elements of the model, we may consider presence through the lens of 'fluid responsiveness' (Denham-Vaughan and Chidiac, 2007). If we imagine, then, that the boundary of each of the components is fluid, expanding and contracting in response to the demands of the situation and in particular to stress, the model becomes a dynamic tool enabling analysis of imbalance and deficit.

Figure 2.2 illustrates the changes that might occur at the contact boundary between each of the component parts in response to trauma. The image of trauma as a black hole arises in the literature (van der Kolk and McFarlane, [1996] 2007; Ataria, 2017).

> There appears to be no better way to describe the traumatic experience than as a 'black hole … whose gravitational field is so strong that nothing, including light, can escape it … For trauma victims, the traumatic event turns into an axis around which their entire world revolves. (Ataria 2017: 180)

While the focus of this chapter is on the situation, we will go on to look at the other aspects of the model throughout the book. Note that the authors of the SOS model are advocating a balance of all parts of the system, which is critically disrupted in trauma. They add a further dimension:

> Vitally, we also use the model to convey a 'felt sense' of the socio-political ethic inherent in a socially inclusive relational paradigm: we are all ultimately interconnected and interdependent. (Denham-Vaughan and Chidiac, 2013: 101)

Figure 2.2 Trauma SOS

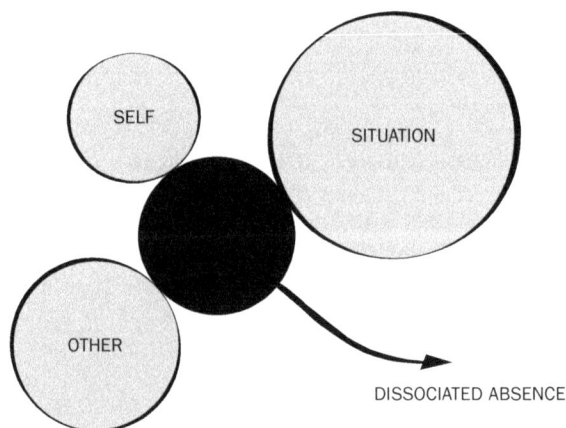

The resources necessary to maintain an attitude of ethical presence denote a position of benign power (Chidiac and Denham-Vaughan, 2020: 24); conversely, I would suggest, that dissociated absence is a reflection of oppression. The SOS model demonstrates how our sense of culture is created at the boundary (Wheeler, 2005: 43), providing a sense of 'the way the world is' (2005: 47), reorganized by trauma. Lewin makes an important distinction, in which he defines the life space – or situation – as a *psychological* field ([1948] 1997: 162), what we might think of as the perceptual, experiential field. In recognizing this, we can begin to see that the kind of attention that is afforded to the experience of trauma is socially and psychologically determined.

Dropping in

Take a moment to consider some of the people, places, or things that help you feel most connected in the world. As you identify each in turn, breathe a little space around the experience. What is your felt sense of this, and what do you notice now in your body?

The idea of a life space through which we move is embedded in the concept of habitus. Habitus, as defined by the sociologist Bourdieu, is

> … a concept that expresses, on the one hand, the way in which individuals 'become themselves' – develop attitudes and dispositions – and, on the other hand, the ways in which those individuals engage in practices. (Webb et al., in Huang, 2019: 48)

The concept accounts for the ways in which those dispositions are incorporated at the level of bodily movements and styles (ibid.). Implicit embodiment is deeply socially conditioned, the total situation in the singular body: 'We internalize culturally learned ways of being, involving the postures, gestures, and movements of the body, that identify us to selves and others' (Caldwell, 2018: 34). In similar vein, Clemmens writes: 'I define the embodiment of culture as a group of people moving together, creating space, knowing each other physically in the same ways over time' (2020: 21). Our culture is expressed implicitly in the ways we move and how we adapt on an embodied level. As a matter of course, we all do a number of things in order to adjust our appearance to a perceived social 'norm' – or our way of being in the world.

Relationship – being in the world – is our first template for survival, sense of safety, and belonging. With the narrowing of focus that an individualist mindset creates, the self can easily be seen as the context of distress. In my experience, this understanding of trauma still prevails and it is interesting to reflect on why this is, and what the systems are that keep it in place. In line with Denham-Vaughan and Chidiacs' thinking, I am proposing that we now examine Self, Other, *and* Situation in the context of trauma. It is important to stress that this does not preclude attention on the individual, but places the emphasis on the individual *within* the whole context.

The subsoil of trauma: Situational structures

> Every trauma that occurs is an individual trauma perpetrated by individuals and experienced by individuals. Every trauma is a social trauma with roots in social institutions and implications for society at large, and every trauma is a historic trauma, fostered by the past and reverberating into the future. (Glendinning, 1994: 126)

When we situate trauma in its wider context, we can recognize the survival needs that are 'anchored in structures of emotional and cultural expectations that provide a sense of security and capability' (Alexander, 2004: 10). It is not too strong a point to emphasize that 'the cultural tissue is most sensitive to the impact of traumatogenic changes, *precisely* because culture is a depository of continuity, heritage, tradition, identity of human communities' (Sztompka, 2004: 162, emphasis added).

'Cultural trauma', then, is a term used to denote aspects of historical memory that disrupt these expectations and 'undermine or overwhelm one or several essential ingredients of a culture or the culture as a whole' (Smelser, 2004a: 38). It may present as a background of trauma that is not much altered by specific events (Fassin and Rechtman, 2007: 1). As one example, Smelser considers that 'The Protestant Reformation qualifies as a cultural trauma because of the fundamental threat it posed to the integrity and dominance of the Catholic cultural worldview' (2004a: 38). There are, of course, numerous other examples across the entire history of humankind – an ecology of trauma (see, for example, Gretton, 2019).

The term 'structural trauma' goes deeper than culture: 'I … use the word structural rather than institutional because I think it is built into spaces much broader than our more traditional institutions. Thinking of the big picture helps you see the structures' (Eddo-Lodge, 2018: 64). The structures refer to what I have also called 'ground trauma' (Taylor, 2018: 446), by which I mean aspects of the ground that hold a history of trauma, sometimes very ancient, which are so intrinsic to 'the way things are' that they become almost invisible: 'It seeps slowly and insidiously into the fabric and soul of relations and beliefs of people as community' (Atkinson, [2002] 2018: 53). While a traumatic event may be long past, systemic trauma is ongoing. Thus the very notion of culture emerges from trauma. 'Without trauma there can be no collective, since trauma is a constituent factor in forming a community and preventing that community' (Ataria, 2017: xv). Indeed, Fassin and Rechtman suggest that trauma is a bridge between cultures, the lowest common denominator of shared humanity (2007: 4).

For the purposes of what follows, we will examine trauma through situational structures and then as situational processes. It is important to bear in mind that none of these structures or processes operates in isolation; they are a part of a complex and intersecting whole. I do not claim to be an expert on any of the aspects under consideration here, but wish rather to give some thought to some of the factors at play, as described in Chapter 1. The list I present is indicative rather than exhaustive.

Dropping in

Before you read through the points that follow, I suggest you take a moment to settle your attention in your body, slow your breathing, and allow yourself to read carefully. Consider where trauma operates in each example, and what connections you notice between Self, Other, and Situation:

Colonialism: Although the height of colonization, or empire, was between the sixteenth and nineteenth centuries, the practice goes back at least to Roman times. 'A *colonia* or colony was a detachment of soldiers who were rewarded with land to keep order among the vanquished' (McIntosh, [2001] 2004: 91, original emphasis). This made land into a commodity rather than an ecosystem sacred to the people who lived and worked with it. Implicit in this is the co-existing relationship between the 'victorious' and the 'vanquished'. The fact that those 'bequeathed' the parcels of land were former slaves who earned their freedom by fighting in the legions ([2001] 2004: 91) gives lie to the emergence of the value of ownership, human or otherwise. However, the claiming of land is not the same as relationship with it, which is the preroga-tive of the traditional and indigenous inhabitants of it. The mechanisms of colonization developed largely through European explorers, who established global trade routes for goods and people. World domination was Eurocentric. It is noteworthy that for all its responsibility in creating empire, Britain is also historically one of the most colonized countries in the world. From that per-spective, it was from the Norman conquest of Britain onwards that a series of statutes brought about the feudal system, the enclosure of common land, Highland clearances, and property rights that are embedded in the British way of life. Similar events took place across Europe (McIntosh, [2001] 2004). Perhaps because ground, place, the land we belong to is so fundamental to ensuring the survival of the human psyche, real-estate became the prize com-modity, and human and non-human living systems became to varying degrees expendable.

> The consequences of colonialism are still persisting in the form of chaos, coups, corruption, civil wars, and bloodshed, which pervade many of these countries, mainly because of the residues of colonization. (Hamadi, 2014: 39)

Slavery: If good land was to be put to making a profit, people would be needed to work it. Labour, too, had an economic value and, for certain people, a very low one at that. The eighteenth-century economist Adam Smith organized soci-ety in terms of 'ranks of people' and the 'natural order of things' (in McIntosh, [2001] 2004: 56–57). Smith argued that slavery would be 'justified if it can effi-ciently generate wealth for owners' (ibid.). Much of Britain's wealth was founded on the profits of slavery; the grand buildings of our port cities, and generous bequests supporting educational and civic institutions were evidence of the status of merchants trading in human 'commodities'. It is sobering to read Eddo-Lodge on the subject:

> Over the course of the slave trade, an estimated 11,000,000 black African people were transported across the Atlantic Ocean to work unpaid on sugar and cotton plantations in the Americas and West Indies. (2018: 4)

Slavery was abolished by Act of Parliament in 1834, when one-sided compensation was paid to 'the 46,000 British slave-owning citizens who received cheques for their financial losses' (2018: 6).

That debt was only paid off in 2015, meaning that most tax-paying British adults like myself have contributed to the payments. Despite legal abolition, we sadly cannot relegate slavery to the mists of history; modern-day slavery, of which human trafficking is a part, remains a huge organized international dark economy. At the time of writing, it is estimated that Western lifestyles are dependent on 'employing' an average of 32 slaves per person, producing our coffee, mobile phones, cotton t-shirts, and other day-to-day 'essential' items (www.endslaverynow.org).

Racism: Colonialism and slavery were only possible because some people – especially people of colour and black, often indigenous people – could be conveniently viewed as a 'lower' rank of humanity. Back American slaves were regarded as less human than their white 'owners', while the horrors inflicted on Aboriginal peoples by the white colonizers of their land were not considered human at all. Using an evocative term, Menakem describes the relationship of white people to black people as 'The Great Othering' (2017: loc 1576). The history of racism has been brutal and has gone underground because it is so enmeshed with preserving white identity. Commenting on 'white fragility' DiAngelo notes that, 'The racial status quo is comfortable for white people' (2018: 14). However, according to Eddo-Lodge, things are not so comfortable for people of colour and black people: 'Looking at our history shows racism does not erupt from nothing, rather it is embedded in British society. It's in the very core of how the state is set up. It's not external. It's in the system' (2018: 56). MacKenzie-Mavinga writes of someone she worked with who 'tells me that when she went into a store in London, she was followed immediately by a security guard. She says people don't believe her when she tells them of this kind of experience' (2009: 83), while Eddo-Lodge describes her experiences of 'the silently raised eyebrows, the implicit biases, snap judgments made on perceptions of competency' (2018: 64). Subtle cues to a sense of difference based on skin colour determine a particular way of being in the world. That I consider myself fortunate never to have experienced this as a white person illustrates my bias – it is inevitable. As Jacobs points out, knowing what it means to be black goes hand in hand with knowing what it means to be white (2005: 231).

Class: Underpinned by capitalist values, the notion of class broadly defines the differences between the 'haves' and the 'have nots'. This refers of course to status, to wealth (inherited or self-made), to opportunity, to rights, to educa-tion, and to social mobility, among others. Privilege and disadvantage are part of the deal. In the United Kingdom, the NRS social grades are a widely used hierarchical system of demographic classification based on the income of the head of household. As McGarvey explains, the 'highest' classification

> is defined as social and economic groups which consist of people who have more education and better-paid jobs than those in other groups … while people in the lower classification are regarded as culturally unsophisticated and parochial in their concerns. (2017: 32)

Among the 6 per cent of British elite, few are from ethnic minorities, many are graduates, and over half come from families who were also of the elite class (source: Wikipedia). Class, inequality, and a sense of inferiority are linked. McGarvey observes, 'the belief [among the working classes] is that the system is rigged against you and that all attempts to resist or challenge it are futile' (2017: 37). A Dutch study found that 'Perceptions of classism were strongly associated with poor physical and mental health and percep-tions of inferiority' (Simons et al., 2017: 438). The British may be uniquely sensitive to class and its meanings, but class appears with varying degrees of 'abjection' in different societies, most inescapably in the Indian caste system ordered according to notions of 'pollution and purification, of the pure and the impure' (Krysteva, 1982: 79).

Scarcity of resources: Trauma theory highlights the threshold of coping strategies, and therefore the therapeutic necessity of developing resources. A correlate of this is that a deficit of resources can be traumatizing. Survival is not only compromised by personal poverty, but by deprivation of other sorts. Famine, drought, and natural disaster are obvious candidates, but so are economic and political factors. Here are just two examples. A 2019 report on the worsening healthcare system in Venezuela states, 'the country is suf-fering from an 85 per cent shortage of medicine, indicating that the entire healthcare system is on the verge of collapse. Hospitals report a lack of elec-tricity, and more than 13,000 doctors have left Venezuela in the past four years in search of better opportunities' (Rhodes and Valencia, 2019). The charity WaterAid cites several reasons which lead to water scarcity for 844 million people across the world. These include lack of financing and political priority; lack of institutions capable of delivering and maintaining clean water supply; lack of effective taxation and tariffs; discrimination, disaster, and displacement (WaterAid, 2018). When water is scarce, so is proper sani-tation, and menstrual hygiene products are in short supply. Inequality finds its clearest expression in poverty. In 2018, 45 per cent of wealth in Britain was held by 10 per cent of households, while the poorest 10 per cent of house-holds held only 2 per cent of wealth (Inman, 2019). McGarvey makes a clear case for understanding the role of stress in creating unequal economic and social conditions:

> The existence of emotional stress ... is one of the most overlooked aspects of the poverty experience. Yet stress is often the engine room that fuels the lifestyle choices and behaviours that can lead to poor diet, addictions, mental health issues and chronic health conditions. (2017: 61)

Ecocide: Although the concept of ecocide is not yet established in international or domestic law, the central premise is that widespread, long-lasting, and severe destruction of natural habitats, involving eradication of species and exploitation of natural resources, is inextricably linked to the structures that derive from colonialism, consumerism, and capitalism (Bednarek, 2018). That this is sometimes intentional, such as the destruction of rainforests for the production of palm oils, or for intensive raising of beef cattle is shocking; at other times, it is an unintended by-product of other events, such as the use of chemical warfare (Greene, 2019: 7). Different forms of ecocide are outlined by Schwegler, including 'air pollution, water pollution, deforestation, the spoiling of land' (2017: 76). The suffix '-cide' denotes criminal activity, and therefore trauma is implicated. The crime is against the other-than-human world, and because, as we will argue later, we are all interconnected, it is indirectly a crime against humanity too. Arguably, there is no bigger threat to our survival.

To this complex and interdependent list, we might add other dimensions such as migration, genocide, war, and misogyny.

Dropping in

And breathe again. Notice the impact that these topics have had on you. How did you receive the words – viscerally, do you feel numb, shaky, disconnected, or something else? What thoughts and emotions go with your experience? And now for a therapeutic example. As you read it within the SOS framework, see if you can identify any indications of the structures that have been discussed.

Dale

For Dale, being a gamekeeper was more than a job, it shaped his lifestyle, his way of being in the world centred around it. He knew how to read the land and the ecosystem of the creatures and plants that lived on it, and his relationship with them. Dale had always lived and worked on a large estate that had recently come into the ownership of a foreign businessman. The land had previously been handed down through the generations of a wealthy titled family who had fallen on hard times, just as his job had been passed down to him from his father and grandfather in turn. He lived in a tied cottage with his wife and children; their way of life was modest and had a regularity, punctuated by occasional family days out. Dale was rightly proud of his ability to provide for his family. He understood his place in this system, everything was well defined and had its own rhythm. One way or another, his ear was always to the ground, to the farm, to the seasons, to the community in which he was embedded; a local self-organizing ecology. Dale was called on to sort out intrusions to the social order, such as travellers, drug dealers, and fly-tippers, until the police warned him not to get involved.

Deeper changes over time in the social structure, the introduction of agricultural tariffs, modern farming methods, and the regulation of foxhunting had a devastating impact on Dale. He mourned the changing rhythms of his existence, alongside the loss of hedgerows as habitats for the native creatures of his environment, and the increasing monoculture of the crops. These rhythms had all provided a resource and satisfaction through his knowledge of them; they were among the absolutisms that had given meaning and context. Dale and his family found it increasingly difficult to sustain their lifestyle in uncertain times. And now, an estate manager, a graduate in agricultural economics, had been brought in, promoting the overstocking of game birds for the owner's hunting parties. The natural order of things had been subsumed by an economic and consumerist paradigm.

One day while out in the fields, Dale heard a crash and a scream and ran to find his oldest son Bobby, aged 12, had overturned his quad bike on a rut in the ground and was lying dazed on the ground. Thankfully, Bobby was released from hospital the same day, but the incident was a tipping point for Dale. He described himself as increasingly wound up, angry for no apparent reason, and less tolerant of the children's noise. He could not sleep as the sound of Bobby's scream continued to haunt him, and he was spending longer in the pub in the evenings, which he could ill afford. All this gave rise to such distress that for the first time in his life, Dale was unable to work, signed off with 'PTSD' by his doctor.

Discussion

Dale's story offers up a window into the interplay of situational structures. Much of the meaning Dale made of his life situated him in terms of class, education, power, and privilege. These messages had been passed to him on an implicit level, and become encoded in the fibres of his being. He learnt how to move in the land and to navigate social spaces according to a set of unwritten rules.

Culturally conditioned messages come to us in diverse ways. I recall as a child watching Punch and Judy shows at the local fair. This traditional and very English form of puppet show depicts Mr Punch creating havoc with all the gusto of the Trickster. He establishes authority by use of violence, humiliation, and

Figure 2.3 Situational structures

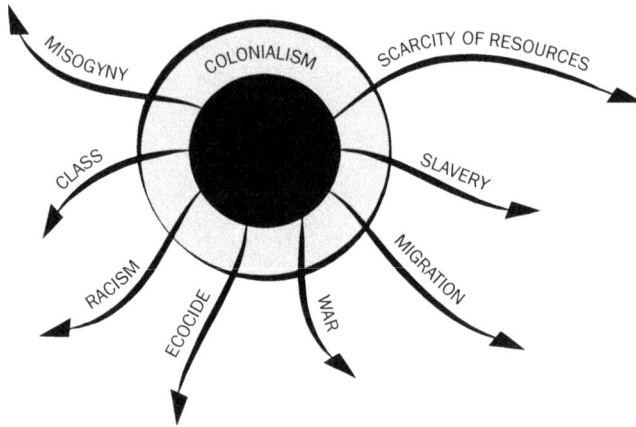

bullying, subjugating his wife and baby, and disregarding the rule of law – and the young audience are 'required' to laugh. This was but one of many ways I learnt about relations between men and women, power and oppression. I remember well the sense of contradiction as I watched, the anxiety and fear that I masked with laughter, because I was witnessing what I already knew from my own life. The political messages were about how I needed to be in the world.

It really is not a big step to consider these intersecting social conditions under the banner of ground traumas. Figure 2.3 attempts to capture the relationships between these situational structures. The breadth, depth, and historical reach of these events is breath-taking and shocking, with profound implications on every level. Even 'what can appear to be an acute natural disaster may in fact have arisen from chronic conditions imposed by men [sic] in their attempts to exert power over and to exploit the natural environment and/or human beings as a resource commodity' (Atkinson, [2002] 2018: 52). Above all, Woodbury posits a paradigm shift in thinking about the current climate emergency. His argument is that climate crisis is not so much a past cultural trauma but a threat to a shared common future (Woodbury, 2019: 4), triggering other contemporary and historical traumas. Thus he defines climate crisis as a completely new order of trauma – a 'superordinate' trauma (2019: 3). Climate trauma is a concept that frames all the foregoing structures, and many of the processes outlined below. We will return to this later in the book.

This supports the proposition that trauma not is only an event or personal experience but a system of enmeshed processes with universal implications; it is 'part of a process-in-system … [since] trauma entails some conception of system' (Smelser, 2004a: 35). A contemporary perspective is of eco-systemic trauma. 'The character of the traumatic response must also be found in the context – psychological or cultural, as the case may be – into which it comes to be embedded' (Smelser, 2004b: 270).

The bedrock of trauma: Situational processes

Historically, in the trauma literature the different classes of events and experiences were initially considered to be discrete and separate. However, by the advent of DSM-III in 1980, 'all the different syndromes – the "rape trauma syndrome"; the "battered woman syndrome"; the "Vietnam veterans syndrome"; the "abused child syndrome" were subsumed under this new diagnosis [of PTSD]' (van der Kolk et al., [1996] 2007: 61). We can apply this same principle of overlapping phenomena to the situational factors above, permitting focus on the processes that they have in common.

Symptomatic of trauma are a number of processes, outlined below, that form a common thread between different traumas; the problem lies in the effect – usually enduring – rather than the event. 'Another phenomenon often accompanying the work of recovery is the mirroring of inner and outer worlds' (Glendinning, 1994: 150). We can look at each of these processes through the lens of trauma, lending weight to the conclusion that they are each trauma responses in their own right. To ground this discussion in trauma theory, we might hold in mind Taussig's view of 'our reality as a chronic state of emergency, as a Nervous System' (2004: 270). There are overlaps between the concepts, but I attempt here to distinguish between them.

These processes include:

Survival: The signal SOS is based on the need to survive in times of danger. Our organism is primed to orient towards survival as a response to trauma (Taylor, 2014: 28–29). However, our threat warning systems cannot distinguish between degrees of threat. Indeed, the same response is triggered when the sense of self is under attack as when the physical organism is threatened. Shame is one particular threat of annihilation of the self, against which we defend ourselves rapidly. Individuals and societies are primarily organized around the need for survival; we protect our borders, become defensive in different ways. 'Only when survival is secured can they proceed to the satisfaction of other imperative human needs' (Fromm, [1956] 2002: 78). Our ability to survive is contingent on the connections we make and sustain. But sometimes that focus becomes excessive, when self-defence, violence, and greed lead people to create their own crisis. As a species, survival has depended on the coherence of our relationships (Ullman and Demaris, 2020: 203). It is helpful to be reminded that survival is a great human endeavour: 'Trauma is both the product of an experience of inhumanity and the proof of the humanity of those who have endured it' (Fassin and Rechtman, 2007: 20).

Safety: The sense of threat experienced by traumatized individuals is usually disproportionate to objective and external sources of danger. When we refer to establishing safety in trauma therapy, we are more interested in the *inner sense* of safety, the regulation that can occur within the window of tolerance. This sense of inner safety is critical for allowing us to grow, fully in relationship with ourselves, others, and the world around us, consistent with the social engagement system proposed by the Polyvagal theory, which challenges how we understand safety:

> By moving the defining features of 'safety' from a structural model of the environment with fences and surveillance monitoring to a visceral sensitivity model evaluating shifts in the neural regulation of autonomic state, the theory highlights our societal values regarding how people are treated. (Porges, 2017: 44–45)

Disconnection: In the face of overwhelming fear, shock, and shame, we simply shut down. Numbing physically and psychically is a protective response to inescapable threat, producing freeze and collapse states (Porges, 2017). As before, we can draw the link between personal disconnection and disconnection within and from the wider field: 'alienation from our vital, sentient bodies and alienation from the rest of nature are interrelated' (Adams, 2020: 81). Ataria explains, 'When the natural body is rejected, the world itself is rejected as well, and that is because we perceive the world through our body' (2017: 90).

I take this to include disconnection from our fellow human beings, creating 'a dominant *culture of isolation* that spreads dehumanizing stories of separation' (Ullman and Demaris, 2020: 199, original emphasis). We can look at dissociation as evidence of oppression in one form or another. Extreme disconnection can be seen as ecological, affecting the multiplicity of current and potential future relationships available to us. Disconnection can be generalized, according to Shaw, who states that 'mass dissociation is possible in any group, at any time, anywhere' (2014: 55).

Power: In most societies, gender is a primary mechanism of power. The need for personal, group, or national survival can come at the expense of others who are seen as 'outside' of the group or system that is, or risks being, threatened. One way of understanding power is that unbearable and uncontainable pain is displaced from one person, group, or bloodline to another. An individual or marginalized group is implicitly called upon to bear the suffering that others cannot. In the fashion of the Trickster, there is an inversion here of what we might consider to be strength and vulnerability, of which we will say more later. Oppression, domination, exploitation, and coercion are inappropriate forms of managing conditions which take us to the limits of tolerance. The subjugation of a person or a group impacts psyche, body, mind, and spirit. Power and fear go together, aligned via the fight response. A sense of loss of control is a psychologically demanding correlate of traumatic circumstances, which may be countered by means of trying to regain control. Social and institutional power determine access to resources, each level of power an aggregate of the layers that went before. Some distinctions need to be made. Power and authority are not the same; it is an over-extension of benign or appropriate authority that creates a power imbalance. 'Power over' and 'power with' are separate concepts that we will return to in Chapter 7; personal agency is power in the service of Self, Other, and Situation; proportional power is therefore relational.

> Man [*sic*] can try to unite himself with the world by having *power* over it, making others a part of himself, and thus transcending his individual existence by domination. The common element in both submission and domination is the symbiotic nature of relatedness. (Fromm, [1956] 2002: 28, original emphasis)

Therefore, an excess of power in any component of the SOS model is problematic, structured according to context. Writing with reference to child sexual abuse, Pilgrim observes that: 'Where there is … a structured power imbalance, then personal exploitation is ever present, as both a prospect and an actual outcome'(2018: 136–137). Misuse of power is not necessarily intentional, but the unforeseen consequence of an act or omission. Power is easier to see when it's used against you than when you hold it and use it against others, and is most pernicious when denied. The case for increasing our sensitivity to how we hold power is clear:

> Power achieved, at least for the well-intending, is power forgotten, power which has receded to ground, power which has become invisible as an organizing context of perception … If you want to know where the power is, or, more importantly, where it isn't, don't ask those who have it. Ask those who don't. (McConville, 2005: 178)

Power, however, tends not to bring peace to those who wield it; built on fear and a deep insecurity, it is never satisfied.

Privilege: Our privilege is often invisible, unnoticed until something contrasting shows up in our awareness. We might see it as the absence of struggle or hardship. The things we take for granted about the way our personal world is organized are markers of our privilege. Unearned privilege is structured into the organization of a culture or society. If you don't fit into an oppressed group, you will be benefiting from it. Conversely, as with power, if you are not in a privileged position, you will know about it. Some privileges are immutable and greater than the sum of lesser ones. For example, white privilege overshadows any privilege held by people of colour or black people (e.g. DiAngelo, 2018; Eddo-Lodge, 2018). Supremacy is a survival strategy, a manifestation of basic efforts to secure primary needs, thus linking it to trauma processes. Dominance and control are an unsustainable attempt to obtain constancy of security for one's group. Privilege and entitlement go hand in hand, likely arising from trauma:

> As an outgrowth of the traumatic experience, the origins of narcissism are not difficult to locate. The satisfaction of one's needs for security, integrity, and communion is truncated, leaving the individual in such a needy state that she can survive only by 'Looking out for Number One'. (Glendinning, 1994: 94)

dehumanizing

Such an individual 'can experience himself as cohesive and alive only at the expense of devitalizing his objects' (Shaw, 2014: 35). *Privileged people are traumatized and then replicate it.* Furthermore, there are costs to holding privilege. True safety is illusory, simply *because* of the disconnection from collective humanity, and *because* unstable identity is founded on dominance. Growth and interdependence are not options. Driven by an equally constant threat of insecurity, the dynamics of social privilege are self-reinforcing. However, it creates a chronic over-stimulation of the autonomic nervous system, which never settles and becomes rigidly defensive. Equally, the window of tolerance model can give context to the experience of oppression, whereby resources are reduced and the capacity to bear is stretched. Both privilege and oppression are thus brittle conditions. Insecurity perpetuates one side of the dynamic, while fear, anger, and mistrust perpetuate the other.

Splitting: It is from the fundamental context of wholeness that we split; compartmentalization or fragmentation occur in response to significant stress (Totton, 2011: 126). The Gestalt concept of polarization, which can be understood as a continuum linking opposites, comes under the umbrella of splitting, but is not quite the same thing. Both are common responses to trauma. Splitting as a less conscious process is an effective way of managing overwhelm, whereby our attention rests on some aspects of experience while others go 'underground'. It is thus harder to bring to awareness. For this purpose, it is hardwired at an implicit, physiological embodied level, but it is also reinforced cognitively primarily through a Western mindset. This can be traced to Descartes' famous dictum, 'I think therefore I am'. A dualistic Cartesian worldview powerfully prevails, perhaps because it is 'not so much as a scientific theory but … an idea – one might even say an ideology – about what aspects of human experience are scientifically tractable' (Bullmore, 2018: 48).

We emphasize thinking at the expense of feelings, body, relationships, and connections, which are all mediated in sub-cortical regions of the brain, beneath the level of the thinking brain. Always 'other'. Words matter: 'they' and 'them' are the language of splits in the fabric of consciousness. Binary processes of alienation and identification help maintain the status quo (Barker and Iantaffi, 2019: 71). We ask ourselves, 'Who is like me or not like me'? (2019: 100). Because dualism has become the dominant cultural paradigm, splitting is encouraged and rewarded: 'Dissociation and numbing are integral parts of late-modern cultures of denial' (Cohen, 2001: 93). We become blind to the costs of this tear from wholeness and interconnection. According to Bednarek, 'The split has become "normal" and therefore does not feature in our therapeutic theories or assessments. The idea that we may share a collective trauma is mainly unexplored' (2018: 11). But by dualist definition there is another side to the 'Cartesian vision of a human body machine', the human condition, 'embarrassingly different to modern scientific and medical minds' (Bullmore, 2018: 48).

Dehumanization: It is impossible to exert power over someone without diminishing their humanity; indeed, we can say that trauma operates beneath the level of human dignity. And yet, as demonstrated by the infamous Milgram (1963) and Zimbardo (see Haney et al., 1973) experiments, the route to treating others inhumanely is paved with incremental steps (see, for example, Carroll and Shaw, 2013; Cohen, 2001; Gretton, 2019; Haidt, 2012; Recuber, 2016). These two psychological experiments created contexts in which ordinary people found it acceptable to administer pain to others; in the case of Milgram, 65 per cent of subjects administered the maximum 450 volts (Carroll and Shaw, 2013: 480). I have wondered often whether in a situation of duress my 'obedient' self would put me in that 65 per cent, or whether the humane part of me would prevail. Milgram clearly created such a conflict in his subjects (Recuber, 2016: 47), and it humbles me to admit that my potential for violence is an aspect of my humanity. In order to cause harm to someone, or some group, whether intentionally or indirectly or not, it is necessary to dis-identify with them, to make them 'other'. 'When we depersonalise other people, see them as commodities, paint others as threats, we can do all sorts of horrendous things to them' (Carroll and Shaw, 2013: 161). Shaw places this in a psychological context: *(share)*

bad/good – projection of bad

> Traumatizing narcissism seems to have been with us since the dawn of humanity. It is the source of all the ways that humans have objectified, enslaved, and dehumanized other humans. It is the very essence of relational trauma. (2014: 580)

For, 'when narrated identity is unbearable, when the boundary between subject and object is shaken, and when even the limit between inside and outside becomes uncertain, the narrative is what is challenged first' (Krysteva, 1982: 141).

Indifference: If dehumanization finds expression in the aggregate of small steps, the final step leads to indifference. Using numerous examples of atrocities, Gretton provides ample evidence that a paralysing numbness replaces the ability to process overwhelming experiences (2019: 488), through which the horrific becomes 'normalized', even banal. Human beings can no longer be seen as suffering individuals, but as abstract, undifferentiated masses. The sheer scale is stupefying. Joshua Oppenheimer's 2012 documentary 'The Act of Killing' demonstrates this chillingly, depicting Indonesian gangster-turned-death-squad-leader Anwar Congo dancing at the site of mass murders. One wonders at the trajectory in his life, the forces of oppression and power that conspired to create this awful destruction. I choose to end this section with some comments on the effects of power, privilege, and dehumanization on the perpetrators. McConville points out that 'any system of privilege not only oppresses the disenfranchised, but *poisons the spirit and diminishes the humanity of those who are advantaged*' (2005: 177, emphasis added), while Pilgrim considers that power 'limits their critical appraisal of what is happening and why' (2018: 155). Finally, from a relational perspective, Carroll and Shaw offer this from Appiah: "'If my humanity matters, so does yours; if yours doesn't, neither does mine. We stand or fall together'" (2013: 101). This notion of interconnectedness is one we will revisit later.

The role of denial

In true Trickster fashion, we need to render visible what is obscured through the operation of denial, appearing in many guises (see Carroll and Shaw, 2013; Cohen, 2002; Pilgrim, 2018). As Herman puts it: 'Denial, repression, and dissociation operate on a social as well as an individual level. The study of psychological trauma has an "underground" history' (1992: 2). Trauma is a controversial subject, sometimes anathema. The study of trauma leads us:

> … into realms of the unthinkable and founder[s] on fundamental questions of belief … [bringing us] face to face both with human vulnerability in the natural world and with the capacity for evil in human nature. (1992: 7)

Internal conflicts created by polarization and splitting are reflected in social groups and between nations, 'some oriented toward playing down the trauma and others in keeping it alive' (Smelser, 2004a: 54). Containing elements of dissociation, denial serves to alter reality to suit individual or group needs, and effectively rewrites history. In collective denial, we observe cultural versions of psychological processes.

Cohen provides some introductory ways of thinking about denial. First, he tells us that 'denial may be *active* (repudiation, rejection, negation, disavowal) rather than *passive* (the mere withdrawal of attention, deflecting the gaze)' (2001: 32, original emphasis). The passive form can be sub-divided further, by either

> … *turning a blind eye* – keeping facts conveniently out of sight, allowing something to be both known and not known … [or] *retreat from truth to omnipotence*, [which] is more insidious and more resistant to therapy or insight. (2001: 34, original emphasis)

Outright denial is a principal form of denial. Brutality, racism, and the denial of civil liberties are meant, in the main, to be hidden from public view (Eddo-Lodge, 2018: 4). Further manifestations of denial, according to Carroll and Shaw (2013: 59), include:

- Denial of facts
- Denial of the implications
- Denial of feelings
- Denial of need to change
- Discredit
- Renaming, in which bullying becomes 'challenging someone' or torture becomes 'fact-finding'

[handwritten margin note: projection is contained in here, eg denial if my part is ?]

- Justification
- Denial of responsibility
- Denial of injury

Miriam Part 1: Roots

I will take this opportunity to bring some of these ideas together in the first part of my own story. Here, some of the terms described in this chapter, including situational structures of class and processes of privilege, splitting, and denial are evident.

I was born in the mid-1950s, the fifth child of a widely spread out family with older parents. There was never a time when we all lived under the same roof. Our home was in an affluent part of London, albeit less well off than many of our neighbours. There were contradictions: we had domestic help when my mother couldn't cope, plentiful food, books, and a grand piano. But my clothes were always handed down, we had no television or car until I was about 10, and holidays were mostly spent at my grandfather's house. Money was always problematic for my mother, who resented people who were more comfortably off than we were. The area we lived in was predominately Jewish, though we were raised Catholic by my mother. While I witnessed tolerance in the community – both ways – I hovered at the margins socially. Education and culture were prized by my open-minded parents, but were not deeply rooted in the family history. My architect father's family had prospered in the early 1900s, establishing a successful manufacturing business on the south coast. Capital and status were relatively recent. A watchful child, I tuned into the subtle ways the family put itself 'on show', trying to accommodate where we didn't sit naturally.

Social class is something that I have long struggled with. I was privately educated, but unlike my siblings, only until the age of 12. Because I was failing to learn, private schools rejected me, and I then had the good fortune to be sent to a state school. Here, for the first time, I found myself trying to find my place among peers from a mix of social classes, children of artists and intellectuals from 'my' side of town, alongside those who were truly and shockingly poor, including black immigrants from the Caribbean. I think this was my first concrete memory of bridging two realities – out of my awareness for years – for I was not as utterly adrift in this glorious mix as you might suppose. My school reflected two sides of my personal world, the one that was on show and another that was to all intents and purposes dissociated. My mother had, through a mixture of serendipity and talent, been given a ticket to flee her impoverished, working-class, and undoubtedly abusive upbringing in South Wales. This led later to her crossing paths with my father. To have been working class was so desperately imbued with shame for my mother she never talked about it. It was only through my school experiences that I could begin to claim my working-class heritage; proud, comfortable, and still puzzled by how I embody it. Academically my schooling was a disaster, but provided an invaluable lesson in belonging and social justice.

Therapeutic reflections

The dimensions we have been looking at are not usual therapeutic considerations, even though psychotherapy has always been interested in the marginalized and underprivileged. And, as Kubesch says,

> We psychotherapists must develop sensitivity to seeing disorders not only as the manifestation of an individual's strategy to survive but also as a manifestation emerging from a historical, cultural and political context. (2005: 69)

Some of these dimensions will take us well out of our comfort zone. To the extent that we feel discomfort, we carry countless layers of unprocessed cultural and intergenerational traumas. We cannot separate the elements of the SOS model, for figures arise always in relation to ground or context (see Appendix A for an explanation of this concept). 'When ground is silent, invisible, figure ends up bearing the weight of ground' (McConville, 2005: 175). Traumatizing systems are self-perpetuating, co-dependent, and interconnected. Trauma fragments appear out of context and deny us the capacity to see and feel the contents of the ground, such that 'an understanding of trauma begins with rediscovering history' (Herman, 1992: 2). How much we can see and admit depends on our cultural backdrop. Trauma theory teaches us that we have to attend to ground conditions in order to heal trauma (Taylor, 2014: 44), and to consider cultural dimensions in this way is simply a matter of scale. Trauma can't be processed without context. We have also seen that psychology, culture, and ethics bump up against one another repeatedly; we will return to these themes later. There is no neutral – we live in a culture that conditions us not to see toxicity and normalizes the absurd. As Carlson and Kolodny remind us 'Whatever is out of bounds … is potentially controlling the conversation. If it's not on the table … it's under the table' (2009: 159).

The relational implications of this are profound. The lone individual is much more open to further threat (Levine, 1997: 88–89), evidence of a traumatic loss of intersubjectivity. When there is no context, meaning cannot be made; when there is no shared language of trauma, it cannot be conceptualized; we cannot reflect on the processes and integrate them. Loss of resources reduces our resilience and our ability to test the world (Scaer, 2014: 5); we become 'experientially groundless' (Kepner, 1995: 94). And to reclaim context makes something more ordinarily accessible and human out of trauma, rather than a pathology – none of which is to deny the seriousness of the impact of traumatic events.

I have found this chapter unusually challenging to write; it has taken many months. The work began in preparation for a keynote presentation at a trauma conference in Sydney in 2019; despite extensive research, I barely scratched the surface. Glimpsing the impact of colonialism on the indigenous peoples of Australia, I noted the irony that I was standing in the shadows of the invading power, invited to offer something, as if I knew anything. I began my talk with a shaky voice as I said: 'I am a colonialist and a racist, not by choice, but by virtue of the way I have been socialized, by the history I have been taught, and by what has been edited from it'. There was a sharp intake of breath from my largely white Australian audience. We just don't name such things. When it came to questions at the end, a therapist of Aboriginal heritage stood and publicly said what a relief it was to hear me admit and honour that. We had both dropped our defences and met in our gaze across the room, tears streaming down my face. Raw, naked, honest – a moment of healing across a divide that changed something profound in me. This is personally a deeply disturbing and uncomfortable journey to be on, as I struggle with what has needed to be articulated and recontextualized. I understand that not everyone wants to do this work, but I have learned that if I don't enter this territory, I maintain the splits that structure trauma in the fibres of society and become part of the problem. I do this painfully, slowly, humbly, gladly.

3 Something in the air

Systemic trauma

In the previous chapter, we considered a number of situational factors and situational processes relating to trauma as though they are separate phenomena. Here we begin to weave them together as interconnected and co-dependent systems. Central to the thinking is the premise that we can see the same patterns and processes replicated on different scales. The outer world is reflected in the inner and vice versa, as we will see time and again in this volume. It is tempting to think of the ripple effect of uncontainable trauma, but larger systems become traumatized in their own right through lack of processing. I think therefore in terms of fractals. Fractal patterns appear in many natural organisms, in which any one part is *identical* to any other part, large or small, regardless of scale, to infinity (Jin et al., 2017). Fractals can be seen as complex, dynamic, non-linear systems. It is relevant also to consider the self-organizing tendency of such systems, which are more or less adaptive according to situational factors (Fryer and Ruis, 2004). The application of trauma theory seems to suggest that overly focusing on one part of a system may blind us to how that same pattern or process is also situated elsewhere in the system.

A vital part of our healing work is to become aware of how patterns in our own lives connect. The notion of intersectionality (Crenshaw, 2017) helps to identify the cultural signifiers that unconsciously shape our place in the world. Intersectionality theory offers a nuanced perspective on the dynamics of power, privilege, and oppression. For example, I can describe myself as: white, British, middle-class, having lived my life as a straight woman. I am a mother and a grandmother, as well as a latecomer in my career. I am currently self-employed and financially secure, a homeowner, and was educated via an unconventional route. I am also healthy and able-bodied, of retirement age.

Dropping in

Take a moment to notice this picture I paint of myself. What does each of these signifiers tell you about relationships? How might I navigate the world? What privileges do you begin to see in me, or conversely do you identify anything I might struggle with? What is either 'normative' or 'different' from how you see yourself? Notice any biases or assumptions you might make (Johnson, 2018a: 105). Notice, too, that a number of these signifiers have to do with how I live in my body. This illustrates how each one of us begins to position ourselves according to our life circumstances. And now, take some time to make a list of signifiers that would apply to you. Pay attention to how you feel in your body as you compile your list and then look at it. Consider the ways in which each of these connects you to the world, where any privileges may exist, any things that you have been able to take for granted in living the life you live.

Our intersectional signifiers speak neither to privilege nor oppression, but to how *both* may operate in different areas of an individual's life in tandem. For example, identifying as a woman will in some situations disadvantage me, but because I am also white, I have privilege over black people. The relevance of this to how our multiply different intersections 'meet' is complex, and will be discussed later.

Trauma-organized systems

A familiar model that sheds light on relational dynamics in trauma is Karpman's drama triangle (1968), in which the characteristics of victim, rescuer, and perpetrator can be seen to interact in enduring patterns, the 'players' shifting quickly between roles which are more or less familiar to each. This provides a useful tool to aid us in stepping back and noticing what is going on in a therapeutic relationship. The drama triangle concept can also be applied on a far bigger scale, for example where there may be unprovoked violence, war, or an emergency response to a natural disaster.

In order to understand what enables and maintains these dynamics, we can turn to Bentovim's notion of trauma-organized systems. An important premise of this concept is that the perpetrator who abuses a child (in the instance the author describes) is also *'caught up in a system that allows the maintenance of abusive action in secrecy'* (2002: 22, emphasis added). Others participate through similarly being caught in a system of secrecy, denial, and blame, thereby perpetuating and maintaining the abuse. Unpacking how this works, Bentovim proposes that features of a trauma-organized system include:

1. The key actors are the victimiser and traumatiser and the victim who is traumatised.
2. There is an absence of a protector, or potential protectors are neutralised.
3. The victimiser is overwhelmed by impulses ... of a physically, sexually or emotionally abusive nature that emerge from his or her own experiences.

(2002: 22–23)

This then leads to a series of psychological binds involving denial, secrecy, minimization, and blaming of the victim, in which their attempts to escape the abuse only serve to justify an increase of violence. Alterations in thinking and perception of reality become distorted, to the extent that the situation cannot be processed. Note also, from the above list, the importance of the perpetrator's own history, indicating a cyclical repetition.

From this analysis, a number of points stand out. First, the issue of *regulation of impulses* – the window of tolerance – is a key driver. This view is confirmed by Bloom and Farragher (2013), who describe hyper- and hypo-aroused organizations. The window of tolerance model (Figure 3.1), conceived originally as an individual phenomenology, can be applied on larger scales and is helpful in understanding the behaviours of organizations. One can imagine the fear engendered by a powerful and out-of-control perpetrator, and the adaptations that are needed to re-establish regulation. Each participant in the system co-creates the situation, likely out of fear and subsequent dissociation. The roles may become part of how each person sees him or herself, assimilated into their identity, which may hold a degree of safety through familiarity. The psychological and cognitive twist in which the victim is made responsible for the abuse is very typical of the people who present for therapy. Defying rationality but yet keenly felt, self-blame as a result of victim-blaming is a significant therapeutic obstacle. The possibility of challenge to the system by calling people to account feels unsafe; it is neutralized along with protection – a resource in short supply. It is not uncommon for whistle-blowers to be threatened with legal action for defamation, or with dismissal, or be required to sign non-disclosure agreements. Note also that professionals may become caught in these systems.

Figure 3.1 The window of tolerance model

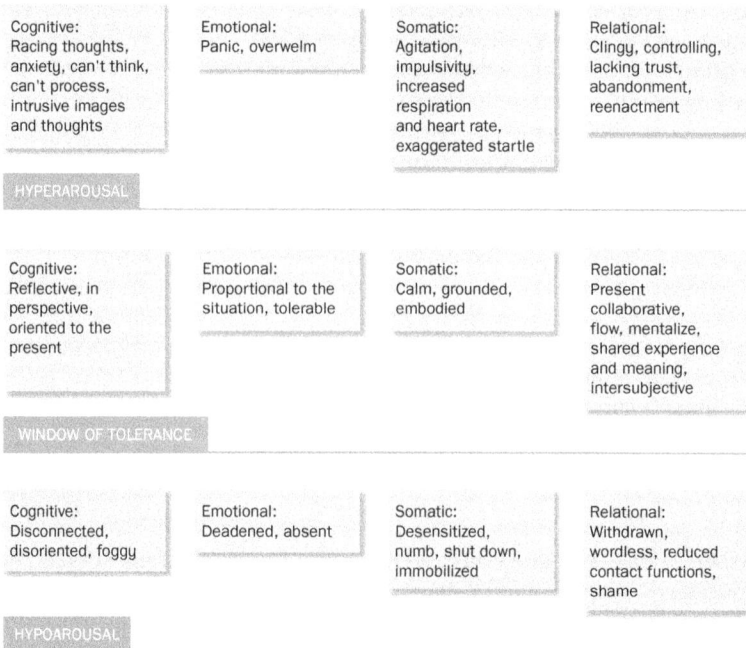

Cognitive: Racing thoughts, anxiety, can't think, can't process, intrusive images and thoughts	Emotional: Panic, overwelm	Somatic: Agitation, impulsivity, increased respiration and heart rate, exaggerated startle	Relational: Clingy, controlling, lacking trust, abandonment, reenactment
HYPERAROUSAL			
Cognitive: Reflective, in perspective, oriented to the present	Emotional: Proportional to the situation, tolerable	Somatic: Calm, grounded, embodied	Relational: Present collaborative, flow, mentalize, shared experience and meaning, intersubjective
WINDOW OF TOLERANCE			
Cognitive: Disconnected, disoriented, foggy	Emotional: Deadened, absent	Somatic: Desensitized, numb, shut down, immobilized	Relational: Withdrawn, wordless, reduced contact functions, shame
HYPOAROUSAL			

With multiple frameworks to shape the following examples, we now examine how elements of ground trauma became evident in four people's stories.

Duncan

After Duncan's marriage ended, his 14-year-old son, Corey, was bullied at school. Greatly distressed by this, Duncan considered it his fault and came to address this in therapy. Duncan was 38, an area manager for a sports retail chain. His childhood had been unsettled; his opinionated and controlling father was a staff sergeant in the army, his mother quiet and distant. The family had moved several times before his parents separated when Duncan was nine. He had struggled all his life to gain approval from either parent. Seared into Duncan's memory were his father's pronouncements about gay men in the forces; seared because throughout his teens Duncan had questioned his own sexuality. He felt a great deal of guilt and shame about his interest in men, to the extent that he squashed down his desire and entered a dull marriage with Jenny. The only thing that brought Duncan to life was his passion for cycling. On the road, the burst of energy that pushed him to greater limits felt soothing, focusing his mind, and numbing his body. This was a welcome distraction from bouts of depression and helped him feel safer. Duncan was an active member of his cycling club, which made him a 'proper man', and he and Jenny were friendly with other couples who were members of the club.

But Duncan never resolved his yearning for intimacy with a man. One evening, fuelled by alcohol, he went to a gay bar in a town where he was working. He described how it had felt, almost as though his decision to enter would mean death. He wanted more than anything not to want this. But he wasn't prepared for how unsafe he would feel, under the scrutiny of strangers who wanted his body. He knew very little of the gay scene and was out of his depth, and it took time before he had a sense of coming home and identifying with anyone there. Having resolved not to give up on himself so quickly, he made it a pattern to stay late after working away, where he would visit gay bars. Duncan had a couple of rough and swift sexual encounters; he felt himself to be abnormal for having been disgusted by these experiences that he so desired. Feeling increasingly desperate and confused, Duncan was drinking more often. Jenny noticed the changes in his behaviour and asked if he was seeing someone else. Duncan broke down and the truth came out. Jenny's sense of betrayal signalled the end of their marriage.

Duncan volunteered to leave the home, and had an honest conversation with Corey about the reason he was leaving. Corey accepted his father's homosexuality, while finding the loss of the father he knew and the breakup of the home difficult.

Coming out to his mother would have been a non-event had it not cut him to the quick; she sighed saying, 'I suppose that means you're bi-sexual' and turned to wondering about her lottery numbers. As ever, Duncan felt unseen by her, and that this most defining moment in his life was irrelevant. Duncan wanted to tell his father himself, which felt again like risking his life. Having been drinking for three days, he went to see him. On hearing the news, his father left the room and was sick. He then subjected Duncan to a tirade of homophobic abuse, telling him he never wanted to see him or his 'gay-boy' son again.

Duncan knew that one of the managers he worked with was gay and confided in him. It was not long, however, that he was outed by this manager in an area meeting, which outraged him, and yet he felt he deserved it and said nothing. What followed confused and pained Duncan. One colleague 'congratulated' him, another said 'I'm still fine with you, I know someone who is gay', and he became aware of others looking at him differently. He noticed subtle changes in their behaviour towards him, and it wasn't long before homophobic banter and slurs seeped into their conversations: 'That's so gay'. The boundaries of the area under his watch were redrawn, bringing a loss of responsibility and a smaller annual bonus. Paralysed with fear about coming out to his friends in the cycling club, Duncan said nothing. When a social event was mooted, he excused himself from it, and later pretended that Jenny had been ill. For some months he lived a double life in respect of this group. The pretence didn't hold for long, because the partner of a club member ran into Jenny in town, and then asked Duncan if it was true. He came out to a few individuals, but the news spread soon enough. Duncan initially felt a bit more relaxed around club members, but those who had been closest to him and Jenny spurned him. He noticed that some members became more competitive with him, and he felt the need to train harder in order to prove himself.

But it was the homophobic taunts experienced by Corey at school for having a gay father that took Duncan to the edge of despair. In staying close to his son, Duncan sought to be the father he had never had. A guiding principle for Duncan was to be a good role model for Corey. Now he felt he had failed as a man, a husband, a friend, a manager – and as a father. He worried now that he had ruined Corey's life and was afraid that he too would come out as gay. Around this time, Duncan met someone he was attracted to, and he did all he could to hide this from Corey. For some weeks Corey refused to talk to him and Duncan took this as the harshest rejection of all. Close to breaking point, Duncan sought therapeutic help.

Dropping in

How did you first learn about gender and sexual relationship diversity? When did you first 'know' your sexual orientation? To what extent do you understand your sexual preferences as either binary or on a continuum?

As you read Duncan's story, what judgements do you make about him or others? How does intersectionality theory help you understand Duncan's situation, in terms of privilege and oppression? What situational processes (Chapter 2) can you identify in his story? If you were to see him in therapy, what assumptions would you make about the therapeutic tasks, and how might these be coloured by how you identify your own sexual orientation?

I invite you also to step aside from this book and do a bit of research. Look up the Riddle Assessment Scale on the internet (www.involved.unl.edu/lgbtqa/safe_spaces/docs/riddleAssessmentScale.pdf), and score your answers. Does anything surprise you or change your responses to the questions above?

Discussion

One of the striking features of Duncan's story is his enduring inner conflict about his sexual orientation. Reinforced by a heteronormative upbringing, such a conflict commonly translates into internalized homophobia. While many gay and lesbian people would recognize the experience of internalized homophobia, the concept can be criticized because it places the focus on the individual's 'pathology' rather than on institutional oppression (Williamson, 2000: 104). A more sympathetic framework is to understand internalized homophobia as a form of minority stress. For example, invisible disabling conditions may be hidden from plain sight because of fear of stigmatization, of being seen as 'different', and because of the fear and prejudice on the part of those in the 'perpetrator' role. Duncan had lived his life within majority cultural 'norms' and the transition towards a minority was fraught with conflicts.

> Homophobia is not something that can be addressed by attending only to the intra-psychic or social field relationships. It is an event at the contact boundary of the self/world shared phenomenal field. (Desmond, 2016: 50)

The contact boundary between elements of the SOS model had shifted. 'The minority person is likely to be subject to such conflicts because the dominant culture, social structures, and norms do not typically reflect those of the minority group' (Meyer, 2003: 676).

People identifying as gay or lesbian stand on ground that is woven through with opposition. From discrimination to extermination in Nazi death camps, to imprisonment for sodomy and chemical castration, there is a long history of brutal anti-gay prejudice. While there is research showing the links between minority stress and poor mental health, including self-harm, eating 'disorders', and substance abuse (Williamson, 2000: 103), there continues to be considerable discrimination within those mental health services intended to help. According to the gay rights campaign Stonewall, 'lesbian, gay, bi and trans people continue to experience these harmful [conversion] therapies' (undated), which are a legacy of homosexuality's inclusion as a 'mental disorder' in early editions of the DSM, only removed in 1973 (Davies, 2013: 14). As Duncan's story shows, discrimination does not have to be very blatant to take its toll; it is easy to overlook 'the role of mundane, everyday discrimination, such as unfair treatment … subtle discrimination is more prevalent than overt forms of mistreatment for minority identities' (Woodford et al., 2015: 143). Contemporary societal 'norms' will extend this treatment to those identifying 'differently' such as trans, non-binary, or bi-sexual.

Far from wishing to paint LGBTQI people as victims, the socially constituted distress of people with minority sexual identities does, however, need to be taken seriously. In a study of prejudice, social stress, and mental health in lesbian, gay, and bisexual populations, Meyer estimated that 'approximately $\frac{1}{5}$ of the women and $\frac{1}{4}$ of the men experienced [overt] victimization (including sexual assault, physical assault, robbery, and property crime) related to their sexual orientation' (2003: 683). A reduced sense of security and increased vulnerability can lead to a range of psychological adaptations such as concealment, heightened vigilance, retroflection of emotion, and self-loathing. From a

lesbian perspective, Hodgson and Skye write about the strain public perceptions and questions make on a relationship:

> We'd tell you about how one silent position intersects with another and how
> exhausting it is filtering out the layers of obstacles, stereotypes, judge-
> ments, prejudices, mockery, tolerance just to access day to day life.
> (2016: 204)

By virtue of existing endlessly, inescapably, in a survival space, such minority
experience falls under the umbrella of trauma.

Luisa

Twenty-four-year-old Luisa came to the UK from her native Portugal during her
master's degree in modern languages. She was pleased to get a job in events
management, in a company that had recently been bought out by an American
counterpart. Luisa was part of a small team led by Phil, who appeared pleas-
ant and supportive, yet she quickly noticed how the other team members
secretly laughed about him and treated him cautiously. One month after she
started the job, the department manager left abruptly and mysteriously. Luisa
and her colleagues quickly realized that this could not be talked about or questioned. The vacancy was unfilled for three months, during which time Phil
appeared more agitated and behaved in confusing ways. First, he became
increasingly attentive and encouraging of Luisa, such as announcing to the
team, 'She's such a great girl, Luisa, isn't she?!', or standing too close and
staring at her. Luisa felt that Phil's compliments were contrived and meaningless. But on the other hand, he was like a closed book in relation to the project
that they were working on, not sharing or replying to emails, and was silent in
response to polite social pleasantries. One of Luisa's responsibilities was to
manage event budgets, and she needed Phil's authorization for expenses. She
was surprised, therefore, when contrary to company policy Phil bought a new
computer for his own use on the expense account – there was no manager to
authorize it. When she asked him about this, Phil smiled disarmingly, saying
that he had earned it by working long hours to bring money into the company,
and maybe it was best not to tell others in case they were jealous. Yet it
seemed that a number of other people were equally uncomfortable with Phil,
citing numerous infringements of company policy. However, despite a lot of
negative office gossip, no one was able to take the problem anywhere as Phil
was highly regarded by senior management. Another team member resigned,
and Luisa found herself with an additional workload, and longer unpaid hours
to manage this. At the same time, Luisa felt trapped in her relationship with
Phil, humiliated by his excessive praise and attention. The company's stated
mission to inspire and empower people through the excellence of their delivery
was not translated into the organizational culture.

In due course, a new department manager, Marga, was appointed, head-
hunted from a rival company. In contrast to Phil, Marga wanted to run a

tight department, but it became clear that she had no experience of managing a department of this size, and her skills and experience did not fit the job description. Noticeably out of her depth and ineffective, Marga interrupted people and vented her frustrations by barking orders to the team, including Phil. Everyone in the office became more tense and Phil grumbled, and was in turn more demanding. At the review of her six-month probationary period with Marga, Luisa was told that her work was very satisfactory, but that Phil had reported that she was not a team player and this would go against her. She needed to make improvements, so her probationary period was extended by three months. When Luisa asked for specific guidance and goals, Marga shrugged and told her not to be so stupid again and just get on with it. During the run-up to Brexit, Phil asked Luisa to check the social media accounts of individuals in companies who were bidding for a contract with them, explaining: 'We need to make sure they are not in the Remain camp, don't we? We are not going to offer contracts to companies with European affiliations. I need you to report back first thing tomorrow'. Palpably upset by this, and cancelling plans to meet her boyfriend, Luisa worked very late that evening. The following day she found a moment to talk to her colleagues about going to HR to complain, but no one was willing to back her in doing so.

Her meeting with the HR manager, Vicky, did not go as she hoped. 'Phil is a very experienced and respected manager, you know. You seem stressed and we need to address that'. Rather than treating Luisa's situation as grounds for a potential grievance, Vicky proposed initiating a new staff well-being programme, with guidance on stress management and lifestyle, and informal monthly team gatherings. 'You'll feel much better when you can learn how to relax'. The logical decision that Luisa faced, to carry on or to press for a formal grievance, brought her to therapy. On an emotional level, though, she was worn down and worried that her capacity to cope was poor and that if she wanted to succeed she needed to work on this.

Dropping in

Is there anything in Luisa's story that is personally familiar to you? If so, how did you contribute to the system, what habitual or new part did you play? What parts did others play in your situation?

I invite you to think about the features of trauma-organized systems and consider how this helps shed light on the dynamics of Luisa's working relationships. What roles does each of the characters play? What situational factors and processes helped shape the situation? Is there a particular point at which you see things deteriorating? In what ways might trauma theory explain what has happened? Can you identify what harm might be done in the wider field of customers, competitors, sub-contractors, and others?

Discussion

Luisa experiences her working environment as unsafe; despite Phil's words, she feels unvalued and stressed. It is a toxic workplace that is at risk of becoming a hostile one (Tastan, 2017: 83). The shadow side of an organization can emerge under certain conditions such as when (Carroll and Shaw, 2013: 309):

- poor performance is not tackled
- conflict is not dealt with
- difficult personalities are not confronted
- rules are not enforced, or are done so unjustly
- we preach what we do not practise
- promotions are not based on merit.

Luisa's story ticks all of these boxes, and more.

Tastan identified two categories of toxic environment: 'behavioural toxics' and 'contextual toxics'. Each of these comprised four variables: toxic behaviours of co-workers, toxic behaviours of managers, toxic social structural factors, and toxic climate (2017: 102). None of the individuals in the organization could be seen to be inherently bad or devious, but there are aspects of the culture that shape their behaviour. With reference to Zimbardo's experiment discussed in the previous chapter, Carroll and Shaw suggest that while he 'was not looking at anything specific' (he had no hypothesis to test), he was 'assessing the extent to which the external features of an institutional setting could override the internal dispositions of the actors in that environment' (2013: 51).

A ground for corruption grows when people are placed in institutional structures that encourage or allow its practice (Tastan, 2017: 87). Characteristics of toxic managers include a fragile or fragmented sense of self, and a preoccupation with their own status (ibid.). We can conclude that they may themselves be traumatized. Groups, teams, and organizations can replicate family dynamics, which leads to activation of unexamined adaptations and re-enactments. This can put managers and leaders into survival mode, leading to the creation of traumatizing cultures for their staff (Vaughan Smith, 2019: 94).

The organization in which Luisa works can be seen as being 'overbound', or hyper-aroused:

> In hyper-aroused *traumatised* organisations, there is generally a palpable sense of speed, rush and high energetic demand ... In organisational/business terms we might expect to observe constant, 'urgent' deadlines, poor time management, almost everything given 'high priority', poor attention, multitasking, excessive task initiation but poor completion, implementation or sustainability. (Denham-Vaughan and Glenholmes, 2019: 225, original emphasis)

Denham-Vaughan and Glenholmes also examine the case of the hypo-aroused organization in which little is achieved (2019: 226). In either case, the operative word is 'traumatized'.

Vaughan Smith explains how teams become traumatized as a consequence of 'events that have a profound impact on all team members and their capacity to continue to do their work collectively. Whatever the cause, those individuals already traumatised by earlier life experience are more likely to be affected than those whose trauma biography is less intense' (2019: 103). She goes on to suggest that, 'One factor alone is unlikely to be re-traumatising. The event responsible for the most trauma survival responses is usually preceded by several other events that disturbed the team's equanimity, attachments, and identity' (2019: 105).

When an organization is configured around unseen trauma, the creation of more crisis will have a familiar feel. Carroll and Shaw (2013: 300) describe how a 'climate like a mist enveloped the organisation and the members breathed in the toxic environments that changed their way of thinking and being'. They also point out that it 'takes more effort to sort out the dysfunctional organisation than to deal with and support the individual who is a casualty of an organisation over time' (2013: 299).

By attention to the 'symptom', in this case Luisa's distress, rather than the cause, the trauma dynamic is reinforced. Luisa is being asked to tolerate increasingly unacceptable conditions and is blamed for her inability or reluctance to do so. We will come back to this point in Chapter 8.

There have been notable examples in which the culture and vested interests of multinational organizations have created enormous suffering. One instance is the Bhopal disaster of 1984, in which an estimated 500,000 people were exposed to toxic fumes and some 16,000 people died as a result. It took five years for the Supreme Court of India to order the company to pay compensation (Gretton, 2019: 340). A second example is the long-standing refusal of tobacco companies to acknowledge the health risks of smoking. Ricard quotes the director of a large tobacco company, who declared in an internal memo, that 'Doubt is our "product", since it's the best way to fight all the facts that are now known to the public', doubt in this instance created by counter-claims of 'research' (2015: 483).

The values an organization espouses are often at odds with its practice: 'Virtually every corporation lists "transparency" at the top of their values, yet of course, unless legally forced to be so, corporations generally want to have their practices kept in the shadows as much as possible' (Gretton, 2019: 164). How pertinent, then, are the words of Cohen:

> At the organized level (perhaps indicating the pervasiveness of lying in public life) more terms are in currency: propaganda, disinformation, whitewash, manipulation, spin, misinformation, fraud, cover-up. (2001: 4)

Once again we are looking at situational processes that can be scaled up from the personal to the collective.

Hugh

Fifty-two-year-old Hugh spent his early years in what was Rhodesia, modern-day Zimbabwe. His father worked for the British Foreign Office negotiating trade deals with large mining companies. Hugh was the youngest of three brothers, and the family enjoyed a secure existence in the suburbs of the capital, Harare. As the country descended towards civil war, the children moved with their mother into the bush, but eventually the situation was so unsafe that the decision was made to send them to school in the UK. Hugh, aged eight, was sent to a rural prep school, while his older brothers went straight into public schools. The boys were under the care of their maternal aunt, who they barely knew, spending half-terms and Easter breaks with her, only returning home to their parents at Christmas and for the summer holidays. Hugh remembered this as a shockingly lonely time, alienated, disconnected from all attachments of family, culture, and place. The only female presence in the school was the matron. So overwhelmed had he been that he forgot, or rather, dissociated, some important details of his time at this school. A painful set of memories only began to surface decades later when the present headteacher contacted Hugh, as part of an investigation into alleged abuse at the school in the 1970s.

In therapy, Hugh began to piece his story together. As a new boy in the school, Hugh often got into trouble for infringing rules he didn't know existed, and socially inept, was laughed at by his peers. By the end of his first month his teddy bear had been damaged and then stolen; big boys don't need sentimental attachments to home or comfort. Hugh also had to run the gauntlet of initiation rites, into a cold shower then sprinting naked across the playing field back to his house to retrieve his clothes that had been snatched away. This was but one of several such humiliations watched sometimes by teachers; he couldn't complain because they were just 'harmless pranks' or 'character building'. Slowly, Hugh noticed his discomfort when talking about his housemaster known as the 'Major': disturbing somatic fragments that caused him to dissociate profoundly in sessions. The Major used to catch Hugh's eye at mealtimes and offer him second helpings before the other boys, or give him extra help with his 'homework'. Most boys were able to go for home leave at weekends, but Hugh and two others were not. Recognizing their 'homesickness' the Major started to invite these three to his flat for 'tea parties' on Saturdays and Sundays. There were 'games' that soon became sexual. This was painful and confusing: Hugh couldn't understand what he had done wrong. He craved the attention and physical touch, but was shocked and disturbed by the violence of what was happening.

Spurred on by his outrage and by the other boys, Hugh turned to his year head, Mr McVeigh, to try to report the abuse. For this, for the telling of 'slander', Hugh was caned. Other teachers treated him punitively afterwards; his failure to complete his maths homework satisfactorily resulted in all boys in the class getting the ruler over their knuckles. He was ostracized by his class mates. Even the school chaplain preached about the special place in hell for boys who lied. For Hugh, there was nowhere to hide except in a soothing bubble of dissociation.

Motivated in part by his innate sense of injustice, an interest in human rights, and in part by his family expectation of following an honourable profession, Hugh was drawn initially to study law. During his time at university, Hugh reported his abuse to the police, where in an interview his sexuality was questioned and a file reluctantly opened; at this time the AIDS epidemic was spreading and the legal status of homosexuality remained controversial. While he waited for his case to proceed, Hugh started having panic attacks. Hearing nothing, and failing to keep up academically, Hugh followed up his report with the police. Initially he was told that the Crown Prosecution Service had probably concluded that there wasn't a case to answer. When Hugh questioned when this had happened, the police told him that the files had been lost so they could go no further. He had a breakdown and dropped out of his degree, much to his father's fury. Single for all his life, Hugh eventually scraped together a living as a freelance graphic designer. His trust in others was low, and he suffered from bouts of suicidal intent. The recent contact from the headmaster made him very fearful of disclosure, despite all reassurances. His sleep was poor and he was troubled by nightmares and weight problems.

Dropping in

Notice, with curiosity rather than judgement, how your body has responded to Hugh's story. Settle your breathing and slowly and mindfully make some movements – stretching, taking some steps with attention to your weight on the floor. As you settle, what thoughts come to mind – any associations that you make, any memories stirring? And what emotions go with this? To what extent do you think Hugh's experiences were a sign of the times? In the different layers of Hugh's story, what is the relationship between privilege and oppression? Can you identify any ways in which Hugh's school is itself a trauma-organized system?

Discussion

Despite the presumed prevalence of physical and sexual institutional abuse, there is surprisingly little written about the subject. This may in itself tell us something about the taboos surrounding the notion that those acting *in loco parentis*, both state and private institutions, do at times cause great harm. As Duffell suggests, 'This is partly because British society, with its inbuilt conservatism, is extraordinarily good at self-policing' (2014: 10). Schaverien adds: 'Sending young children to boarding school may be considered a particularly British form of child abuse and social control' (2004: 683). She does, however, qualify this by holding in mind that for some it is a positive experience, even a respite from an intolerable home life (2004: 685). The experience of boarding school may hide in the shadows of other presenting issues in therapy; loss of secure attachment may show up first as long-term relationship difficulties (2004: 686). The privilege of boarding school creates a considerable double bind for those who have been harmed: 'even though you are unhappy you really appreciate how good it is for you' (2004: 686).

Pilgrim is one writer who tackles the subject of institutional abuse head-on, perhaps controversially. In making a clear case for systemic failures and deliberate obfuscation of the facts, he inevitably gets pulled into a polarized position, a parallel process. However, his voice is one that needs to be heard. His 2018 book catalogues detailed research into numerous instances, and is one of the most depressing I have ever read. Relevant to this discussion, Pilgrim states that:

> There is an inner working of power, where a 'nod is as good as a wink' to colleagues to keep a group secret. Complicity with wrongdoing and strong group loyalty within the power elites then become opposite sides of the same coin. (2018: 14)

The need to turn a blind eye is unspoken, embedded in the hidden fabric of social convention. Providing varied accounts of police complicity, collusion, systematic destruction of records, and forms of cover-up in cases of child sexual abuse, Pilgrim notes that:

> Because so much of criminality [the police] encounter is linked to the economic powerlessness of the 'underclass', they may be insecure when, much more rarely, they have to deal with the rich and the powerful and are expected to confront them about serious crimes. (2018: 11)

From this perspective, the protection of the law is biased towards those with privilege, and, we may conclude, is weighted against those of the so-called 'underclasses'.

We do well to take into account the long-term social and economic impact of sexual violence. For some, under-performance in employment, and reliance on state benefits is part of life, while others drift towards substance abuse or criminality (Atkinson, [2002] 2018). Scaer, for example, based on evidence from the United States, estimated that the annual medical cost per child abuse survivor for symptoms related to somatization averages $4,700 (2014: 111). Added to this is the cost of substance abuse and mental health provision and ongoing implications for future generations. It is a hidden epidemic.

Alesha

The first contact the counselling charity had with 14-year-old Alesha was through a series of silent phone calls to their helpline, spread over several weeks. A number of volunteers tried to engage her gently in conversation, and the agency was alert to potential risks in doing so. The helpline coordinator, with the agency managers, despite requests, failed to put together a plan for a consistent response should she ring again. In due course, however, Alesha agreed to attend a face-to-face appointment with the trainee volunteer counsellor, Hayley, who was stepping out of her usual role to see her. Alesha was of mixed heritage; her friendly and mature presentation was incongruent with how she had been on the phone. It was only with hindsight that it became evident that Alesha was emotionally cut off. The story she told was of the sudden death of her white Irish father a year before, since when her mother, a British born black woman, had immersed herself in seeing spiritualists and mediums to 'get messages' from him. Her mother's ability to care for Alesha was severely impacted, as her grip on reality slipped away, and supported by her aunt, her mother came under the care of mental health services. Hayley sensibly enquired about other support available to Alesha, and she was reassured to find that she enjoyed babysitting for some older friends.

In counselling, Alesha began to explore her feelings about the loss, effectively, of both her parents. It was a surprise to Hayley to learn of Alesha's very poor school attendance and that a move to a Pupil Referral Unit (PRU) was planned. Identified as a young carer, Alesha was allocated a support worker. Hayley took this to supervision, and it was noted that there was a pattern of things not quite matching the story Hayley was hearing. Hayley also noticed that Alesha was being dropped off for her sessions by an older man, and picked up after. 'It's fine', Alesha told her, 'It's just my boyfriend; he likes to make sure I'm not getting into trouble'. Hayley needed the support of her supervisor to raise this with Alesha – but she didn't want to tell her supervisor that Alesha was a person of colour and her boyfriend was black in case she was seen as racist. The following week, Alesha's mobile phone rang in the session; she tried to ignore it but answered when it rang a second time. She apologized, explaining: 'Tyrone worries if I don't pick up; he really loves me'. Alesha sounded a bit more cagey and defensive. She insisted that she was fine, but didn't arrive for her next session.

The next time they met, Hayley wondered if she saw some faded bruising to Alesha's face, but wasn't sure because of her skin colour, and was that a shadow on her neck … or something else? Uncomfortable, but not knowing how to broach the subject, Hayley kept quiet. She didn't say anything about this to her supervisor immediately, either. Alesha's attendance became more erratic. Hayley noticed her pupils were dilated, she seemed tired, and began to allude to 'rough sex' with Tyrone. Now Hayley talked in group supervision. The counsellors complained of tiredness and were listless, and the supervisor shortened the session because she developed a severe migraine. It seemed she was tuning in somatically to Alesha's unvoiced experience. Hayley then received a text message from Alesha, saying that Tyrone was 'passing her round his mates for money', asking if it was normal. The agency thus had a dilemma relating to child protection, and the manager made some 'hypothetical' enquiries of social services, also failing to mention Alesha's ethnicity. The matter was passed directly from social services to the police, with a concern for gang-related activity, and the sexual abuse of a minor was overlooked because Alesha was in a relationship with Tyrone.

Dropping in

Place a hand on your heart and allow yourself to breathe into it; take as long as you need with this. Is there anything that resonates for you from your personal life? And professionally? Did it cross your mind that the agency was becoming 'traumatized'? At what point was this evident? What difference does race make in Alesha's story? What are the implications for the agency and for Alesha that race is avoided? What conclusions do you draw about Tyrone and his friends? Could earlier intervention have been possible? What about the other professionals who have crossed Alesha's path? How do theories of systemic trauma account for what has happened to Alesha?

Discussion

The evidence points to Alesha having been groomed by Tyrone as part of a gang culture, involving drugs, sex, and money; child sexual exploitation (CSE) in other words. Gill and Harrison cite McAlinden, suggesting that grooming entails: (1) the use of a variety of manipulative and controlling techniques; (2) with a vulnerable subject; (3) in a range of interpersonal and social settings; (4) in order to establish trust or normalize sexually harmful behaviour; and (5) with the overall aim of facilitating exploitation and/or prohibiting exposure' (2015: 35). The most common definition of CSE is this:

> The sexual exploitation of children and young people under 18 involves exploitative situations, contexts and relationships where young people (or a third person or persons) receive something (e.g. food, accommodation, drugs, alcohol, cigarettes, affection, gifts, money) as a result of performing, and/or others performing on them, sexual activities. (2015: 35)

In Alesha's case, advantage was taken of her vulnerability and young age, in particular exploiting her need for affection. How is it that Alesha is initially so wary of talking, so protective of her boyfriend? She has developed an emotional bond with Tyrone, akin to 'Stockholm Syndrome', a concept related to hostage situations but which can be applied in other circumstances such as inescapable abusive and violent relationships (Eaton and Paterson-Young, 2018: 14). Alesha wants to be loved, sexually desired even, a complex process that 'involves both individual pubertal development and the absorption of social images and pressures which celebrate the objectification of women and girls' (2018: 16). Importantly, Alesha does not recognize that she is being abused, so certain is she of Tyrone's love: 'Children ... do not always recognise that what is happening to them is abnormal or harmful – even when they are experiencing daily violence, aggression, manipulation, and threat' (2018: 33).

It is not unusual for serious trauma to have a ripple effect as it did in the agency Alesha came to; trauma can be extremely hard to contain. There was a fluctuation between both hyper- and hypo-arousal, and powerful parallel processes within the implicit field. This is a clear example of a trauma-organized system, situated in a cultural context in which minors and people of colour are discriminated against, and assumptions made which obscure the facts. Hayley, as an inexperienced counsellor had blind-spots and low confidence; many trainee counsellors are plunged in at the deep end with complex people and are soon out of their depth. Some dissociative phenomena were missed, including the supervisor's somatic response. These factors might explain some of the missed opportunities to step in and protect Alesha. In a fragmented system, the net which might have caught her sooner had large holes, and, crucially, key questions were not asked – or were avoided.

While attention was focused on the criminality of Tyrone and the gang, protecting Alesha and prosecuting accordingly was overlooked. This, again, is a common dynamic; the problem lies with the victim. It is not easy to cut through the protestations of a terrified girl, in love with her abuser, to recognize the situation Alesha is in. The final thought here comes from Pilgrim's exploration of organized criminality in large British towns, which:

> Traditionally has used the sexual exploitation of women and children as one of its many 'rackets'. These child victims were a source of money like contraband cigarettes, heroin or crack cocaine. It was ever thus, at least in modern times. Why are we surprised when gangsters act like gangsters? (2018: 96)

Concluding reflections

There are a number of common threads between these four stories. In each case there is an apparent focus on the difficulties of the individual, in which the individual carries the burden of larger systemic issues. We see an interweaving of the situational factors and situational processes outlined in Chapter 2, organized around power, privilege, and oppression. It requires a small step to recognize that in each case, and on different scales, traumatized systems are a constituent of the experiential ground many of us stand on or are involved in. Most organizations, schools, businesses, statutory institutions, and welfare agencies revolve around invisible trauma, mirroring the processes related to cultural or ground trauma (Chapter 2). Emotionally and cognitively complex situations cannot easily be seen as a whole, and thus elements disappear from full sight. In this, the shape-shifting tendency of the Trickster comes into play (Chapter 1). In any social group we see the enactment of a complex interface of original family dynamics, multiplied by the number of participants. Trauma becomes a ubiquitous part of the life of the group.

The theoretical frameworks I have described offer a way of seeing more clearly what is obscured through denial and dissociation. Clearly, there are overlaps between them and therefore they complement one another. Any of the lenses they provide can be helpful in enlarging our ability to contextualize what is happening. It follows that the next step on the road to reforming trauma is to name it.

Before and during my early training I had three jobs in the self-advocacy movement, supporting people of different oppressed and marginal demographics to speak up for themselves. In each job, when I got close to uncovering an instance of current abuse – sexual in two cases and financial in another – I was either shut down or criticized for my attempts to bring into the open the experiences of the oppressed, which is precisely what I was paid to do. As one manager told me, 'We mustn't talk about things like that'. Power denies power to those who need it.

4 Do no harm

After 17 years under the care of mental health professionals, I had become a great deal sicker, both physically and psychologically. I felt I had lost 17 years of my life … How could a system I had turned to for help have harmed me like this?
– Sue Irwin, 2019: 178

It is the case that sometimes the provisions that are in place to protect the vulnerable and distressed end up doing more harm than good. In reviewing the literature on this subject, I notice that, as in the case of Pilgrim mentioned in Chapter 3, feelings run high and can feel extreme. The factions in the arguments about mental health and its accompanying services are often pitted against one another; you are either 'pro' psychiatry or 'anti' it. One reason for this may be a strong reaction to the prevailing 'normative' discourse in which mental health professionals and especially psychiatrists are endowed with the privilege of authority. The power dynamic is so entrenched that people push harder against it. And the same carries over into allied mental health professions, including psychotherapy and counselling. The 'psychotherapeutic encounter is just one more instance of an unequal relationship, just one more opportunity to be rewarded for expressing distress and to be "helped" by being (expertly) guided or dominated' (Chesler, [2005] 2018: 167).

By definition, people who fare well in statutory mental health services are less likely to present for therapy, so the clinical experience I draw on is weighted accordingly. However, it would seem that 'patient' satisfaction is low, and the voices of those who are retraumatized within the system deserve to be heard. In this chapter, we will examine some of these controversial issues, *not in order to take sides but to see more clearly what is often implicit* and to question some of the foundations our work as therapists rests on. The aim is to present critique rather than be oppositional. We will do this through a case example, interwoven with discussion.

Stella Part 1

Rather than go to university, Stella moved to London and signed up with a modelling agency. With classically striking features, she was used to being a 'head turner'. Stella's adoptive father was proud of his 'little mouse', and while her mother exaggerated her success, she was also jealous. Although Stella was naturally reserved, she was secretly ambitious to make it onto the catwalk and the pages of prestigious magazines. Despite some difficulties settling into independent life, Stella drew on her own reserves and had never had an emotional crisis requiring medical attention. She worked hard in the first few years, modelling makeup and high street fashion. Rather than exciting and glamorous, it was a gruelling existence, waiting for the next shoot, sometimes earning very little, cold, hungry, and lonely. But she developed a pleasing portfolio and was well respected. A social life grew around people she worked with over time. Although Stella was cautious, drinking together and some cocaine use after studio sessions became routine, a part of the deal.

Marcus was a photographer Stella worked with from time to time, and he took her to cocktail bars alone a couple of times. He showed interest in her, and asked about her plans for the future. A bit less inhibited, Stella told him her dream. The next time they worked together the atmosphere in the studio was tense and cold. As the shoot was finishing, Marcus suggested that she stayed on with the crew to have a drink together, and he opened a bottle of something fizzy. As she went to the bathroom, she saw one of the crew locking the door and felt uneasy. Stella's memory of the sequence of events was blurred, but she had a recollection of Marcus leaning towards her with a glass in his hand saying, 'Let's break you in a little, shall we?' Stella recalled that at least three of the male crew present raped her that evening. She came to in a taxi which Marcus ordered to take her home. Early the next morning Marcus phoned Stella, offering her some lucrative work – telling her that she had a lovely body which she wouldn't want to hide. Shocked, but realizing that this meant work in pornography, Stella caught a train back to her parents.

Dropping in

If you will, call to mind a soothing image – a flower, a sunset, a pet, a child. Bring all your attention to whatever is most vivid in this image. Does anything change in your breathing, your heart rate, your muscle tone? What sensations go with this image? Are there any thoughts that arise now in relation to Stella's story?

Discussion: The lived and the unlived body

Since the time of Descartes in the seventeenth century, the mind and body have been viewed as separate. The Cartesian split is problematic from an ecological perspective, and highlights a disconnection suggestive of trauma. Kepner (2002) describes dissociation as withdrawal of the energy of awareness, a fleeing from embodied life, the absence of the black hole of trauma. The conceptual leap we have made in trauma therapy is to distinguish between events and experience. From a Gestalt perspective, this requires attention to what we call 'process'; the phenomenological fabric of our lives. Thus Kennedy asks: 'Is my process identical with my lived body – a recognisable *style of being*, totally special to me yet totally dependent upon the support of the world about me?' (2003: 77, original emphasis). Our lived experience is mediated by cells, organs, bones, a nervous system. In agreeing with Kennedy's proposition, I suggest that lived embodied experience is fundamental to our cohesive sense of self; disconnection from it becomes the existential challenge of working with trauma.

The ways in which the body carries the weight of unmetabolized trauma are now well documented (e.g. Ogden et al., 2006; van der Kolk, 2014). Oppression of the body, which exists on a continuum with trauma, is endemic in Western societies. 'Scholars in the field of nonverbal communication have identified the body as the primary locus of social control and dominance' (Bennett Leighton, 2018: 25). Women in particular have borne the brunt of dominance and control through non-verbal embodied communications, 'a man, for example, touching a woman he doesn't know on the arm without her permission and the woman smiling demurely and averting her gaze in response' (2018: 25). Women's bodies have become a matter of clinical significance, from gendered self-harm and eating distress to body-image. Women are socialized to conform, whether they are feminists or not (Chesler, [2005] 2018: 333). This is not to say that men are not socialized to conform, but that they do so according to differently gendered 'norms'. 'Male conformity … implies conformity to action, struggle, thought, mobility, and pleasure; female conformity implies conformity to inaction, resignation, emotionality, and unhappiness' ([2005] 2018: 329).

Objectification of the body is widely recognized and criticized. What may be of more importance, though, is to see that objectification is not the end of the story, but the dehumanization that is inherent in it (see Chapter 2). This moves us from the cognitively based I–It towards the heart-based I–Thou; a person within and beyond the physical body; a person in relationship. How has Stella's experience affected her sense of her own humanity?

Stella Part 2

On her return home, Stella withdrew into a passive, numb state, in which she became quite uncommunicative. She didn't tell her adoptive parents why she had returned. Her mother's open frustration with her daughter was barely tempered by her father's helpless concern. Some two months later, Stella found herself bleeding and in pain; it dawned on her that she had missed a period and that she might be having a miscarriage. She broke down in incoherent tears and began hitting herself uncontrollably, which frightened her parents. They took her to the doctor who prescribed a course of antidepressants; Stella didn't tell him either about the rapes or the bleeding. Stella shut herself in her room, crying and shaking, and refusing to eat. A few days later, her parents found her confused, drowsy, and agitated, and called an ambulance; intending to end her life, she had taken an overdose of the antidepressants. Stella was admitted to the psychiatric ward of a general hospital.

Looking back to this time, this is what Stella had to say about it: 'It was just awful, terrifying, out of control. My brain felt treacly, blank, I couldn't think at all. Everything was in a thick fog, like I would need to make an enormous effort to reach through it. That was impossible, I didn't really want to try, I felt sort of safe in a bubble. I couldn't think about telling anybody, if someone spoke to me that's when I felt really out of control, like they were going to take over. I kind of wanted someone to know, and to make it better, but all they did was tell me that I should get a grip and I didn't know how to. That was worse, no help at all. I thought I couldn't possibly survive the pain, so I took the pills'.

Discussion: Framing suffering

The first question to ask here is whether, having been hospitalized, Stella is indeed ill. Clearly, she is suffering greatly, to the degree that she cannot bear to go on living with such distress, and has resorted to coping strategies that are not uncommon among people who have been traumatized (Fisher, undated). How we answer this question depends in part on which of several models of mental distress we subscribe to. The medical or disease model most adhered to in general psychiatry assumes that there is an identifiable underlying pathology for mental illness, comparable to a broken arm or diabetes. However, no such pathology exists or can even be tested for (Davies, 2013: 40). Mental distress is frequently attributed to 'chemical imbalance'. Bullmore, an NHS psychiatrist, writes of a conversation with someone he was assessing for depression, describing it as a serotonin deficiency:

'How do you know that about me,' he asked, 'how do you know that the level of serotonin is unbalanced in my brain?' We both immediately knew that I didn't have an answer to that question. I didn't even have a clue about how to find out the answer. (2018: 106)

Furthermore, the medical model supposes that rather than being an expression of the human condition, distress means that there is something wrong with you. The medicalization of human difficulties with everyday life conditions is of concern (Davies, 2013: 44).

Another model, the biopsychosocial model, at least in name recognizes that diverse factors contribute to emotional distress, although the emphasis in practice remains on the biological. Embedded in the culture of traditional mental health services, the psycho-social elements are often used in a tokenistic manner (Denham Vaughan and Chidiac, 2013: 103). The links between 'bio', 'psycho', and 'social' are not discussed often and the model remains relatively obscure (Cromby et al., 2013: 4). Davies cites Dowrick: 'The biopsychosocial model has little substance beyond the descriptive, and in everyday general practice is viewed mainly as necessary rhetoric' (2013: 223). It seems the approach is conceptual and fragmented at best, not based on any empirical understanding.

A neurobiologically informed basis to working with trauma has held much promise in the last decade. I could not work without a firm understanding of some of the insights provided by neuroscientific research, as I explained in

Chapter 1. What seems incontrovertible is that as a species we have evolved with hardwired ways of responding to threat and of ensuring our survival. (See Appendix B for an overview of some of the more useful neurobiological models.) There is a broad set of fairly predictable responses governed by brain structures, neural pathways, and neurochemical changes that are features of trauma. This points to these being *normal responses in abnormal circumstances*, beyond conscious control; adaptations that any healthy person might develop. Is it right, therefore, to assume that someone experiencing a constellation of these 'symptoms' is ill? Furthermore, some of this research is not generalizable. It simply shows what is happening in the brain of an individual, devoid of any kind of context, at a particular moment in time.

However, if we decide that Stella is traumatized, rather than that someone has hurt her, the spotlight remains on her. Thus, I question how useful it is to apply the language of trauma too liberally. By focusing on the suffering of the individual who has experienced trauma, we take our eye off the perpetrator and the society that has engendered such violence. Incorporating the SOS model into our thinking about distress proposes a 'radical paradigm shift … [in which] … this individual focus is not automatically the outcome of contact with mental health services, including counselling / psychotherapy services' (Denham Vaughan and Chidiac, 2013: 103). Denham Vaughan and Chidiac continue: 'In many cases, however, more than one single element of the SOS model will need to be addressed if the change intervention is to be both successful and enduring' (2013: 103). To be truly trauma-informed, we need to take many things into consideration, including ground traumas, race, gender, class, and other implicit oppressions that are part of an individual's shared existence.

The second question that arises in relation to Stella is, 'Since she is in hospital, what is wrong with her?'

Stella Part 3

During her hospital admission assessment, Stella was quiet, slow to respond and trembling. Stella's mood and thought processes were discussed, but not her history. Given that over half of people within the psychiatric system have been abused (Filer, 2019: 131; Pilgrim, 2018: 135), it is astonishing that it is not common practice to inquire about this (Caplan, 1995: 105). Stella is unable to speak of what happened, and no one is asking. Neither was there any consideration of her strengths and wishes. Her initial diagnosis was that of a 'major depressive episode'. Because she had only recently started on antidepressants, it was decided that she should stay on them at a higher dose, in the expectation that she would feel better once they had taken effect. She did not sleep for the first three nights, and was additionally prescribed Zopiclone to help. When she was found to have been cutting her stomach and thighs, Stella was put under strict 24-hour observation. Losing control, and physically restrained from banging her head, she ran away from the hospital. Four hours later she was found by police walking along a canal, and returned to the ward. She was then placed under Section, and a further diagnosis of 'bipolar disorder' was proposed.

This is what Stella said about this period in her life: 'I was so, so scared, I couldn't understand what was going on. It was the darkest time. I hated hospital, I hated myself, I hated life. The place was like hell, people screaming, staff talking about me in corridors, nowhere to hide. Every time someone came near me with medication I just froze; it was the way the drugs made me feel – spaced out – I had no control over it. When they held me down, well, you wouldn't treat a dog like that, would you? I kind of fainted when they did that. I don't think the staff really cared, they didn't seem that interested, except in keeping the peace. Was I depressed? I don't know what depression is, I just accepted it, it kind of felt better to have a name for it, but it didn't feel great. It was as though I had a label stuck to my forehead, so that everyone could see I wasn't right in my head. Humiliating, that's the word for it, and I couldn't figure out where I had gone wrong. It didn't help at all that they couldn't agree what was wrong with me. I felt I had to just roll with the punches and gave up. I felt helpless like I was in prison. I didn't care anymore. Well, part of me still hated it, cared a lot, and that's when I kicked off, but I was always squashed back down when I did. Like I was punished for wanting something better. Every time. I was trapped in a cycle I couldn't escape from. My parents, my mum especially, made a huge fuss with the doctors about the diagnosis. I think she was ashamed of me, like she might catch it. She kept telling her friends that I had a chemical imbalance in my brain, which really annoyed me. When I was home, people started looking at me, like I was being judged. That was really the worst thing for me, I felt like an outcast. There was nowhere to go except into a big empty hole inside me'.

Dropping in

Place your hand over your heart and breathe 'into' it deeply. Do you think of yourself in terms of any negative labels? How do you feel when you use those terms to describe yourself? Have you ever been negatively labelled by other people, family, friends, or professionals? In what ways does that feel different? How has any label, whether positive or negative, in your life put you in an opposite power relationship with others? Have you ever been given a psychiatric diagnosis, or do you know someone, maybe close to you or someone you work with, who has? Try to remember the impact this had on you. What difference did it make to you to know this? Do you think Stella is mentally ill or does she have problems in living?

Discussion: Labels and formulation

Since the 1950s there has been a huge surge in the number of people being diagnosed with so-called 'mental disorders' (Davies, 2013: 39); I shall say some more about this later. However, as Davies goes on to say, 'there are still no objective tests that can confirm the validity of any psychiatric diagnosis, a fact supported by the continued low diagnostic reliability rates' (2013: 40). Furthermore, as Stella's changing diagnoses suggest, there is no consensus about psychiatric diagnosis (Filer, 2019: 82). More accurately, there has been a great deal of controversy about psychiatric diagnosis, the ways in which thresholds for inclusion in the *Diagnostic and Statistical Manual of Mental Disorders* (DSM) have been determined across five editions to date. A significant part of the debate has hinged around defining the point at which 'normal' human suffering becomes 'disordered'. Both Davies (2013) and Caplan (1995) have written detailed and critical accounts of the ways in which these decisions have been made. There remains a lack of objective science to support these arguments, and yet people's lives are greatly impacted by the decisions that are made about them. Published in 1980, DSM-III was especially contentious for its inclusion of two 'diagnoses' relating to women. 'Pre-menstrual dysphoric disorder (PMDD)' was hotly contested for its pathologization of a normal female bodily function; do many women really 'go crazy' once a month? (Caplan, 1995: 122). In addition, so-called 'self-defeating personality disorder' (SDPD) ran the risk of pathologizing women whose ability to think for themselves has been eroded by the coercive control of others:

> To call people self-defeating for behaving in self-denying, self-effacing ways in order to *avoid* punishment and rejection – and in order to receive approval and love – is to insist that their behavior be regarded as pathological. (Caplan, 1995: 104, original emphasis)

These diagnoses were recommended for inclusion in DSM-III on the basis of a single study (1995: 109), which runs contrary to a rigorous scientific approach. Furthermore, as Caplan provocatively argues, they were proposed without a correlate for male dominating and delusional behaviour driven by fluctuations of testosterone (1995: 168).

Receiving a diagnosis increases access to state benefits and to 'treatment' pathways in the UK, and can fit chaotic and dysregulated experiences into something of a pattern, which makes them simpler to manage. However, for many people, the costs of being diagnosed far outweigh the gains, and the question of whether diagnoses can do harm has not been addressed (Caplan, 1995: 140). It is important to keep in mind that the experiences that come to be diagnosed as illnesses started out as creative adaptations to difficult circumstances, and as such serve a purpose (Lynch, 2019: 147). From a trauma perspective, I believe that it is crucial to recognize that 'symptoms' need no longer be seen as signs of illness, but as *survival strategies* (Johnstone, 2019: 17). The challenge is to work with the person to understand that purpose and whether it still has currency.

Stella's account shows that she is aware of the stigma attached to her diagnoses; she has become 'other' to important people in her life. 'Stigma is the shadow of the asylum, the birthplace of diagnosis, with its roots in moral treatment' (Fox, 2019: 42). A diagnosis of 'borderline personality disorder' (BPD) has always carried particular stigma. Now often renamed emotionally unstable personality disorder (EUPD), it very often comes in the aftermath of abuse. Shaw contends that:

> Whatever an individual has suffered – rape, abuse, homophobia, poverty – the linguistic category of 'BPD' states that the cause of their distress exists within them. The individual – rather than the traumatic experience, the family, the society – becomes the problem. (2019: 80)

How would it be instead to validate the phenomenon of so-called 'borderline' processes as survival strategies, involving courage and creativity, rather than as a 'disorder'? An important dimension on the recreation of abusive relationships is offered by Stolorow:

> To attribute the affective chaos or schizoid withdrawal of patients who were abused as children to 'fantasy' or to 'borderline personality organization' is tantamount to blaming the victim and, in doing so, *reproduces features of the original trauma*. (2007: 11, emphasis added)

It is likely that without diagnosis, the stigma associated with the expression of suffering would not be the problem that it is. Self-stigma presents as a passive acceptance of diagnosis, bringing a sense of loss of control over symptoms, and an absorption of cultural stereotypes of mental 'illness' (Read and Magliano, 2019: 100).

There are other ways of approaching the problem. The Gestalt view is that assessment is an intrinsic part of relationship. This would take into account an individual's patterns of being 'in process', considering their relational patterns and field conditions (Joyce and Sills, 2014: 59–64). An alternative to psychiatric diagnosis is the use of formulation (Johnstone, 2019: 13), developing with the designated 'patient' a narrative about their difficulties over time, and the meaning of them. As early as 1995, Gestalt therapist Jim Kepner conceptualized the consequence of abuse as, 'I feel bad about what was done to me' (1995: 38). The Power Threat Meaning Framework (PTMF; Johnstone and Boyle, 2018) developed by professionals and 'service users' (Johnstone, 2019: 19) is an alternative approach to understanding distress. A set of four core questions provide an entry point for the PTMF:

> 'What has happened to you?' (How is **power** operating in your life?)
> 'How did it affect you?' (What kind of **threats** does this pose?)
> 'What sense did you make of it?' (What is the **meaning** of these situations and experiences to you?)
> 'What did you have to do to survive?' (What kinds of **threat response** are you using?)
>
> (Johnstone, 2019: 20, original emphasis)

Two supplementary questions complete the picture:

> 'What are your strengths?' (What access to **power resources** do you have?)
> 'What is your story?' (How does all this fit together?)'
>
> (2019: 20, original emphasis)

The PTMF seeks to identify the patterns of responses to the negative impacts of power, 'to go beyond a series of individual narratives and identify broader regularities in people's expressions and experiences of distress', patterns which importantly are organized by meaning rather than by biology (2019: 20). Johnstone links social distress – the situational structures we have already considered – with processes of neglect, violence, and abuse, creating a more integrated picture. She comments that: 'Ideological power is central to all other kinds of power. From a PTMF perspective, imposing a psychiatric label on someone is a very good example of the operation of this kind of power' (2019: 19). Or as Caplan points out, giving something a name is an act of power (1995: 273), in this instance a use of power which is potentially retraumatizing.

The PTMF is gaining traction across the world among so-called 'service users' and professionals alike (see Watson, 2019; A Disorder for Everyone, www.adisorder4everyone.com), but has yet to break through into mainstream psychiatry. Its popular success demonstrates the need to listen to the voices of people who are 'expert by experience' and for critical psychiatry, which is not to be confused with the anti-psychiatry movement. People are beginning to question the validity of their diagnoses and their medications, sometimes sadly only to be told that their disagreement is clear evidence of their illness. There seems to be little awareness of the double-bind this places them in, or of the power play involved.

Stella Part 4

Over the next two years, Stella was admitted to hospital three times and her diagnosis revised once more to that of 'EUPD'. More medication was added, antipsychotics and benzodiazepines. On ward rounds, she was asked what improvements she felt, and when unable to respond positively, her medication was changed or the dose altered. These adjustments were so frequent it seemed as though her body, her nervous system, was not allowed to find a way to settle, was being constantly interfered with. Stella was assigned to two 'therapy' groups, one for coping skills and the other for relaxation. She was so terrified of being 'found out' in the first that she froze and could not speak; in the second she felt increasingly anxious because she felt she was doing it wrong. She soon refused to go to either group, and was deemed non-compliant. On her second admission, Stella was prescribed electroconvulsive therapy (ECT), which was administered five times. She suffered from headaches, loss of concentration, and poor memory after these 'treatments'. ECT was only stopped when Stella was able to report, falsely, that she was feeling better.

Between spells in hospital, Stella moved from her parents' home into a small flat. She was supported by the Community Mental Health Team, and began a degree course in psychology, which she soon dropped out of. In a suicidal crisis once more, the Crisis Intervention Team became involved, visiting her three times a day to oversee her medication. It was terrifying for Stella to have strangers come into her home in this way, hugely increasing her sense

of unsafety. Returned to hospital under compulsory Section after another suicide attempt, Stella finally told her female psychiatrist the story of her rape.
The doctor was caring, but told her: 'We don't know how to help you for that',
and referred her to the Complex Needs Team. Multiple features of Stella's
experience of the psychiatric system might be reframed as retraumatizing.

Discussion: Pills and other interventions

The third question that arises from Stella's story is this: 'What interventions are
helpful for someone with a psychiatric diagnosis?' Drawing on a medical, biological model, the first line of treatment is invariably to prescribe medication.
A critical view of this inevitably raises some interesting issues. Many so-called
mental illnesses are considered to be long term, and the possibility of spontaneous recovery is rarely taken into account. A diagnosis of 'personality disorder' is likely to be regarded as lifelong, without hope of recovery. The 'condition'
is managed through psychotropic medication, or often a cocktail of drugs
which might typically include one or more antidepressants, antipsychotics,
mood stabilizers, and benzodiazepines. A cynic might suggest that these are
used to control the occasional emotional outbursts of people like Stella. These
drugs appear to reduce suffering by suppressing the emotional range and cognitive function of the person who is prescribed them. A 2009 study into the
side-effects of antidepressants, cited by Davies, showed that

> Most participants … described feeling emotionally detached or disconnected
> from their surroundings. Most also described this detachment as extending to
> a detachment from other people … Almost all participants described not caring
> about things that used to matter to them. They cared less about themselves,
> about other people and about the consequences of their actions. (2013: 107)

Furthermore:

> Numbing things isn't curing things, or even, in the long run, helping things.
> It's just providing a temporary and superficial distraction, and one that may
> store up problems later along the line. (2013: 100)

It is also a way to disown responsibility for harm that has been done, or of the
potential re-enactment of such harm (Fellows, 2020b).

Psychiatry is slow to recognize dissociation, and especially the correlation
between iatrogenic dissociation and some antidepressants and antipsychotics
in people diagnosed with 'BPD' (Pec et al., 2018). From a therapeutic point of
view, it can be argued that instead of numbing the pain, what *people really need
is to be able to experience the fullness of human emotion without becoming
overwhelmed*; I will return to this idea in later chapters. While psychotropic
medication does certainly help some people, there is a lot of evidence that
shows that it is not as effective as we might hope it to be. First, the side-effects

of some medications are considerable and can outweigh the benefits (Filer, 2019: 195). Withdrawal from long-term use of antidepressants, antipsychotics, and benzodiazepines can be painful and slow and creates significant problems for people, but they are rarely warned about this before taking them. Once started, you might as well stay on them, not that they necessarily do much good anyway, for example: '85 to 90 per cent of people being prescribed antidepressants are not getting any clinically meaningful benefit from the drug itself' (Davies, 2013: 67). An increase in suicidality has been recognized as an effect of some antidepressants.

Randomized control trials (RCTs) are seen as the pharmaceutical industry gold standard, providing the needed 'evidence base' for the National Institute for Clinical and Care Excellence (NICE) to authorize prescribing in the UK. However, there are problems associated with RCTs in mental health. These include the selection of participants who may already be on medication, 'unblinding' in which participants recognize side-effects and so can tell if they are on a drug or a placebo, medication withdrawal, analysis and presentation, and publication bias (Cromby et al., 2013: 163). It has been common practice among pharmaceutical companies to suppress negative findings of research, skewing perceptions of their efficacy (Davies, 2013: 145). Universities are dependent on research funding from the very same companies whose products are being investigated, creating a complex screen which obscures the real science.

The ECT which Stella underwent is also contentious: 'There has never been any evidence that it is more effective than placebo' (Read and Magliano, 2019: 97). The ethics of conducting RCTs with a 'blind' control group are questionable. They follow a medical model which assumes that the 'problem' lies within an individual. Stella's side-effects are typical. Crombey et al. cite Read and Bentall: 'The very short term benefit gained by a small minority cannot justify the risks to which all ECT recipients are exposed' (2013: 172).

Gender, power, and psychiatry

While what happened to Stella is fictitious, I have worked with a number of women who have had similar experiences, and who have been involved over many years with statutory mental health services. The details of Stella's story are typical of them, including diagnoses of 'personality disorder' and, interestingly, her study of psychology. None, I repeat *none*, has found the services of general psychiatry to have been helpful, and some have been harmed by them. It has been a different story for some of those who have been able to access specialist trauma or complex needs services. But all were glad to find an alternative in trauma-focused psychotherapy, which was not offered to Stella. I cannot pretend to know how or why things improved for them, but all have, over time, disengaged from psychiatric care, reduced their medication, and begun to lead more fulfilling lives. I know that being listened to helps. I believe also that being asked about their strengths, survival capacities, joys, and interests makes a difference by putting their experiences into a different perspective. I do not treat people as though they are ill because if 'we talk sick, our clients will – beyond their own already confusing and frightening experiences – think sick or have it confirmed that they are sick, and are more likely to feel sick and act sick' (Johnstone, 2019: 28). Looking beyond 'symptoms' and validating the experience of trauma is crucial. The sample is small, and this is no RCT, but anecdotal evidence is still evidence.

Although trauma is clearly *not* an exclusively female experience, women have suffered in particular ways, and disproportionately within mental health services. Freud's rebuttal of accounts of sexual abuse as 'hysteria' and 'blame it on the mother' serve to shape mental health provision through underlying biases and implicit assumptions about women, which we will examine further in the next chapter. In psychiatry, the culture is one in which reason is placed over emotion, and embodied life is mistrusted, with echoes of colonialist control. There exists a gender bias in this, a male-dominated profession working with a 'compliant' female population. Caplan notes that Freud's legacy persists today, and although not limited to women, there can be a disbelief which often extends to anything that people, especially women, might say (1995: 24). It is therefore a culture in which many layers of historical 'norms' are perpetuated and perpetrated and are slow to change. Because of the investment in the status quo of the power imbalance, positioning professionals as the 'well and rational experts', the culture is not only slow to change, but is resistant to change. The term and strategy of 'change' within services is more often than not used to mean a reshuffling of the same deck of cards. This is experienced by frustrated staff and patients as an attempt to placate and silence; and only serves to undermine trust and the hope for more meaningful experiences of healing in the system (Fellows, 2020a). Indeed, in Stella's story we can clearly see a systemic re-enactment and perpetuation of violence, violation, and silencing of women's bodies within the mental health system that follows on from such dehumanizing treatment.

There are a number of situational structures as well as situational processes at play in mental health services. Implicit misogyny is one, and implicit racism another. Mental distress is culturally specific and there is an over-representation of black and people of colour within the patient population (e.g. Cromby et al., 2013: 72). Doctors representing the educated establishment are endowed with automatic and often unquestioned authority, creating another binary of privilege and oppression. 'Doctor knows more about this than I do' or 'I know what's best for you' – these are positions that also carry overtones of a colonialist mindset. While the role of professionals may be endowed with some legitimate and expert power, it can tip into the power to reward or to coerce (Carroll and Shaw, 2013: 170). A system that is set up to be evidence-based requires outcomes and this exerts considerable pressure on services, which does not correspond to the slow unfolding of increased well-being we have the benefit of working with in talking therapies. Available resources are scarce. The decontextualizing of the individual within the medical model increases the possibility of blame. On the assumption that people with a 'personality disorder' cannot recover and that medication will manage symptoms, there is a degree of indifference which stands in the way of listening. In the psychiatric literature there is an absence of discourse about empathy. Psychiatrists' self-report perceptions of their level of empathy were found to be higher than the ratings given them by the people they worked with, which is unsurprising. Relational skills such as building a therapeutic alliance, meaning-making, managing co-transference, collaboration, and negotiation skills were also classed as aspects of empathy in a 2017 study by Ross and Watling, skills which are taken for granted in psychotherapy. A propensity to fit the person to the 'disorder' rather than vice versa is equally concerning in terms of power.

Situational processes appear in other forms. Psychiatry has a difficult relationship with trauma, a blind spot that typically operates in the Trickster. It 'both blinds us to something (that's hiding in plain sight) and blinds us to our blindness. We can't see something and *we can't see that we can't see it*' (Bullmore, 2018: 177, emphasis added). Trauma is greatly under-acknowledged and mis-diagnosed. In a study by Floen and Elkit (2007), only 7 per cent of patients with a history of trauma received a diagnosis of post-traumatic stress disorder (PTSD), and more women than men were given it. It is not easy to explain why the profession is so defensive about this. Watson attributes it to status and superiority (2019: 232), which suggests some sort of underlying fragility. If you are at the top, the only way is down, especially in a very hierarchical and competitive profession. Because it has so far failed the test of science, mental health also has a difficult relationship with physical medicine. Mental health services do not sit comfortably in the world of healthcare.

Talking therapies in context

The extent to which psychotherapists and counsellors are embedded in this system is a necessary consideration. The matter is relevant when we work with someone who is, or who has recently been, in the care of statutory services, and where we may work in tandem – or at cross-purposes – with psychiatric provision. A diagnosis can colour our ways of thinking about and meeting a person, and, as Watson points out, puts us in a position of 'colluding with state-sanctioned power structures that serve to perpetuate the very factors that are bringing clients to our counselling rooms. How is that ethical?' (2019: 228).

The second instance in which we might directly rub up against mental health services is when in a crisis we are required ethically to refer someone to other mental health services. My professional experience has been that this tends to escalate matters rather than create increased protection, and may place the individual concerned in a split between therapist and doctor. We more commonly work with people on medication which we have no influence over, and which may be making matters worse. In terms of status, psychotherapists are way down the pecking order, and the central approach of listening does not sit well alongside therapeutic approaches that privilege 'doing something'. Rather than collude with this state of affairs, we need a more ecological approach, which will be explored in Chapter 10.

But we must not be blind to parallel issues within the talking therapies. Privilege is reflected in what is often self-funded training, and through the dominance of white practitioners. While this is a largely female occupation, more men write, present, and teach. That is, men become more visible and prominent. There is a hierarchy between agency and private practice, and between counsellor and psychotherapist, practitioner and supervisor or trainer. Access to long-term free therapy is the exception. Private practice in the UK usually attracts those who by virtue of their own privilege can afford to pay for therapy, a myopic position which cuts me off personally from some of my roots and plays into some of the assumptions that we will consider in the next chapter. It is a commercial transaction on which my livelihood depends.

Different modalities within the profession can be tribal, risking an over-certainty that comes with ascribing to particular theories or ways of doing things. Do we intentionally or unintentionally deceive ourselves or the people we work with about our ability to help? (Caplan, 1995: 21). It is the women like Stella who have confounded my most precious theories, compelled me to listen, and been my greatest teachers. The beginner's mind has served me well, of which I will say more in Chapter 8. Working relationally and in-depth can boost my self-esteem by co-creating moments that feel special, even exclusive. To say it is my privilege to work with people has more than one meaning.

Of course, therapists bring their own history of narcissistic vulnerability to the situation, as we will examine in more detail in Chapter 6: 'Analysts are often fulfilling deeply cherished, idealistic aspirations in choosing their profession, aspirations that transcend narcissistic concerns regarding power and prestige' (Shaw, 2014: 65).

Powerful people sit on our regulatory bodies and ethics committees. This structures power in the profession in particular ways, associated with the particular role we take. We will look at another issue, of relational power, later. Power can be grossly misused without regulation, and even with it when it goes unchallenged or unrecognized. Prominent psychiatrist Ewen Cameron, for example, attracted worldwide recognition for his writing, senior positions, and for his personal warmth and vital concern for the well-being of others (Lemov, 2011: 61). That he was also the mastermind behind a series of barbaric experiments involving brainwashing, designed to eliminate so-called schizophrenia, financed by the CIA from 1957 onwards, is less well-known. The cult-like experimental methods used destroyed the lives of over one hundred Canadians, with an expectation of establishing total control over them (2011: 69), possibly in a bid to win a Nobel prize for his contribution. This shows an altogether darker side of Cameron's personality, with reports of his coldness and being 'the dark figure of ultimate manipulation' (2011: 77). We are compelled to ask, 'What were the embedded institutional, personal and political structures that allowed the peculiar operation of his experiments to go forward as if nothing was amiss?' (2011: 81). Hosemans argues the need for widening the contextual frame clearly, suggesting that psychology embedded within a positivist paradigm 'has served, directly or indirectly, to strengthen the oppressive structures, by drawing attention away from them and toward the individual and subjective factors' (2020: 37).

Finally, I want to consider the concept of 'symptom pools'. This proposes that there is a 'pool' of legitimate culturally appropriate ways through which, out of conscious awareness, a culture may 'choose' to express its distress. This helps to explain why expressions of distress vary between cultures, changing fluidly, and perhaps why there has been an exponential increase in psychiatric diagnoses in the West.

> This idea implied that certain disorders we take for granted are actually caused less by biological than cultural factors – like crazes or fads they can grip or release a population as they enter or fade from popular awareness ... people seem to gravitate unconsciously to expressing those symptoms high on the cultural scale of symptom possibilities. (Davies, 2013: 238)

Trauma has clearly entered the 'symptom pool' of early twenty-first-century Western consciousness. A whole industry has evolved around this trauma symptom pool, involving technologies, research, protocols, psychometric testing, writing, teaching, and delivery of therapy. I am very much a part of this system! While I defend my need to earn my modest income, this leads to a question about who profits from trauma, and what our ethical response should be (Fassin and Rechtman, 2007: 27). Furthermore, to what extent has my own interest in trauma been shaped by the symptom pool, and to what extent does my interest in turn shape and sustain it?

Part 2

The Space Between

Trickster story: Subverting reality

In ancient days when Mawu lived here on earth, Legba was her obedient servant. When he did a good deed the people ignored him and thanked Mawu, but when he did an evil deed the people blamed him directly, as if Mawu had nothing to do with it. Legba complained of this arrangement. Mawu replied that in governing the world it is best if the master be known as good and the servants be known as evil.

'Very well,' said Legba.

Now Mawu had a yam garden and Legba told her that thieves were planning to steal her crop. So Mawu assembled all the people and announced that anyone who stole from her garden would be put to death. That night Legba stole Mawu's sandals and, wearing them on his feet, stole all her yams. When the theft was discovered, Mawu assembled the people and searched to find a foot that matched the footprints in her garden. When none could be found, Legba asked if Mawu herself might have come in the night and forgotten about it.

'Who, me? That is why I do not like you, Legba. I will measure my foot with that footprint.' When Mawu put her foot down, it fit the print exactly.

The people began to laugh and shout. 'The owner herself is a thief!' Mawu was humiliated. She left the earth. She didn't go very far, though – only about ten feet up. And Legba was still her servant: every evening he would come to her and give an account of the day's activity and receive his instructions for the day that followed.

And again, whenever Legba did something wrong the people would blame him, and Mawu herself would join in the reproach. Irritated, Legba conspired with an old woman. Every evening after she had washed her dishes, this old woman would throw the dirty dishwater up into the air and soak Mawu with it. Angered, Mawu soon departed. Now she lives on high and Legba, her son, lives here on this earth.

– Lewis Hyde, 2008: 173

5 | **In the face of trauma**

Portions of this chapter and the next are drawn from my 2019 paper titled 'In the face of trauma: Relationship, ethics, and the possibility of presence'.[1] Another section will appear in Chapter 10. This paper confronted some core issues in working with trauma which deserve to be expanded on. These chapters take us into the Self and Other dimensions of the SOS model.

Having situated trauma within the wider implicit field in which we are all embedded, we turn our focus now to the relationship within the therapeutic dyad. We can call this the situated therapeutic relationship. Both this chapter and the next should be taken together. The title of this chapter draws on Levinas:

> There is a commandment in the appearance of the face, as if a master spoke to me. However, at the same time, the face of the Other is destitute; it is the poor for whom I can do all and to whom I owe all. (1985: 39)

For 'destitute' we might substitute 'traumatized' or 'suffering'. Levinas was a Lithuanian Jew, a philosopher, a seer perhaps, whose family perished in the Holocaust; he knew trauma. A Levinasian approach would be to consider trauma as a moral injury, a human rights issue. Thus his commandment draws us into the territory of ethics, for our responsibility to the Other shapes how we come into relationship with them. In this way, the commandment begins to open up the question, 'Who am I, as therapist, in this?'

Dropping in

What does this 'commandment' evoke in you? A sensation, a thought, an emotion, a memory, an image? How do you receive it and does your body respond? And what is your impulse to do in response? Does your response call upon a familiar or otherwise subtly traumatized response of flight, fight, freeze or collapse? (Taylor, 2014: 60).

When I first presented this paper in Toronto in 2018, I was asked a question about Levinas. My response was that I don't know how to *think* about Levinas; I don't pretend to be a philosopher and indeed am pretty baffled by much of what I have read. I tend to become over-focused in the effort of trying to unravel Levinas' sometimes obtuse, almost prophetic language, which rather obscures the message. This is not about thinking or doing, but about experiencing and being, requiring a shift in attitude rather than a practice. A thought inserts itself into the intersection between Self and Other, turning the Other into an object of concern, reducing presence. Recall, if you will, that at the centre of the SOS model presented in Chapter 2 sits ethical presence, turning into dissociated absence under traumatic conditions. This dissociated absence shifts us out of our bodies and more 'into our heads'; we try to think our way out of an experience that needs to be felt.

However, as Levinas acknowledges, some thoughts cannot be assimilated easily: 'The putting into us of an unincludable idea overturns that presence to self which consciousness is' (Levinas, in Hand, 1989: 175). My preference therefore is to *feel* Levinas. Despite my extensive reading, I have felt my way into this chapter as readers might, and this seems to be entirely consistent with what Levinas tells us.

Echoing Levinas to some degree, the language here is at times dense and sticky; this is a reflection of the themes herein. The Other draws us into a dissociated field, which we recognize by its felt sense rather than through observation (Bromberg, [1998] 2001: 193). There is a mystery in the face of the Other and in our encounter with it that essentially captures and recreates the lived experience of the Other's suffering. The capitalization of 'O' personifies the Other; gives them a name. The effort to grasp the Other in recognition is not to be confused with the *idea* of otherness ([1998] 2001: 64), which pulls us back into our heads. Levinas describes being taken hostage by the Other. Why, then, would anyone want to be taken hostage by trauma, to stare into the face of extreme suffering, to hear stories of the worst atrocities that humans can inflict on one another? It is at best an odd choice to put ourselves *in the face of trauma*, and at worst it is risky. Our primal need for regulation and sense of safety is challenged in the presence of traumatized Others.

Stephanie

I want to introduce you to one of my lovely people who I will call Stephanie, though it's not her real name. Stephanie is one of those people whose dissociation is so extreme and enduring that they are hard to reach. Clearly, there are things she doesn't want to know about her experience any more than I do. This, she tells me, includes her fear of knowing that she is afraid. Her dissociated, usually silent self-state is an example of *unformulated experience* – that which has not been symbolized by thought or language and is not yet knowable. The experience is not able to be reflected upon without threatening the integrity of her self (Straight, 2013: 24).

On one occasion a little way into our work, Stephanie was evidently triggered into a flashback during a session. I had, as I often did, been over-thinking. Rather than work with a tight focus to guide her back into the present moment, I sat back in the chair and opened myself to the feeling tone of what was in the room. As I did so, wave after wave of nausea arose in me. Up until this point, I think I had been defending myself against this, but on reflection, it seemed as though our relationship was ready for it. Where my defences had been up, I could now tolerate, allow in, some of Stephanie's experience, and, I suggest, she was also giving me permission to share her feeling state. I gave my experience back to her: 'It feels as though something really sickening is going on', at which Stephanie nodded and 'came back' more into the room. The conversation that followed took us to new and more clearly articulated territory, more formulated experientially, one to which we could both be differently present.

Knowing and not-knowing

Trauma by nature drives us to the edge of comprehension, cutting us off from language based on common experience or an imaginable past.
– Bessel van der Kolk, 2014: 43

Just as I tell myself I don't really want to know about this, there is also something about trauma that doesn't want to be known – it can be described as an absence, as something that we just can't grasp; it is based on the *destruction* of coherent patterns. Rather like treading water, there is no sense of direction or intentionality, to use a phenomenological term; nevertheless, it requires an immense investment of energy to stay still. To not know is to preserve innocence, and it carries a vulnerability, of which we will say more in the next chapter. These are processes that often don't have any discernible experiential or sensory origin, that have the qualities of the Trickster, the shape-shifter. A natural tendency to seek patterns and meaning makes the uncertainty and confusion in their absence difficult to tolerate, and so we seek comfort in landing on what seems at first to be a certainty. The Trickster can fool me into thinking I am doing something right.

Revisiting my inner chorus from Chapter 1, I want to offer an extended segment from Laub and Auerhahn:

We all hover at different distances between knowing and not knowing about trauma, caught between the compulsion to complete the process of knowing and the inability or fear of doing so. It is in the nature of trauma to elude our knowledge, because of both defence and deficit. The knowledge of trauma is fiercely defended against, for it can be a *momentous, threatening, cognitive and affective task*, involving an unjaundiced appraisal of events and our own injuries, failures, conflicts and losses. (1993: 288, emphasis added)
Reprinted by permission of Taylor & Francis Ltd,
on behalf of Institute of Psychoanalysis

These are such very human responses, aren't they? And when our defences come up, as they will, who are we really defending? Bear in mind here that protection is the flipside of defence; the defensive manoeuvre of distancing may protect us from intense emotion, intimacy, confluence, or fear of 'contamination'. Part of that defence is, I think, to do with the sheer energy that gets tied up, retroflected, in trauma, particularly in frozen people such as Stephanie, and our implicit fear of this being unleashed in our face. The face of trauma is one that holds intense emotions.

The notion of hovering that Laub and Auerhahn refer to implies that there is no right way to be in relationship to trauma, no distance that we strive for. Our response is both personal and situational, and may hold remnants of our own enduring relational themes (Jacobs, 2017; see also Chapter 7) in an effort to protect our differentiated self from annihilation (Bromberg, [1998] 2001: 63). In the distancing is a dynamic tension, the black hole that we simultaneously gravitate towards and resist, and there is often a very fine line between the two. In the territory of what lies between Self and Other is dissociated absence, fear, uncertainty, shame, knowing and not-knowing simultaneously. Krysteva describes this eloquently:

> Suffering is the place of the subject. Where it emerges, where it is differentiated from chaos. An incandescent, unbearable limit between inside and outside, ego and other. The initial, fleeting grasp: 'suffering,' 'fear,' ultimate words sighting the crest where sense topples over into the senses, the 'intimate' into 'nerves'. (1982: 140)

We cannot begin to make sense of meaningless cruelty and suffering; instead, we shift from cognitive to sensory experience, which is of the essence of what the traumatized Other brings into the room. Importantly, this sense of absence can, paradoxically, be unavoidably present, most acutely felt by the therapist. Of course, the absence is and must be present.

Dropping in

Settle your breathing quietly and call to mind an instance, if you can, in which you pulled away from someone, perhaps someone you work with. Feel that pulling in your body. How did you experience it? What was happening in the moment before you pulled away? How did it help you to pull away? What was different once you had done so?

However, this is more than a one-sided situation. The state of 'knowing and not-knowing' about trauma is co-created in the therapy. It is not possible to apportion the ways in which the trauma 'belongs' to an individual or the ancestral or systemic ground. What can be admitted to personal, mutual, or collective consciousness is determined by fear of consequences. These fears may revolve around our capacity to respond appropriately to that which we now know, primarily our capacity to tolerate and still survive this knowledge. Once we look into the face of cruelty that people inflict on one another, we cannot not know; we are exposed to uncomfortable aspects of the human condition that we share. The knowing changes us and our worldview (Perlman and

Saakvitne, 1995: 282). We may be confronted by atrocities on a different scale from anything we have experienced before – ritual abuse, torture, paedophile rings – that stretch our credulity to its limits. Knowing about trauma therefore challenges our collective and personal identities and narratives about the safety of the world and the structures of society we may have taken for granted (see, for example, Gretton, 2019; Pilgrim, 2018). We come up against both the 'obscenity of the act and the obscenity of the silence' (Gretton, 2019: 440), individually and collectively, which hold us in thrall, and can lead to moral corrosion (2019: 518). Used creatively, however, the condition of not-knowing can be seen as an opportunity for learning, growth, and assimilation.

A collective knowing and yet not-knowing is described by Gretton, for example, in his account of Jorge Semprún, a survivor of the concentration camp at Buchenwald who reminded the townspeople of Weimar that they had lived for years, complicit, under the shadow of the camp:

> 'Your pretty town,'… 'so clean, so neat, brimming with cultural memories, the heart of classical and enlightened Germany seems not to have had the slightest qualm about living in the smoke of Nazi crematoria!' … The old men looked away, clearly unwilling to listen to any of this'. (2019: 843–844)

Absence

In Chapter 2, the concept of 'dissociated absence' at the heart of the traumatic breakdown of the contact boundary was imagined. It is a property that organizes the traumatized field. The feeling tone is of a different vibration or wavelength from my everyday tangible reality, which is one way of describing unprocessed trauma.

Three forms of absence are described by Francesetti. First, the absence of 'not being constituted as subjects' (2012: 8), the negation of selfhood that is characteristic of trauma. In the best of therapies, there will be moments, shaped by our own relationship to trauma, in which such negation occurs. There is nothing; it is unknowable. Related to this is being absent, or anaesthetized, to our own senses: 'Here it is difficult to define ourselves through a process of co-creation and therefore the potentialities of the field are only partially embraced' (2012: 9). 'There is something but I don't know what it is'; it is sensed but not yet knowable. The third form of absence is described as more marginal in therapy, for it is 'the experience of an absence that has no sense of the suffering of the other. It is the sense of those who, having no sense of suffering, inflict it' (2012: 10). The absence of the first two forms occurs at the boundary or intersection between Self and Other, the potential of contact.

> The in-between is the common ground which we constantly co-create at the contact boundary. It is the fabric which connects us to the world and to life moment by moment … The in-between is no longer a meeting place. (Francesetti and Roubal, 2013: 441)

Although these authors are writing about depression, the loss of shared ground equally describes the disconnection of trauma. It is 'impossible to form a figure of contact … nothing reverberates in the therapeutic *in-between*' (2013: 441, original emphasis). What is experienced as shapeless, un-form-ulated arising from the traumatized ground, can also be understood as a difficulty in figure-formation (Taylor, 2014: 43), in which undifferentiated figures of interest may present. (See Appendix A for further explanation of these concepts.) In either case, there is no clear focus for attention. The Trickster quality of this is that no sooner do we sense that we have grasped something, it eludes us once again: 'Now you see me, now you don't'. The Trickster is not where we look for it, and we catch the essence of the not-known less by looking full on or searching for it, but by coming at it sideways, almost as if by accident. And yet, something demands to be known in some shape or form, for without this it cannot be assimilated. A constituent factor in trauma therapy is always a striving to know what can't be known and to forget what is already known.

In our encounter with the traumatized Other, there will be an everlasting absence that can never be overcome. This is the absence of the protective Other, the loss of which must be mourned. Recall that in Chapter 1 the contem-porary definition of trauma I offered is that it is something that cannot be sur-vived *alone*. The absence of relational supports at the time of the traumatic experience seems to foreshadow enduring effects and lasting damage. For those who arrive in our consulting rooms, there may never have been any kind of 'relational home', to use Stolorow's (2007: 26) evocative term. This absence of relational ground is something that can be felt by both parties; we might feel into it but not know how to breach the gulf. We then find ourselves staring into an abyss of terrifying loneliness in the person we are with, reverberating with our own existential longing for protection or sanctuary. In the space between we risk both intimacy and pain. Facing the trauma of abandonment may do me harm, for the person who sits before me abandons me, and demands that I don't leave. The face of trauma traumatizes us. We are helpless in the face of suffer-ing, which is intolerable (Gantt, 2000: 11). 'Suffering always implies and is always experienced by more than one person, by more than the individual sub-ject' (2000: 17).

Prior to connection must come recognition of the absence. Held hostage by the black hole we surrender to it, stepping into the river. There is not yet energy for filling the void, and we must not foreclose on the current lived experience. This is how it is now, in order to prepare ground for the next (Spagnuolo Lobb, 2013). 'In a healthy situation, such an abyss is also present as a polar potentiality, as the other side of the potentiality for meeting the other. Such a possibility of a total abandonment is present in the situation' (Roubal, 2019a: 71).

The negative space of such absence shapes the figure, as can be seen in this work by Escher (Figure 5.1). Naming it as an observable absence helps, staying phenomenologically close to experience. When I did this, one person agreed: 'It's empty … dry … parched … cracked', opening a way towards exploring the meaning of these words for her. 'The energy required to traverse [the abyss]

Figure 5.1 M.C. Escher, *Sky and Water*

comes to appear impossible. However, the very fact that its apparent absence causes such acute distress demonstrates that intentionality is actually present. It is present in the very pain which derives from the perception of its absence' (Francesetti and Roubal, 2013: 443). We need to discern this intentionality for the kernel of energy and growth that lies within.

There may not be a story, or much of a story that makes sense. Absence of narrative is sometimes seen as a problem by therapists. For therapists who need to make sense, the absence of narrative need not be the concern that is supposed. Van der Kolk goes so far as to caution against the 'voyeurism' which is fed by stories (2014: 253), for the retelling will create the retraumatization and objectifying distance we wish to avoid. The embodied, implicit, and visceral nature of traumatic memory does not lead towards coherence of story. More helpful is to learn to read the stories that the 'symptoms' – or creative adjustments – are telling, including an understanding of the ways in which the body gets involved. For example, a freeze response can be observed in rigidity of muscle tone, informing us of terror, and a collapse response may indicate helplessness. What can be grasped may be splinters of a story, which are nonetheless laden with sensory experience. The story may present in the content of nightmares, the dream world acting as a shield against knowing in waking life. Most probably, we tune into a recognizable pattern of traumatized existence which speaks through the silence, the known but not yet known. In the stilling of the collapsed or rigid body, the averting or glazing over of the eyes, or the withdrawal of the energy of contact lies a story of terror, of abandonment, of resistance, and of survival. 'The narrative yields to a *crying-out theme* that, when it tends to coincide with the incandescent states of a boundary-subjectivity that I have called abjection, is the crying-out theme of suffering-horror' (Krysteva, 1982: 14, original emphasis).

Dropping in

Colloquially, we might call it the elephant in the room, the thing we can't put into words but we know is there. It may or may not be sensed clearly. Settling yourself, call to mind a time when you had a feeling that there was something missing, either in a personal relationship or a professional one, the sense that you didn't quite 'get' someone. Pay attention to your felt sense of this memory, how your body responds, your emotional tone, any thoughts you might remember about the situation.

The 'thought without a thinker' is a concept proposed by Bromberg (2006: 65); that there is not yet enough of a coherent sense of Self that can be summoned to think it. Similarly, Bollas (2017) introduces the related concept of the 'unthought known'. Although not yet realizable – and it may never be – the unthought known is not to be confused with presupposing or preconfiguring. Neither does it precede contact in a Gestalt sense, which would carry some impetus towards intentionality. We are trying to grasp something more of the essence of the unthought figure, pre-conscious in its existence. Prior to knowing comes being and experiencing (Bollas, 2017: loc 3953), being directly exposed to being (Levinas, in Hand, 1989: 39). Knowing is not always a shared knowing, at least not at the outset. What we may share at any one moment is contingent upon the capacity to remember through experience, to feel into the self-state of the Other, the knowledge being existential rather than cognitively apprehended (Bollas, 2017: loc 542). It is a complex task to track and sustain focus in the fog of such absence, and it affects our sense of who we are in the encounter. Bridges speaks of the difficulty that clinicians experience in maintaining attunement to affect, particularly traumatic affect, on the basis of what this stirs up in the subjectivity of the clinician's self, life, and experiences (cited in Straight, 2013: 73). The work of staying with knowing and not-knowing calls us to infinite patience, trust in the emerging process, courage and humility. The experiential worlds of the people we work with become so personal to us that we may pull away.

Luke holds up a mirror

This brings to mind a young person, Luke, whose story was the stuff of nightmares, and how I slowly became increasingly unsettled by his disclosures of extreme violence in his earliest years. On one occasion, I needed to slow right down and put some plans on hold in order to attend to what disturbed me. In so doing I realized that Luke needed me to process some of his story and give it back to him. I also understood that, for completely different reasons, a terror-filled part of his story overlapped subtly with my own. It was only when I had identified this for myself as the source of my disturbance that I was able to formulate both his story and my own which intersected in the context of our relationship. The next time we met, I told Luke that I had understood that he needed me to process some of his story, and he replied 'Yes, you're spot on'. I suggest that this is a part of our obligation to the Other: 'It is the fundamental responsibility of the therapist to suffer-with and suffer-for the client' (Gantt, 2000: 12). I will return to the impact of this work on the therapist in the next chapter.

Paradoxically, we may have to experience disjunction in order to realign more deeply (Straight, 2013: 224). The Trickster runs in chaotic circles rather than in straight lines. The difficulty of navigating chaotic circles prompts our need to withdraw. This may feel like a misattunement, when it may in fact be an attunement to the dissociated states of our people, a dissociative attunement (2013: 233). Dissociative attunement can be understood as being 'neither intrinsically therapeutic, nor intrinsically traumatizing. It is simply an implicit knowing of information within the therapeutic relationship that may or may not be available for mindful awareness' (Hopenwasser, 2008: 358). It may be felt as a rhythmic relational encounter (2008: 349). According to Bromberg (2006: 142), becoming caught in the dissociative 'bubble' with the people we work with may be a necessary aspect in work with dissociation. I cannot know the river without getting wet. Disengaging from the dissociative bubble we might create the distance, or the intersubjective space, in which we might find a way to meet the Other, through shared experience. It is helpful to really know the difference in our bodies between reacting, resonating, and responding. Each has a different energetic quality and sense of direction.

Dropping in

Take a moment to sit back and check if you can tell the difference, from your experience, between getting caught in the dissociative process of another person and a reactive resonance, which is a differentiated position. How does this register in your being?

British body psychotherapist Shoshi Asheri writes about the presentation of disorganized and dissociated manifestations of trauma:

When a client enters the therapy room ... they inevitably enter into a relationship with a part of the therapist that would rather remain dissociated than feel the unbearable feelings that an engagement with such trauma can evoke, particularly if the therapist carries a related trauma of his or her own. (2013: 73)

How we establish the capacity to bear the unbearable is a major therapeutic endeavour for the both therapist and the person they are working with. This is what summons us to turn dissociated absence on its head and awaken to the possibility of ethical presence.

One of the dichotomies I would like to highlight and deconstruct is that of alienation and identification. Trauma leads us face to face with splits and the problem of otherness, including our inner sense of otherness. By this I mean the disowned, including those aspects of experience that may be dissociated within ourselves, which we make 'not me'. This relates to the quote from Parlett that I introduced in Chapter 1:

> 'Identification with' is to be aligned with, or to join together; while 'alienation from' involves distancing from 'the other'. *And with this distancing goes a small, subtle, and yet discernible reduction in the personhood of the other, or others … All of us are part of this phenomenon of identifying and alienating. It takes an enormous shift in consciousness to transcend this dynamic, to step outside it, to recognise it, and to avoid being caught in it.* (2015: 124, emphasis added)

Notice the echo here of the 'momentous task' emphasized in the earlier quote from Laub and Auerhahn, which we will come back to later. The alienation in trauma involves psyche and soul as well as body and flesh (Fassin and Rechtman, 2007: 187). Just as I begin to grasp this, paradoxically it seems to turn on its head, the modus operandi of the Trickster. Alienation and identification are the underbelly of human dignity, connection, and reciprocity, and the shifts are small and subtle as we will examine further in Chapter 7.

The processes of alienation and identification raise a question about how we meet one another in our differences without alienating others or closing ourselves off. As the evidence of the Milgram experiment reminds us (see Chapter 2), there is much of the human condition that we might well want to dissociate from, including our personal capacity for violence, or the brute genocide of indigenous peoples. 'The theoretical problem is not "why do we shut out?" but "do we ever not shut out?"' (Cohen, 2001: 249). How do we meet trauma, with all our very human resistances and defences against knowing, hearing, feeling – about ourselves? This is the challenge of consciousness, presence, and connection.

Bisi

After qualifying as a doctor at the University of Lagos, Bisi went to work in maternal health in northern Nigeria. Despite being frequently overstretched in her capacity to treat the women and children in her care, Bisi was committed to her work. She was confronted daily by terrible systemic poverty, disorganized health provision, and a lack of resources. The region she was in, however, was unsettled by attacks during the insurgency by Boko Haram. Bisi regularly treated the injuries of women and children raped in front of one another, horrific and sickening events. She tried to intervene on the behalf of victims, but as a woman, a professional, and a non-Muslim, her position was risky for complex cultural reasons. When her own life was endangered, she fled, leaving via Lagos for the UK, where she was offered a post in a British hospital.

Two years later, Bisi came into therapy because she had not settled well in Britain. She was an angry woman. Having grown up with the idea that Britain was some sort of promised land, the reality came as a shock to her. I sat with her as she raged week after week about the coldness of British people, the discrimination she experienced, about feeling unwelcome, too visible, not belonging. She railed at me for being white and British, despite the welcome I hoped I was offering; it felt as though I was standing in for all British people, all white people. I could not see myself in her attacks and resented being seen as white and unwelcoming. And yet I recognized that some of 'my people' could behave in such ways. Very slowly, the cold realization of the legacy of British colonization of Nigeria, embedded in Bisi's story and in our relationship, dawned on me.

At times reeling from shame, I experienced a deep helplessness at being unable to reach Bisi in her terrifying loneliness. I was fearful both of my incapacity to meet Bisi and of being cast out of her experiential world. This conflict created in me a small and subtle distancing in the face of her attacks. My reaction felt of a greater proportion to what was being articulated, already present, and yet I could not identify directly with her experience. A period of painful self-reflection tuned me into a darkness masked by Bisi's anger, which I recognized as a dissociated defence. With a sense of foreboding, I had to accept that there was yet more to come. It felt inescapable and inevitable, signals that there was a deeper layer of trauma present in the room. What other narrative was being masked by her experience of being treated as Other? This enabled me to wait more patiently for this unknown and nameless 'absent presence' to reveal itself.

And thus, out of layers of disconnection and confusion some words came to me: 'Bisi, no matter how much you may want it, I can never be a black African woman like you'. Bisi stopped and looked directly at me as if seeing me for the first time. Our eyes met, we smiled and breathed more slowly together. Bisi's anger subsided and we began to edge towards the as yet unformulated other terrors in her life.

Dropping in

Centre yourself and bring into focus the gap between you and others, however you experience this. Take a few breaths. As you inhale, bring more of others into that gap. As you exhale, extend more of who you are into that gap (adapted from Nepo, 2000: 199).

Into the intersubjective space come shards of traumatic memory, one a time. 'We have been drip-fed traumatic narratives; we are watched [by the people who come to see us] to see if we retaliate, get ill, give up. Only when we show that we are still standing is it possible for the next drip to be given' (Sinason, 2008: 84). The people who come to see us take the lead in reading us, faster and more essentially than we read them. There can be constant fear of being too much, of the implicit understanding that we must be in the river together. Without this joining in the experience, the sufferer is once again lost and abandoned, making them highly vigilant to our capacity to stay present. I know; I have knowingly 'drip fed' a therapist myself. As a therapist, I need the humility to accept that I don't know it all.

Implicit bias

Before people arrive in our consulting rooms, we undoubtedly already hold attitudes and biases, often out of awareness, that will preconfigure the relational field. These biases can be part of our identity and reflect our position of power and privilege, the ways in which we make people 'other', not me, and are formed in part because the human brain is wired to notice difference. Beyond our natural defences or compulsion in relation to trauma, we all make judgements which colour our way of perceiving the whole picture. Quite naturally and inevitably we will adopt the positions that most fit our comfort zones, that *don't* challenge our own preconceptions. For example, thinking in particular ways about what it means to be a 'victim', we might make allowances for the chronically ill mother who colluded with an abusive father, or we might overlook the fact that someone's partner employs trafficked people in his construction business, implicitly becoming passive bystanders in the process. Enduring cultural myths – prejudices even – about the nature of trauma, of child abuse, sexual violence, and recovery also inform our stance. Can we really hold unjaundiced attitudes about whether someone can 'ask for' a violent sexual assault, or, perhaps like Alesha in Chapter 3, 'enjoy' abuse by an adored older person? These ethical questions are so sensitive that we easily get pulled in one direction or the other, and we position ourselves accordingly. How, then, might such perceptions and avoidance play into our own patterns of identification and alienation, and then play out in our consulting rooms? When does our hope for recovery turn into over-certainty in our approach? When do we have a 'plan' and find that, in Trickster fashion, it goes awry?

Implicit biases are 'typically characterised as automatic associations, of which we may not be aware, that are difficult to control and *may conflict with our professed beliefs and values*'(Holroyd et al., 2017: 1, emphasis added). A conscious avowal of non-discrimination may preclude self-reflection of how this is imparted in actuality: 'I am a feminist, and therefore I don't have to look at the subtle ways in which I treat men differently, or at how I treat black, trans or disabled women'. These kinds of biases operate not only individually but at all levels of society, in healthcare, in criminal justice systems, education, and the financial sector (access to loans or mortgages) as suggested in Part 1.

Because implicit biases are usually embodied, held out of awareness and culturally enforced and repeated, the harms may be particularly damaging (Holroyd et al., 2017: 2). Bear in mind, if you will, that a bias against some group or individual will have its corollary in a positive bias towards some others.

Dropping in

Put aside this book and log in to a computer. Search for Harvard University's Project Implicit (www.implicit.harvard.edu/implicit/takeatest), where you can choose from a range of tests to check your own bias in different areas. Each takes a few minutes and is revelatory. I suggest you take at least two of these and note what surprises you or confirms what you already believed about yourself. What do you learn about your self-awareness in difficult areas? And what might you feel obligated to do or change as a response? Which of the categories reveals either your oppression or privilege? What do your biases tell you about your culture and what is 'normalized' within it?

As you will have seen in these tests, the biases and assumptions we make are frequently associated with body image. Johnson (2018a: 105) describes an exercise in which she invites her students to make inferences, often remarkably astute, about her own social identifiers such as religion, sexual orientation, class, and age from their observations of her posture, gait, attire, and facial expression. There is a correlation here with the concept of intersectionality considered in Chapter 3.

Aside from the assumptions you may hold about who is 'Other', the issue of responsibility is relevant to the issue of bias. First, a distinction can be made between the *cause* of the wrong and how *blame* may be apportioned – the moral responsibility (Holroyd et al., 2017: 3). I have written elsewhere about the linked concepts of shame, blame, and responsibility (Taylor, 2014: 153), looking at boundary organization and co-creation. I have personally found the notion of blame to be more associated with shame, and therefore suffering, while the taking of responsibility is softer, more nuanced, and more relational. ⌐ check

A further consideration is that of reparation, defining who can or morally should be accountable and make amends. Is reparation an individual responsibility or a structural one?

> Therapists feel responsible for the change, for a result in the therapy, for helping the suffering person in front of them … Therapists either put this responsibility on themselves, and then they become frustrated by themselves, or they put the responsibility on their clients, and then they become frustrated by them. (Roubal, 2019a: 11–12)

According to Levinasian ethics, our responsibility to the Other is total and primary, a non-symmetric summons to commit ourselves to the suffering before us. Welfare systems and compensation for victims of injustices indicate collective responsibility that is not always primary. Systemic repair does not absolve individuals from offering themselves in the service of the suffering Other. Arguably, the only duty we have is to be there and to witness.

The ethics of being in relationship

The ethical questions raised in the face of trauma are not concerned with codes or the practicalities of setting of boundaries and fees. The questions here are the ethics of being in relationship, emerging from and intrinsic to relationship. If you are not in relationship with, and cannot see the face of the Other, you cannot feel obligation (Gretton, 2019: 806). The responsibility to witness sits neither with the therapist nor the person they are working with. Roubal's (2019b) proposition is that responsibility lies one hundred percent with one, and one hundred percent with the other. An ethics of a different order is proposed by Bloom (2013). This he calls 'situated ethics', the ethics of the human situation, 'a structure of the phenomenal lifeworld in which all of us can be *human beings*' (2013: 132, original emphasis). It is this situated ethic that is the basis for contacting, for reorganizing the breakdown at the contact boundary. Every intervention we make, even choosing to remain silent – and for how long – involves an ethical decision about the possibility of presence and the space from which a new knowing might emerge. This is an ethic of choosing. The balance between maintaining enough flexibility to exercise choice and becoming ossified by the fixed Gestalts of traumatic material requires constant attention. In any walk of life, and most certainly in the psychotherapy profession, 'I know that by not deciding, I have decided. I know that by not committing to a position, I have committed. Not making an ethical decision is, itself, an ethical decision' (Carroll and Shaw, 2013: 19).

Denham-Vaughan and Chidiac position the SOS model as an ethical premise: 'It is important to realize that, in balancing the threefold elements of self, other and situation, the focus shifts away from simply prioritising meeting the immediate needs of the client; the issue of impact is also directly addressed' (2013: 104). We will return to this concept of impact in the next chapter. Here, the ethical consideration is not one of intention or focus, but of taking into account the effects of one's actions – or inactions – and therefore is deeply relational. Consistent with a humanistic orientation, we do our best: 'Of course, our intentions are always "good". It is difficult for us to do deeds with bad intentions' (Carroll and Shaw, 2013: 242). However, recognizing that *intent does not equal impact* is critical; the implicit bias tests demonstrate how impact may be the very opposite of good intentions. We may cause the Other pain just by staying with them in this space. As Smothers rightly asks: 'What are we to do when the other standing before us wishes to become known, yet the act of being known reminds her of traumatic intrusion?' (2016: 253).

This is also an aspect of the Trickster playing in the relationship: be careful what you wish for because you will surely get it; however, what you get might not be what you want, but it will most certainly be what you need. Understanding impact thus becomes a necessary condition for dialogue. Regarding our intent to meet difference in the face of the Other, McConville says: 'But good intentions … are not enough. And in so far as they blind me to the impact of my behavior on the other, good intentions are indeed part of the problem … if I am going to wade into the sensitized field of diversity … good intentions are the only thing I can count on' (2005: 180). The theme of the motives underlying our work is explored in detail in Chapter 6.

In locating ethics within a socially conscious paradigm, it becomes possible to think of ethical decisions as a systemic process (Carroll and Shaw, 2103: 20). Indeed, the ethical turn in psychotherapy in the last decade sprang from the study of the trauma of Holocaust survivors in particular (Goodman and Severson, 2016). Orange describes the vulnerability of being taken hostage by the Other as an 'ethical subjectivity' (2016b: 61). Hence, as Wheeler suggests, the greater difficulty comes 'not from the overt clash of beliefs and isms but from a much deeper, more paradigmatic level of assumptions' (2005: 47), which colour our attitudes to 'Other', gender, change, history, and trust, for example, and which may not be in the awareness of either party. Some of these dynamics were very evident in Bisi's story, above.

The commandment Levinas entrusts us with draws us so inexorably towards pain that it is easily construed as masochistic; no other profession demands this of anyone. To regard this as masochism, however, is a misunderstanding. Making a distinction between the submission that is commonly associated with masochism and surrender, Orange says this: 'Suffering without ego, without intention, with sincerity, does not seek pain; it simply suffers it for the sake of the Other. To surrender is not to seek pain or punishment' (2016a: 58).

My concern is not about me but about my responsibility to the Other. Ghent also offers some pertinent thoughts about this surrender: 'Faith, surrender, the beginnings of creativity and symbol formation all intersect in the world of transitional experiencing' (1990: 108). Likening the surrender to the Other to sexual orgasm, Ghent implies that surrender leads to intimacy. In the absence not yet formulated into realizable experience, we are in a transitional space full of creative potential. In the setting aside of ego, we come to a more immediate form of intimacy. 'The superstructure of defensiveness, the protections against anxiety, shame, guilt, anger are, in a way, all deceptions, whether they take the form of denial, splitting, repression, rationalizations, evasions' (1990: 109). The commandment exhorts us not to so much to submit as to yield to the witnessing of suffering without resistance. Ghent suggests that deep down we may long to give up our evasions so that we might be known by the other. We will return to the theme of masochism and therapist well-being in the next chapter.

Absence becomes presence

Various writers attest to the complexities of working with traumatized people. For example, Kylea Taylor (1995: 37) speaks of the particular ethics that are summoned in the presence of non-ordinary states of consciousness in the people we work with, states such as dissociation, because those states seem to change ordinary pitfalls into quagmires, which rings true for me in my clinical practice, such as where things have 'slipped' the memory of one party or the other. We *both* enter into and emerge from states of dissociation. We looked earlier at two contributions which admit to the difficulty of becoming conscious. Laub and Auerhahn described the 'momentous, threatening, cognitive and affective task' of knowing trauma, of bringing it into awareness, and Parlett named the 'enormous shift in consciousness' needed to transcend the splits associated with 'Othering'. In order to be true to the spirit of Levinas, we take on the ethical responsibility of fostering presence for ourselves, as we shall see in following chapters. If we neglect this, we avert our eyes from the face of the Other, dehumanizing them. It is through our senses that the intentionality of contact becomes manifest. Orange speaks of 'ethical seeing', with eyes and ears open (2106a: 94), stressing that seeing is the very core of ethics (2016a: 124). Recognition is re-cognition, the knowing that is waiting to be realized.

A development of the concept of ethical presence at the heart of the SOS model considers the co-emergent properties of the implicit relational field. Here, power is seen as a moderator of the situation, giving rise to the question of whose needs are dominant. The very presence we offer carries a risk of dominating (Chidiac and Denham-Vaughan, 2020: 26). In the presence we summon to sit alongside absence, we offer not a cure, but a welcoming of wounding (Orange, 2016a: 26), giving dignity and validity to the pain. Whose pain, though? We must take to heart the imperative to take care of our own deepest and most vulnerable places. 'The best yardstick for the enormity of the trauma lies in our own incapacity to bear witness to it; or in the level of dissociation that listening to it inflicts on the witness' (Sachs, 2013: 25). The corollary of this is that the best yardstick of healing trauma lies in our capacity to bear witness to it, and in the level of presence the witness can bring to the endeavour. These themes will be picked up in the following chapters.

I suggest that it is in the therapist that lies the first knowing of trauma, guided perhaps by the recognition of the Trickster, who nudges us to being awake enough (Bromberg, 2006), aware enough to know. Returning to my example of Stephanie, waking up to her suffering was a risk I had to take in order to face her trauma with her. In that moment, also was my recognition of several elements: an acceptance of my limits; that I cannot change her suffering or the course of her life; and that she might meet me in return with gratitude, indifference, anguish, or anger.

Note

1   Published in the *Gestalt Review*, and reproduced here with permission.

6 Me voici

This chapter follows closely on the previous one, bringing us to the heart of an ecological approach to therapy, by examining the position of the therapist within the traumatized relational field. In previous chapters, we have considered ground trauma and issues of power and privilege that implicate every one of us, whether therapist or not. We looked in the previous chapter also at the implicit biases and assumptions that we bring to the work, and the impact they may have. 'Relationships are about others, but they are always about ourselves in relation to others' (Carroll and Shaw, 2013: 114). The ethical lens through which we considered Levinas' commandment positions us in relationship to trauma. The title here comes from Levinas: 'Here I am'.

To frame the discussion, a caution is provided by Pearlman and Saakvitne in the following quote, which I introduced in Chapter 1:

> Trauma therapy profoundly changes the therapist. We give up our familiar ways of being and beliefs about the world when we embark on this work with survivors of traumatic life events. These changes are both inspiring and disturbing, involving gains and losses. (1995: 279)

We will return to this towards the end of the chapter.

The key question

A number of the clinical examples I have drawn on so far highlight a primary question in working with trauma, one I invite students to reflect on and work with over time. *I consider the most important question to be about our own relationship to trauma.* This involves three aspects: our ancestral story, including cultural and ground trauma; our personal history – the backstories that tend to pull us in the direction of helping others; and our current position in relation to traumatic events. The latter aspect may include fascination, compulsion, excitement, voyeurism, distance, contempt, or disgust as our personal responses, often based on the assumptions, biases, and myths we hold about trauma, as suggested in the previous chapter. What, for example, do we believe about the nature and gender of a so-called 'victim' or a 'perpetrator'? I have felt many things at different times and generally my own relationship in the face of trauma has changed over the years. This question is important because it shapes how we position ourselves, either helping or hindering the therapeutic relationship.

Dropping in

Taking each of the three parts of the key question in turn, write about your relationship to trauma. You are not going to show this to anyone, so let yourself run free with it. To prompt your thinking, I reproduce here some specific questions from my earlier book:

- 'What is your response to someone who becomes helpless and assumes the victim position?
- What of your persecutory or rescuer parts?
- How do you manage your need for contact when your client is disconnected and dissociated?
- What personal history do you share with your client? How do you regulate yourself around this?
- What are your own experiences of love, hate, aggression, longing, sexuality, grief and terror?
- What are your feelings towards those who hurt others, especially children?
- How do your gender, race, religion and other cultural factors bias your responses?
- What is your response to difficult intense emotions? What is your experience of working with them or of resolving them? Try and think of concrete examples and write about what happened.
- What response do you have to hearing stories of appalling abuse, torture and suffering? Shock, denial, shame, anger, blame, or dissociation may be among them.
- What of your own need to be comforted or regulated by your client?'

(Taylor, 2014: 176, 178, 180)

Fields of mutual influence

The foundations of relationality centre around communication, both verbally and non-verbally. According to Lichtenberg (2001), there are four corners of contact, to which I have added two more here in italics: (1) I am; (2) *You are*; (3) I react to you; (4) I want you to tell me who you are and what you want; (5) I want you to tell me how you react to me; (6) *I want to show you who I am, what I want and how I react to you.* This hexagram of contact (Figure 6.1), if one might call it that, reflects more accurately the mutuality or reciprocity of a contemporary relational approach. Relationship cannot exist without impact, as was implied in Chapter 5. Alter one aspect of this hexagram and the quality of possible contact changes, and will be re-shaped by both parties according to the support available in the moment. This is a concrete way of interpreting Sander's concept of fields of mutual influence (1977). Like two stones tossed into a pool, the ripples we create intersect with those of another. In a relational

Figure 6.1 The hexagram of contact

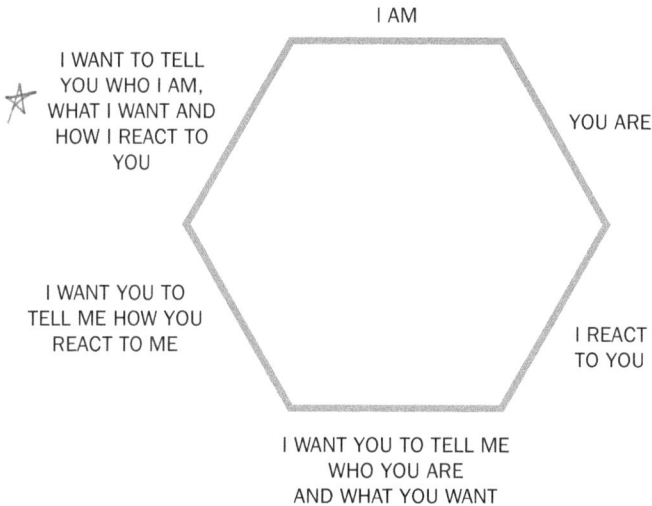

I AM

I WANT TO TELL
YOU WHO I AM,
WHAT I WANT AND
HOW I REACT TO
YOU

YOU ARE

I WANT YOU TO
TELL ME HOW YOU
REACT TO ME

I REACT
TO YOU

I WANT YOU TO TELL ME
WHO YOU ARE
AND WHAT YOU WANT

therapeutic paradigm, *we influence the field every bit as much as the trauma-tized individual influences us.*

Stewart Perlman addresses the personal impact of this work: 'More than any other patients, sexual abuse and trauma survivors provoke deep emotional responses and raise unresolved issues in the therapist' (1999: 25). To resonate with such provocation is not – *is absolutely not* – a failure.

> Our vulnerability to one another is an integral part of our biology, not a sign of weakness or lack of professionalism … When we are in the presence of a traumatized person our brains become activated in the same ways as when we are traumatized ourselves. (Cozolino, 2004: 192)

Our response is as involuntary as the trauma responses of the people who come to us.

Kepner suggests that 'our own body process is an intrinsic part of the trans-action with the client' (2003: 11), emphasizing that intersubjective arousal is a primary transaction. I suggest that it is the autonomic nervous system that we register and resonate with most clearly when we are in the presence of some-one who is traumatized. We join with them or create distance according to our own relational patterns and histories; we are drawn into states resembling chaos and rigidity.

What we ignore or hold out of awareness ourselves may be picked up acutely by the people who come to us, and herein lies a key point: *'The inner state of the therapist* strongly influences the response of the client' (Geller and Greenberg, 2012: 59, emphasis added). My proposition is that greater aware-ness of implicit processes and the dynamics of Trickster states is in itself a major therapeutic intervention, increasing the possibility of presence. Geller and Greenberg link presence to mindful practice, not by teaching the people who come to us to be mindful, but by becoming more mindful ourselves (2012: 13). I can give you two examples of this. Recently, Stephanie reported seeing me as a mindfulness teacher though we'd never talked about it. Another person, Holly, came into the room one morning and was immediately on alert and saying that something was different. Nothing had changed in the physical environment, but she had instantly picked up something in me. I had tripped and fallen the evening before; with no more than some impressive bruises, I was still shaken and was not taking enough account of that. I told Holly about my fall and that helped settle her agitation. What feels like an individual problem is isolating and needs to be reframed as relational. In that context we can make meaning.

There is a currency about avoiding vicarious trauma and secondary trauma in the helping professions that troubles me, and is a theme of this chapter. These concepts seem disconnected from a field perspective and reductionistic, as though one party is doing this to the other in the exchange, and as a shortcoming on the part of the therapist. I don't for one moment believe this to be the case. We cannot avoid being part of the traumatized relational field of which we are all part. I am much more comfortable with Gartner's (2017) notion of counter-trauma, which at least begins to move towards our own trauma responses having a part in our own inevitable embodied resonances. Taking Levinas into account, we make a choice to experience these co-creations. Yet, as Pearlman and Saakvitne remind us, 'Rarely do therapists enter the field of trauma therapy with full understanding of the implications of their choice' (1995: 279).

Taking responsibility

Levinas (1985) asserts in his commandment (Chapter 5) that it is the traumatized Other 'to whom we owe everything'. We have to feel this, he seems to insist, and to bracket our own interests. This is a challenging ethic particularly because Levinas intended it to be asymmetrical. Rabbinical scholars Zweifel and Raskin advise as follows: 'To raise a man from mud and filth … it is not enough to stay on top and reach down a helping hand … You must go way down yourself into the mud and filth' (2008: 211). For many therapists, this is second nature, the relational ground on which we stand. One student told me: 'Taking on responsibility for everyone else's suffering – that's the role I took in a family that couldn't feel anything'. Here lies the potential to over-identify with as much as to raise defences – *a dichotomy we need to seek to overcome for ourselves* if we are to meet in the mud and filth.

Set against this, Orange questions whether our welcome of suffering is in fact (to use her term) an 'unanalysed moral masochism' (2016a: 52). She goes on to ask, 'Should we be setting better limits, for our own sakes … and for that of the client as well? Better limits according to whom, though? … How do we decide what is service to the other and what is masochism?' (2016a: 52). It can be extraordinarily difficult for therapists, raised like my student, to take responsibility to learn to say 'no', especially in times of high demand and scarce resources. Working as clinical lead in a young people's service many years ago, we were challenged by long waiting lists that grew with no hope of helping the people on them. One of the hardest decisions to make on rare occasions was to close the waiting list, and signpost people elsewhere; it simply didn't seem realistic or ethical to ask them to wait indefinitely. The limits we set were clearly in the interests of taking pressure off the service, and it was more comfortable (in a deeply uncomfortable situation) to argue that it helped the young people. I still don't know if we did the right thing.

To be honest, it hurts to see so many therapists suffer for their work, and I invite students and supervisees to think clearly and realistically about their limits and what nurtures them. As just one example, a workshop participant, an experienced mature trainer herself, told me: 'I'd lost hope of ever finding nourishment for myself again', which left me concerned about how she could possibly sustain her work from a position of such deficit. What enduring relational themes (Jacobs, 2017; see also Chapter 7) were playing out in this, I wondered, and what were the implicit messages being held in the relational therapeutic field?

my cutting off

The mission

I work on the assumption that many of us become therapists to deal with our own wounds, and therefore that there will be much personal and collective trauma among my readers. I honour and acknowledge what it takes to come to this place, and join with many of you in saying, 'Me Too'. We are in this together, becoming part of the context in which we work. Our good intention to bring healing into the world may have grandiose proportions: a Messiah Complex. Louis Cozolino has something to say about the unconscious motives that bring us to this work, often in the service of preserving our own sanity or that of our family:

> Many of us grow up being told what good listeners we are, how well we mediate family conflict, or how we manage to regulate the emotions of those around us … we can be better therapists when these missions are identified, understood, and factored into how we experience our clients. (2004: 14–15)

Without this, he says, we risk turning our career into drudgery. That mission may be to heal some wounds from our past by attending to those of other people. Up pops the problem of over-identification.

Among positive and worthy motivations, there may also be a darker, unconscious side. These might include using our professional status as proof of our 'sanity'; becoming preoccupied with rescuing others having felt unable to do so in the past and which has led to a feeling of worthlessness we need to defend against; or to establish the moral high ground in a current power struggle with a significant person in our life (Shaw, 2014: 65).

my being 'human'
↳ be good   to connect deeply

Marie Adams published her doctoral research under the title of 'The Myth of the Untroubled Therapist' (2014). For our parts, some of what we bring to the relational field carries distinct hallmarks of our personal trauma. We do well to take ourselves seriously as participants in the traumatized relational field. How would it be to slow down for a moment and consider how our own histories, dichotomies, certainties, indifference, the things we can't bear, our victim, perpetrator and rescuer states, our potential for violence may all mirror, even subtly, the conditions in which relational trauma gets played out? Adams asks the question, 'Why did you become a therapist?' (2014: 10). My answer to this might be along these lines: *Because I care deeply about people who are hurt, because I am outraged by the damage that one person inflicts on another, and because I believe that the suffering can be alleviated.*

Dropping in

Why did you become a therapist? Write a few bullet points about your response.

Adams tells the story of one person who said in her first session, 'This will begin being about me, but will end up being about you' (2014: 80) – a smart, prescient comment indeed. 'But why did you *really* become a therapist?', insists Adams (2014: 80). Well, here I have to be really honest: because I had an uncomfortable relationship with myself, with my body, with being in my own skin; because of the millions of threads of shame that made the cloak I wore; *because I believed the lies people had told about who I was in the world. Like many of my readers, no doubt, I had lived a hard life and hoped for something easier.* What I have come to recognize is that by continually addressing my answers to the second question, I became less idealistic, less deluded by the Trickster that manifests in my answers to the first question.

Needless to say, we do not enter this profession with an explicit intention to heal our own wounds – any gains by the therapist are secondary to the needs of the people we work with. The ethics we bring to bear about the use of self-disclosure are necessary to protect those people from entering a therapy that is *set up*, even out of awareness, to be about the therapist or their healing. However, we can also use this ethic as a screen for our own vulnerability, the human suffering which we share with the people we work with. This then creates a distance between us.

Although I have never shared my own story with anyone I work with, it is present in every moment of my life, and continually informs my work. I believe, therefore, that some selective sharing, *in the service of the Other*, rather than in a self-serving way, can be of benefit. I go so far sometimes to let people know I have been hurt, that I too know this place. The more that I am willing to be open about this, the more others open up, and this is one way of flying in the face of the secrecy and denial that surround trauma. The story I tell here is one I used to feel ashamed of, masking my vulnerability, but that is no longer the case.

Miriam Part 2: Seismic shifts or the making of a therapist

My late arrival into my large family (see Chapter 2) was difficult. My understanding is that the family was already under enormous pressure, like a familial narrowing of the window of tolerance. Unspoken and unprocessed were my mother's childhood trauma, likewise my father's Second World War experience in which he was present at the carnage at Monte Cassino. A surprise baby was likely a threat to the very uncertain stability of the system. My mother had a 'psychotic' breakdown when I was three weeks old and she was hospitalized for six months. Working through my abandonment in therapy, my somatic memory was like existing in free-fall, relationally and experientially groundless. My baby-self registered her homecoming as the arrival of a disturbance. My mother's hatred of me was visceral: 'Look what you've done to me' delivered an implicit message about my value. Criticism was a constant. I could have been blamed for an increase in the price of bread, so meaningless and comprehensive was her level of insult. As much as she lobbed scorn at me, I caught it, and carried it. That she sexually abused me over many years took her vitriol to a whole new level. She said it made her feel better, made me thank her for hurting me, and passed me on. The most harrowing set of fractured memories I have of this time are of being – for a thankfully brief period – abused in a group setting, during which I was forced to watch another child being hurt: 'Look at what you made us do'.

While my mother was volatile, unpredictable, dangerous, and exciting, my father represented a different order of terror. He was cold and rigid, exercising control through his lack of emotion. He was capable of some staggering cruelty, taking no responsibility: 'Look what you made me do'. I felt as though he – we – lived in a glass dome, and that should I mis-step and break it, a terrible violent rage would be unleashed. There was no laughter in our home; any occasional light-heartedness was berated as 'sentimental'. The permissible emotional range was zero – with the exception of my mother, of course. To live and survive this was simply devastating and annihilating. By the age of eight I was taking medication for chronic insomnia; I had no comfort, not even a teddy bear. One of my sisters made me a rag doll when I was about eleven, a doll without a mouth: 'You can't speak'. Indeed, I became mute for a period of my teens, when I was also truanting and self-harming.

Just as my mother had needed to escape family, so did I. I married young and moved away. Two years later, I was raped at night by a stranger who broke into our house while my husband was away for work. I decided this was worse than murder, because I was going to have to live with this. Reporting immediately to the police left me in an alternative universe in which clear evidence was distorted; I was initially accused of breaking my own kitchen window and fabricating my numerous superficial injuries. Doctors treating me obliterated the experience, obliterated me: 'I suggest you don't go getting into any more fights' one admonished me in a public waiting area. In the blink of an eye I had turned from being a woman asleep in her own bed to being seen as a trouble-maker. How did that happen? Of course I felt duly ashamed, not knowing what I had done wrong. Never 'Why me?', the cry from my soul was simply 'Why?'

> The legal process did not bring a sense of justice; a plea bargain meant I did not have to be cross-examined but resulted in a lesser conviction for assault. My relational field was too fragile to support me. Friends and family tiptoed round me for some time with an uncertain respect, but didn't know what to say. My mother told me it was my fault; why wouldn't she? My fault for being a woman, for being alive. As far as I was concerned, there was also a cultural element. The man who raped me was black, and I believed instinctively that race was a factor. Rape was a sure way a black person could gain power over a white one. I had difficulty reckoning with this; could I, 'should' I, be angry with a black man? I felt like collateral damage in the long history of slavery: 'Look what I made him do'. The reverberations of my rape were long-lived. But live with rape was exactly what I did, and it proved to be an awakening, as we will see in Chapter 10.

The story I have told you may be shocking, but for me the real shock lies not in the detail or how personal it is, but in recognizing how grindingly common such stories are, as any seasoned therapist will know.

> **Dropping in**
>
> Why did you *really* become a therapist? I invite you to take this opportunity to unpack some of the conditioning in your personal story that led you to this place.

Listening to many supervisees, trainees, and workshop participants, they often tell complex, ambivalent, and overly responsible stories of their relationship to their work with traumatized people. This has led me to an interest in the subject of altruism and how it plays into the relational dynamic in therapy. Interestingly, the word 'altruism' shares it roots with alterity, Otherness, or 'autrui', as Levinas would term it.

Altruism

The desire to help others is a clear driver for those who choose to work in caring professions. An altruist is primarily motivated by the reduction of suffering, counteracting the forces that cause harm to others. Altruism, as a cooperative act in service of the well-being of others, is a fundamental aspect of social cohesion. Ricard suggests that altruism is a unifying force against individualism, competition, and consumption (2015: 9), and that it determines the quality of our existence (2015: 12). Charitable giving, fair trade initiatives, and humanitarian aid are all predicated on altruistic motives, regardless of the underpinnings of imperialism and superiority in some instances. The social and relational implications of altruistic behaviour can be viewed through the lens of the SOS model (Chapter 2).

> Altruism has been defined as 'unselfish concern for the welfare of others' ... this definition implies that concern for self and or for other are distinct psychological states and, indeed, that the psychological boundary between self and other can be demarcated. (Li and Rodin, 2012: 138)

In the best of worlds, altruism and our perception of it are grounded in the ability to rise above self-interest, to be context-sensitive, and to be comfortable with ambiguity and radical uncertainty (Halifax, 2018: 28).

Dropping in

What do you think are some of the benefits of altruism, and how might these benefits be distributed between the different elements of the SOS model? Take a moment to think this through. Does anything surprise you?

Altruistic behaviour has social, genetic, ethical, relational, biological, and implicit dimensions. To a large extent, acts deemed to be 'good' or 'harmful' are determined culturally, and change over time. For example, in the West we no longer tolerate the public executions or torture that were acceptable in the past. To some extent, altruism is innate; to raise infants successfully, parents must put their own interests to one side. Serving others is most clearly seen in family and kinship groups. We are more likely to risk our life for the benefit of a number of others to whom we are tied genetically (Ricard, 2015: 155). In some circumstances, we extend our altruistic behaviour to strangers. Blood or organ donors, for example, do not know the recipients of their gifts, potentially including those of whom we might not otherwise approve. Importantly, however, altruism is more concerned with intent than impact.

Given that there may rarely be completely pure motives, it is helpful to consider the benefits to the donor: 'Altruistic behavior has been demonstrated to have numerous benefits for the altruist, including better physical and mental health, and increased fitness' (O'Connor et al., 2012: 15), and we can imagine that the benefits are multiple and implicit. First, we can probably agree that it feels good to help others, thus supporting our sense of self and regulating our own distress at the suffering of others. Sometimes this can be tainted by hubris. In classical psychotherapy, altruistic behaviour was understood as a defence against inner conflict related to self-interest, aggression, or envy (Li and Rodin, 2012: 148). Pro-social behaviour may heighten our own sense of belonging through a sense of connection with 'other'. Additionally, it can mediate a sense of helplessness, of knowing what we could do but being unable to do so (Ricard, 2015: 327). Such helplessness is a typical response to trauma, which we will look at further in Chapter 7. Being aware, to some extent, of the personal benefits of altruism increases choice and reduces the risk of burnout. As in the earlier quote from Pearlman and Saakvitne, there are both gains and losses intrinsic to this work.

It might appear incontestable that altruistic acts are good and 'selfish' acts are bad. This, however, is evidence of deep relational wounding, carrying the belief that our attention to our own 'self'-hood may diminish the other. Interestingly, there are situations in which an unreflective excess of altruism creates difficulties for the donor. Halifax defines altruism as an 'edge state': 'Altruism that is sourced in fear, the unconscious need for social approval, the compulsion to fix other people or unhealthy power dynamics easily crosses the line into harm' (2018: 22). The term that is given to this in social psychology is 'pathological altruism', which has dramatic appeal (Li and Rodin, 2012: 142), but which might more comfortably be understood as a form of *non-relational caregiving*, an I–It dynamic. Here, the unacknowledged cost to the giver is not taken into account, with potential detrimental consequences for the intended beneficiary. An extreme example of this might be animal hoarding. How many stray animals can be accommodated with care without tipping into harm for all? All edge states have their tipping point, which can only be defined in relation to their context.

Altruistic behaviour commonly has a number of characteristics that have something in common with trauma processes. Worthy of mention here are the dependence on 'other' for our well-being and identity; an oversimplification leading to blindness to the diversity of consequences; an unreflective compulsivity; and an inability to process information.

The notion of cost is taken up by Ricard, which is often framed as being a sacrifice of time or money; however, 'this external cost does not correspond to an internal cost ... if this act is experienced as an inner gain, the very notion of cost evaporates' (2015: 77). There are risks involved: 'Persons who are pathologically altruistic are so selfless that they are prone to being used, exploited, and victimized by others' (Widiger and Presnall, 2012: 87). More typical, though, is the situation in which caregiving becomes compulsive, the donor ignoring their own needs and over-identifying with the 'Other'. Unchecked this can lead to burnout: 'Most people suffering from burnout underestimate the influence of their environment and overestimate their share of personal responsibility' (Ricard, 2015: 327).

It is common for caregivers to consider it to be selfish to take themselves into account in their work. We are socialized to help and often to take more than our share of responsibility, especially when things go wrong. Consider, then, the proposition that the opposite of altruism is not selfishness but individualism. The lone wolf has little to offer and can be seen as a threat to the safety of a society or group. Furthermore, I suggest that selfishness is not always a bad thing, in that it implies the formation of self, and an interest in one's own well-being; who, after all, wishes to suffer? At some point, however, caregiving can tip over into self-sacrifice, begging the question: 'How is it better to give than to receive?' We might then question how it comes to be better for some to give and others to receive, and how this is determined.

The role of empathy as a precursor to altruistic behaviour is clear; we need to observe and resonate with the suffering of another in order to behave self-lessly towards them. Just to make things more interesting, there are problems associated with empathy. Klimecki and Singer (2012) argue that we need to replace the concept of 'compassion fatigue' with that of 'empathic distress fatigue'. Empathy involves feeling some distress in the face of the suffering other, and these researchers have found that an over-focus on the 'Other' increases the risk of burnout. Ricard tells us that 'among most people, empathy felt when faced with another's suffering is correlated with entirely nega-tive feelings – pain, distress, anxiety, discouragement. The neural signature of empathy is similar to that of negative emotions' (2015: 61). Compassion, on the other hand, has more of a self-focus, in which the *self is experienced as different from the one who is suffering*, and this reduction in identification with them reduces the risk of burnout. 'The realization of being different from the suffering person without being indifferent toward him or her is an import-ant prerequisite for the development of prosocial behavior' (Klimecki and Singer, 2012: 378).

In Gestalt therapy, we don't really have a concept of empathy. Instead, we lean into Buber's ([1923] 1958) notion of 'inclusion', in which we are able more explicitly to stay with our own experience while at the same time going over to, or including, that of the suffering other. I include myself in order to include you. In my experience, this distinction is crucial to my capacity to hold and hear and stay with intense pain without giving away too much of myself.

In my experience, the compassionate practice of inclusion changes every-thing; I am including compassion for myself in the encounter. This perspec-tive is supported by Neff, who writes: 'Research shows that self-compassion allows us to feel others' pain without becoming overwhelmed by it' (2011: 191). Is this selfish? The capacity to tolerate is central here, which we will come back to shortly.

Dropping in

This is a practice of loving kindness. Read each of these four statements slowly, repeating them out loud for yourself:

> May I be kind to myself in this moment
> May I accept this moment exactly as it is
> May I accept myself in this moment exactly as I am
> May my compassion bring healing and growth

Germer (2009: 28) offers a helpful step-by-step model for the development of compassionate acceptance:

Aversion: resistance, avoidance, rumination
Curiosity: turning towards discomfort with interest
Tolerance: safely enduring
Allowing: letting feelings come and go
Friendship: embracing, seeing hidden value

This moves beyond simple tolerance, and is a process that unfolds over time and with practice. We will turn to a different application of this model in Chapter 8. According to Ricard, 'people who have more control of their emotions behave more altruistically than those who do not' (2015: 255). Mindful self-compassion is a key to creating this considerable shift in orientation to suffering, both our own and that of others (Germer, 2009; Neff, 2011). There is evidence that this practice changes the structure of the brain in measurable ways: increased cortical volume and reduced activity in the amygdala have been observed (Ricard, 2015: 254–255). The reflective capacity created by these changes provides a space in which we can consider our position and motives, accept that we benefit from behaving altruistically and can see the complexity of the consequences of this. Most importantly, perhaps, we can have a kinder appreciation of our limits and vulnerabilities, and set better boundaries. Three factors seem to be of clear importance: that altruistic acts need to be considered for their motives and possible consequences; that they serve better when they are specific rather than general; and that *there needs to be a correspondence between our capacity to give and the demands of the situation*. For me, this begins to resolve the painful dilemma posed by Levinas' commandment considered in Chapter 5. We will take this further in Chapter 10. For now, however, it is a small step to conclude, with Epstein (2017: 34), that self-compassion is ultimately altruistic.

Beyond self-care

I want to say a word here about self-care. In the popular discourse of these times, self-care gets rather glibly paired with vicarious trauma without sufficient critique. My take on self-care is that it is something that needs to go right to the heart of our relational ground and our vulnerabilities. An accounting for our own wounds within the relational field is the polarity of oppression and therefore therapeutically necessary. We need a self-care that goes far beyond consumption or strategy. In creating a life I don't need to escape from, I am unapologetic about the many resources which support my presence in sessions with traumatized people (Taylor, 2014: 196). I propose that a life that is predicated on defences against fear is not enough, and recreates an implicit trauma dynamic. I regard attending to myself – not in a narcissistic or egocentric way! – as a *first* intervention in my work. Moreover, a balanced lifestyle requires *constant and daily attention:* try balancing a pencil on your finger for a moment and notice the repeated fine adjustments you make to keep it in place. This is no easy task, and for some, kindness requires that we embrace pain. We become dogged in our efforts. I believe that this is what people pay me for – to be sufficiently resourced emotionally, physically, and spiritually to be able to tolerate their wounds. They do not, cannot, pay me for the quality of the relationship I offer them within the session.

> **Dropping in**
> Centre yourself and focus on a physical or emotional pain that is with you. As you inhale, bring in all that is larger than your pain. As you exhale, release the pain into the larger air that is pain-free. As you repeat this, focus on the moments that are pain-free, and invite them to expand into your body.

A Zen story gives a valuable perspective. Two acrobats were performing in the street, an old man and his granddaughter. Their act was for the grandfather to balance a pole on his head, up which the little girl would climb. He told her, 'I'll watch out for you and you can watch out for me', to which the girl replied, 'No, Grandfather, I'll look out for myself, then you can look out for yourself, and then we'll both be alright'. She was a wise little girl. The idea that watching out for someone else in order to stay safe is unbalanced, and once again reflects a relational dynamic that often has its roots in trauma.

This relates closely to a relational, co-created window of tolerance which is shown in Figure 6.2. (For a description of the basic window of tolerance model, see Appendix B.) Implicit in this revision of the model is the need for therapists to take care of their own level of arousal which is shaped by their internal wounds. Our autonomic nervous systems need healing attention too. Embedded in this interpretation of the window of tolerance model is the recognition

Figure 6.2 The therapist's window of tolerance

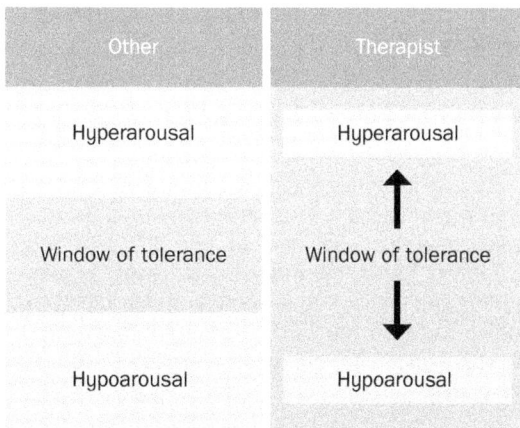

that our level of arousal can be influential in reorganizing the arousal of the people around us. A crucial perspective is offered by Geller and Greenberg: *'The inner state of the therapist strongly influences the response of the client'* (2012: 59, emphasis added).

Imagine for a moment that you come into a room in which two people are having an argument. You register the atmosphere in your nervous system, just as readily as you register the inner calm of the Dalai Lama. It is better that the people who come to see us pick up on our regulated state than a fearful, distancing, or over-identified state. Those who are hypervigilant to signs of safety will know this about us, and adjust their disclosure of themselves accordingly. For Geller and Greenberg, presence is a *reciprocal* process that promotes a sense of personal well-being (2012: 9). But in addition to this, and importantly, I suggest, is the notion that our therapeutic presence becomes an invitation to our people to enter into a more present state within themselves. 'Client's presence can be activated by therapists' presence both by being deeply met by the therapist as well as intersubjective sharing' (2012: 61). Presence becomes mutual when I include my own trauma and can stay in relationship to my people's trauma. The principle of mutual regulation then becomes a central organizing factor in the therapeutic relationship. I propose that it is this crucial change in the relational context that makes recovery possible.

Carroll adds this:

> The therapist's self-regulatory capacity within the relational context of psychotherapy is critical to their ability to consciously and non-defensively calibrate their interventions ...The ability to regulate depends upon the therapist being anchored within their own body, able to bear and attend to sensation, and allow spontaneous automatic shifts to occur. (2009: 102)

This has much to do with the capacity to maintain therapeutic presence, to remain non-defensive in the face of challenge, and to find a therapeutic distance that is adaptive to the situation. By taking care of our presence we become more able to bear the unbearable, to sit with it and restore the relational connection that has been breached by the experience of trauma. We will pick up these crucial ideas in Chapter 8.

Dropping in

Thinking about your own resources, here are some questions for you from my Well Resourced Therapist workshops. Choose three or four of them that interest you:

Reflections: Where do you go, what do you do ... To find colour? To feel aimless? For laughter? To feel the wind on your face? To feel a sense of awe? To be creative? For spirituality? To let go? To move freely? For touch? For a sense of belonging? To lose yourself? To stretch? To play? For beauty? To be vulnerable? For connection? To feel most yourself? For a sense of grace and wonder? For simplicity?

Some 11 or 12 years ago, I undertook Sensorimotor trauma training, which radically changed the way I work and think. It was not only that I had a model for understanding trauma that was highly compatible with Gestalt theory and practice (Taylor, 2013), but I found experiential learning about embodied resources to be transformative in my personal life and work. This gave rise later to my key chapter titled 'The well-resourced therapist' (Taylor, 2014). It is highly likely that my increasing access to a resourced state myself created a significant shift in my contribution to the dynamic relational field. While I discovered that somatic resources such as breathing and grounding were invaluable, Orange (2016a) writes also about the need for inner resources, such as the 'voices' of inspirational thinkers and mentors; I offered some of my own in Chapter 1. Without the capacity to respond to the face of the suffering Other, we are both lost: '*I am he who finds the resources to respond to the call*' (Levinas, 1985: 20, in Gantt, 2000, emphasis added). Perhaps, in meeting so much resistance in myself and in others to this message I become guilty of overstating the importance of developing resources, which could be misconstrued as an ideology of consumption, with a direction away from compassion. To be sure, we need lots of resources for all the right reasons, but enough to keep the balance between being over-resourced and under-resourced.

Marie Adams writes of the shame of needing support, of taking self-care seriously. If we feel threatened by the idea of needing help, recovery, or comfort, we put ourselves above the people who come to us (Adams, 2014: 125), a small and subtle act of privilege that reduces their suffering. The power imbalance in this becomes, in my mind, an ethic of self-care. Cognitively, it is common for therapists to recognize the argument in favour of increased self-care as persuasive, while at the same time deep down being unable to apply it to themselves. If this is the case for you, it may be a good reason to seek extra therapeutic support. There is nothing quite like trauma to bring therapists' own vulnerability to the surface.

Can I take the risk of my people knowing my vulnerability rather than my defendedness?

> A relationship in which one member is expected to change and grow, and the other considers himself exempt from those processes, is a relationship in which the one expected to change is being subjugated, to one degree or another, by the one claiming exemption. (Shaw, 2014: 38)

This is not a binary proposition of either vulnerability or invulnerability, as Aron (2016: 24) reminds us, but that we need to ground our ethics in the experience of vulnerability. It is arguably in our owning of vulnerability that we become strongest. This is a re-evaluation of Levinas. This might translate into considering exactly how much vigilance, openness, distance, or closeness is appropriate in this here-and-now situation, and making choices accordingly. It's not defending ourselves from trauma that's the problem but doing so uncritically, without awareness and 'unchoicefully'.

The compassion and tenderness that we must bring to our own wounded places is not a quick fix or a luxury we can't afford but an *intrinsic intervention in the relational field*; it's about the therapist's capacity to look into the face of trauma. According to Halifax (2018: 134), respect for others is a reflection of the respect we have for ourselves, as well as for ethical principles. It can only be thus. Self-compassion is not an indulgence but, according to Epstein (2013: 153), is instead about restoring balance and making sure that we are not consumed by over-identifying with either emotional overwhelm or negative emotions. It is my contention that therapists' self-compassion as a necessary dynamic therapeutic intervention allows the possibility of integration of the dichotomies of alienation and identification. People need contact with the emotional core of therapists while they are in the throes of reliving their trauma (Perlman, 1999: 27), and surely it is best – ethical indeed – that this core is a compassionate one?

Fitness to practice is embedded in many professional codes of practice, but the stipulation is neither prescriptive nor definitive. How we interpret this is a matter for discussion in clinical supervision among other things. Fortunately, this leaves some room for our personal vulnerabilities. My personal view is that so long as I am not in crisis, acutely unwell, or over-extending myself chronically and without reflection, I will continue to proceed with caution. There may inevitably be harm, paradoxically, because when we hold resources that our work depends on, we also are in a position of privilege (Chidiac and Denham-Vaughan, 2020: 26). The concept of fitness to practise implies a relational component; the harm that we might do unwittingly to another if unfit. My fitness or lack of it has an impact on the relational field. Critically, when understood as a relational aesthetic, I believe that *self-care is an example of situated ethics* (Bloom, 2013; see Chapter 5). Ethics is the science and art of well-being in the world, which in turn provides support for the environmental field (Lee, 2004: 25). It is our reply to the suffering of the world (Staemmler, 2020: 14). But there is never space for complacency, as we shall see in Chapter 7. Like anyone else, I can be prone to over-extending myself.

On being a wounded healer

Buber is quoted as having said, 'Certainly in order to be able to go out to the other you must have the starting place, you must have been, you must be with yourself' (in Rotenstreich, 1967: 127). To do so requires a 'balance between different consciousnesses, while maintaining the capacity to be responsive from that place of internal and external connection' (Geller and Greenberg, 2012: 55). Such a holding of different consciousnesses is containing and ultimately integrative. In order to do so, these writers call for us to cultivate a sense of inner presence first for ourselves. 'Can I accept that I too am wounded? Can I sustain my hope while doing this? How do I begin to accept my limitations and the impact of these limitations? … We are fragile human beings … and we have to be able to accept our frailty and limitations' (Carroll and Shaw, 2013: 25).

A compassionate stance in therapy is not a relationship between the wounded and the healer but a relationship between equals. This challenges us to reconsider what it means to help others. The dominant narrative in some areas of the helping professions suggests that a personal trauma history is incompatible with the role of a therapist. How do we resolve the dichotomy that implies that if we have been broken by the actions of other people against us, that trauma is unrecoverable, and yet still continue to work to restore our people to full recovery? This plays heavily into cultural stigma and victim-blaming, which are also aspects of the narrative around trauma. This leans on an implicit narcissism within the helping professions, in which we therapists need somehow to be more-than-human (see also Chapter 4). And, to the extent that we don't value our vulnerability, our trauma histories, and our need for support, we objectify ourselves. This creates an environment in which some professionals are scared to speak out about their experiences of abuse. How have we allowed this to happen?

Although I was always open about the broad brushstrokes of my history, I clearly remember a time as a trainee when some aspects of my early experience felt unmentionable, because I would surely be unfit to practise if they were known. The unaskable question on our training programmes may be, 'How fucked up can I get away with being?' Of course, trainee therapists need to be seen to be in good mental health, as we need to be fit to practise, but how the line is drawn remains very unclear. Eventually, I felt unable to complete my training without being open about more of my story, because to qualify without being 'known' would have felt fraudulent. It was a risky conversation, because from my perspective my entire future career hung on it. I guess the answer I got is evident enough or I wouldn't be in the position I am in today! I am eternally grateful for that. And I know that I'm by no means alone in having had such concerns; I see recognition and relief in people's faces when I name this vulnerability within the profession. In my experience, training often ignores the self-care of the therapist. There is rightly a focus on clinical resilience, but not on what I am calling 'clinical vulnerability', which needs to be paired with it. Does clinical resilience exclude our histories of abuse, neglect, and abandonment, or welcome, honour, and embrace them? Can clinical vulnerability be resourced and present? In Chapter 10, we will look once more at the issue of vulnerability.

My identity as a psychotherapist is not separate from that of 'victim' or 'survivor' – I can't cut off parts of my identity and still carry on working. Marie Adams reassures on this point: 'It may be from the position of vulnerability that we do our best work' (2014: 17), and I can't help but feel there are instances of this in many of our professional lives. As in the example I gave you of Luke in the last chapter, we may only arrive at an understanding of our resonant responses because we have already known it ourselves, and sometimes we have to dig deep into our own mud and filth to find it. 'Identification was the only way in which I was able to really understand and empathise with these patients' (Van Deurzen, 2019: 59). However, I wish to stress again that *the personal story I have included above is one that I have never shared explicitly with anyone I have worked with.* It simply informs the implicit interventions that I choose.

It is my honour to work with many therapists as a supervisor and trainer. All too often I hear stories about their shame, helplessness, fear, dissociation – the four primary organizers of traumatic experience (Taylor, 2014). While these may accurately reflect the processes of the people who come to us, and are part of the journey if we hold them in awareness, these are the ways I recognize the Trickster entering the stage. I frequently hear of a compelling sense of responsibility that takes therapists way beyond their limits: 'Is it possible to ever end therapy with this person?' In this, we deny the power and self-agency of the people we work with (Pearlman and Saakvitne, 1995: 84). And thus we recreate unwittingly the dynamics and dichotomies of the original traumatized relational field.

I said earlier that therapy can be risky, indeed, it can do violence to the therapist in ways we need to take seriously. I think here of a local outlet of the British National Health Service where therapists are paid by short-term results. The fewer the sessions (three, for example) that the work can be 'completed' in, the higher the rate of pay. Anything over six sessions is rewarded by the lowest rate of pay. What is of concern to me are ways the therapists working for this service consent to this structure, and I wonder what personal or cultural conditions drive such a questionable ethic. It is my sense that in less overtly oppressive ways, it is not uncommon for therapists to consent to working in conditions that are dehumanizing for them.

The Trickster can fool me into assuming that I am okay. After all, I'm the professional here, I've done my training, personal therapy, and have years of experience. According to Totton, 'when we become someone's therapist we become part of the relational field, *part of the problem and part of the attempted solution*' (2011: 188, emphasis added). Assumptions of expertise, of robustness, contain a potentially troublesome power dynamic: if I know what's right and I'm okay, then what does that say about you? There is a pact I make with the part of me that is vulnerable and the part of me that wants to help. My altruistic part nudges my wounded self out of the way and reduces my presence. That's a split I often want to disown, and in doing so I make part of myself 'Other'. I suggest that the Other which is reflected back to us in the face of the people who come to us is one we also must face in ourselves, and one to whom we also owe everything. I can't state this enough: in a retake of Levinasian ethics, *we equally owe our own vulnerable and wounded selves everything.* If the window of tolerance model is in essence a call to wake up, to become present, we do well to consider how this applies to ourselves within the wider traumatized relational field.

If coming in to the heart of suffering is of the essence of trauma therapy, we need to bear in mind also that there is another paradox here. Alongside the pain we need to understand how our people have managed to survive the impossible. The need to survive is the primary function of the autonomic nervous system and associated threat circuitry of the brain. No one sitting with us has failed to survive, even where the cost of survival has been considerable.

Honouring of that cost and the adaptations that have been a necessary part of survival is a necessary part of building the resilience that comes with connection. Such honouring challenges the belief systems that reinforce traumatic memory and the associations that over time become triggers. It is an essential part of the work that we recognize human resilience alongside vulnerability. Within the window of tolerance (for a description see also Appendix B) is an increasing resilience and adaptability to current rather than past reality, and it brings us to a less binary state.

There are multiple other ways in which I embrace the vitality that the Trickster might try to deny (see also Chapter 10). My choice – my ethic, if you will – is to live a sustainable life in order to sustain my work, and not the other way round. This is a radical departure, the Trickster tipping things on their head, thereby making more conscious processes that could not previously be formulated. And yet, I can only be present to the face of trauma to the extent that I can tolerate it one moment at a time, incrementally widening my own window of tolerance much as I hope do with the people who come to me. I am resilient and present only as far as my vulnerability lets me be. And I start afresh with each new person who comes to me.

Dropping in

The reference at the beginning of this chapter to Pearlman and Saakvitne (1995: 279) invited a question about the gains and losses of this work. We have looked at many of the losses and risks associated with this, and will continue with this in Chapter 7, but for now, I invite you to list some of the gains of the work.

So why do I really do this work? I take to heart Levinas' commandment. Yes, and for me, this ethic can at times feel burdensome. A friend and colleague told me: 'It falls to you to do this work'. But the burden lessens whenever I embrace the ethic of self-care and self-compassion and live my life accordingly. One of my most precious resources is my strong connection with the Earth, alluded to in my first book and more explicitly in my workshops with my colleague Vienna Duff called The Well-Grounded Therapist. The natural world has made a significant contribution in transforming some of my Me Too moments. We will come back to this ecological widening of context in particular in Chapters 9 and 10.

7 Walking the line

The relationship that is needed to heal from trauma is the very thing that is most fraught with difficulty: 'What a double edged sword relationships are: Trauma stems *from* them. Recovery depends *on* them … Relationships are both poison and antidote' (Muller, 2018, loc 49, original emphasis). We become like magnets that both attract and repel at the same time. I referred earlier to the fine line that we navigate in tracking, moment by moment, the state shifts or florid figure formation of people who are in the grips of a trauma response while simultaneously attending to our own stream of responses, experiences, and thoughts. It only takes a small shift in the balance we seek for things to get messy, the mud and filth referred to in Chapter 6. A relational construct shows that being deeply embedded in the traumatized relational field, we respond similarly, and in this chapter we look at some of the ways in which trauma itself can shape those responses.

Co-transference and enduring relational themes

Gestalt therapy has to some extent carved a different path from classical notions of transference and counter-transference. Consistent with a relational field model, we consider instead that the relationship is mutually shaped or co-created (Joyce and Sills, 2014: 131). We tend not to think of transference in terms of a meeting of two separate subjectivities, but of something new that is created in the moment of meeting. Thus, as do other approaches, we speak of co-transference. 'If the patient goes away from a session feeling bad about him or her self, attributing negative thoughts or feelings to the therapist, this is an event in which the therapist plays a part' (Yontef, 2005: 94).

Furthermore, we appreciate how the therapist plays a part in *every* moment. What each party brings to the encounter is shaped by their personal histories, attachment style, biases, and intersectionality, as discussed previously. Such relational shaping occurs in the meeting of contact boundaries; it is in the 'space between' that relationship occurs (Spagnuolo Lobb, 2013: 165). Having said this, however, 'There are times when it can be useful for the purposes of understanding, to separate out the co-transference and identify the contributions of the client and the therapist in order to help a client understand his experiences more deeply and the ways in which he constellates his world' (Joyce and Sills, 2014: 132).

A more recent development in conceptualizing transference comes from Jacobs, who introduces the concept of 'enduring relational themes' (2017: 7). This proposition looks at the temporal nature of transference phenomena. Transference is usually understood as a re-creation of something that is past as though it is not based in the actual experience in the present moment (2017: 8). Furthermore, quoting White, Jacobs adds that transference phenomena '*are not unique to the therapeutic situation but occur in all relationships*' (2017: 9, original emphasis). A more interesting question, then, is to consider 'how this so-called transference reaction *does make perfect sense, at this time, in this relationship, in this situation*' (2017: 9, original emphasis). This leads to an understanding of the repetitive nature of enduring relational themes, of which Jacobs says: 'They are what we have learned from our past, they continue to be reinforced through repetition, and they *prepare us to move into our future*' (2017: 10, original emphasis). This inevitably includes how personal relational traumas have patterned our ways of working with trauma. Do we as therapists, perhaps, tend to lean towards what was missing relationally in our own trauma history?

Enduring relational themes may relate to any of the elements of the SOS model (Chapter 2): how I see myself; how I compare myself to others or expect to be treated by them; and how I see myself in relation to the world. This last might be to attribute motives to people in general: 'Everyone is out for themselves', or 'It's too dangerous to get close to people'. These may be rigidly held 'foundational' relational beliefs that are fairly intractable, arising especially in complex trauma or 'totalistic' environments that are inescapable (Jacobs, 2017: 12). Thus, they are meaningful ways of organizing our way of being in the world. A therapeutic requisite is to seek to understand that meaning for the person we are seeking to help. 'Even the most brutal [enduring relational themes] support our organisation of experience. They support our regulation of ourselves, however narrowly' (2017: 13). Having understood our own defences and the nature of trauma does not immunize us from the impact of being with people who are deeply relationally traumatized. Far from it, we are vulnerable to being drawn in. Our own trauma history does not require disclosure but nevertheless shapes the enduring relational themes of our lives and informs the interventions we choose.

Dropping in

Taking each of the lenses of the SOS model in turn, I invite you to reflect on your own enduring relational themes, how you learnt them, and how they support you. What embodied adjustments do you make in relation to each? Looking back over your life, have any of your foundational beliefs about relationships changed, and if so, in what ways? What enabled any changes to your enduring relational themes?

The intersection between our enduring relational themes and those of the people we work with creates interesting positions in the therapeutic relationship, colours our attitudes towards one another, and may obstruct our compassion (Orange, 2011: 83). Both parties will enter the relationship with assumptions based on their respective beliefs, creating a fogginess around the potential closeness and trust that might develop with one another as indicated in Chapter 5 and elsewhere. How, for example, might your belief that 'most people have good will' rub up against one of 'people who seem good only want something from me'? I might be cast in the role of the perpetrator in such ways that I don't recognize myself; conversely, the person I am with may be profoundly disorganized by my transparency as a therapist (Taylor, 2014: 175). However uncomfortable it can be to acknowledge this, *we both carry the positions of victim, rescuer and perpetrator in us,* and according to Davies and Frawley (1992: 30), they are intrinsic to work with adults who have experienced childhood abuse. The drama triangle (Chapter 3) is a co-created dance, moment by moment, which we bring into the explicit process in order to raise awareness, mentalize, and create narrative. 'The more we try to avoid becoming the oppressor, the more it is forced upon us' (Totton, 2009: 19).

Stephanie revisited

In my first book, I identified four factors that accompany most experiences of trauma. They are usually intertwined but remain a helpful way of understanding the experience. They are: fear, helplessness, disconnection (dissociation), and shame (Taylor, 2014). In the following vignette and transcript from a session, these four factors are present in both me (MT) and Stephanie (S), the person who has come to me for help, and illustrate the subtle ways in which they can manifest. They are underlined in the commentary which accompanies it.

Stephanie keeps her eyes to the floor as she enters the room, slowing as she stands by the sofa (dissociation). I notice her intake of breath. Suspended for a moment in which I too feel unsure (fear). I steady myself, connecting my feet to the floor as I ease myself into the chair. I feel slightly unbalanced (dissociation). I take note of her movements as she sits, resigned, helpless, hopeless even. Knees raised to her chest, a cushion held against her, she turns her face away from me, her long dark fringe and straggling hair covering her eyes and the side of her pale face. She is not looking at anything, she's away from the light. I see the dark, the hidden, the uncovering. In this largely silent space, we navigate half-finished sentences and the spaces between them. Her need for control is written into her frozen muscles, and I register also how she hands control to me. The following exchange takes the remainder of the 90-minute session:

I wait before making a comment about how still she looks. Silence, a thick sticky silence fills the room. It feels slightly nauseating, something I don't want to breathe in. I feel constricted around my chest (fear). I adjust my position and cough as if to clear my throat. My voice is slow and even throughout.

MT: 'It is hard for you to see me, and I can see you'. *She shrugs ever so slightly and turns abruptly away from me, as though startled (*disconnection*, fear); now I can see little more than her shoulder. I notice how impatient and rejected I feel in this moment; 'Why do I have to sit through this excruciating session? I don't want to be here, I don't want to be left alone' (*fear*). I'm a little light-headed and my gaze wanders out of the window (*dissociation*). I have lost my body, and remember that I have an embodied anchor in the small of my back. I try breathing into that place, and can't connect. Focusing again on the woman before me, I have a sense of a small fragile girl drawing me towards her. I note her flimsy clothing, how thin she is. I take a deeper breath and she starts to shiver. This is hard work (*dissociation, helplessness*). I resist even as my energy becomes more accessible, a push and pull within myself. I feel as though I am being summoned to reach into a void, and I haven't the energy for it. I am scared that it will cost me too much (*fear*). A vibration ripples down my spine, a moment that reminds me that I am alive. I can breathe more fully into that. I turn a fraction towards her and as I do so I become interested in my experience of her edges, which appear very porous right now. My intuition is to envelop her and I know that might be too much, reaching too far into the space between us. I don't want to intrude. I check what I know and downgrade the intervention I am forming in my mind.*

MT: *Slowly, tentatively:* 'What's asking for attention just now?'

Stephanie: *She tightens again (*fear, disconnection*) ... Long pause*

MT: 'Maybe you could start with what you don't want?'... *Long pause*

S: 'I don't want to be under a microscope' *(*fear, helplessness*)*

MT: 'Oh, of course you don't' *(*fear*) ... I gather myself ...* 'and I wonder how does that happen here?' *Although I am enquiring about the impact I have on her (Chapter 5), this comes from my head, so to speak; I'm not fully invested in the answer yet. I imagine a spell being cast, and feel myself being drawn in. How do we co-create this? I am slightly *dissociated *and am compensating by investing more energy into the intersubjective space. I withdraw my attention – looking at the lining of her coat across her knee. Long pause.*

S: 'I don't want it to come out wrong'. *This is familiar, a *fear *of punishment for being 'wrong'. In this moment, I sense that she is trying to protect me. She isn't able to tell me that I am wrong and retroflects.*

MT: 'I wonder, would you be able to play with finding a form of words?' *I am a bit more interested and offer a provisional way of trying to express herself, to loosen the fixity of the 'right' words. Long pause.*

S: 'I guess it's inevitable really' *(helplessness)*

MT: 'It feels like we're on territory that is so much part of your world that we can't avoid it' … 'I know I have some thoughts and beliefs about focusing on details microscopically, and I'd like to know how that's unhelpful at present – you're the expert here'. *I drop my theoretical belief about working phenomenologically. I am seeking to give her some agency in determining the process. We have a long-standing push and pull in our relationship about who takes the lead. I try to offer her choice in sessions and she resists by shutting down, leaving me with more 'power' than I feel comfortable with. Long pause.*

S: 'Sometimes when you look at me I feel trapped – not always'. *Being trapped is an old story for this person, and we have done a lot of work on how she also traps herself by freezing, which is her instinctive way of making herself feel safer.*

MT: *(Fear, shame)*, *tightening my body in response.* 'Would you be willing to help me understand what it is about the quality of my attention sometimes that is so difficult for you?' *My intervention is very provisional: 'Would you be willing to tell me?' is less of a demand and more of an invitation to collaborate. Long pause.*

S: 'It's not just you, it's anybody, I know it's irrational'. *(Shame)* *She's walking round the edges of telling me and I feel frustrated and unwilling to leave it at this. I gather my energy and drop my attention to the base of my spine, to my feet on the floor, and look back at the lining of her coat, re-calibrating my focus.*

MT: 'I'm guessing you're saying there's no evidence that this is bad but it feels that way? I suppose this is taking you back to old stuff, but there's a hook in the present, something that is actually about me that you hook into'. *Traumatic memory is only ever experienced from the now of the situation. I feel less shame when I can begin to own my part in a process; I don't have to push it away. I can now adopt a stance of genuine curiosity. I know something difficult is coming my way and feel some energy rising at the prospect of open communication between us in the moment. I feel less defensive than I might. Shorter pause.*

S: 'I guess'. *This is a huge step towards increased relationality with me. I imagine that my acknowledgment of the hook in the present has been supportive. My dropping of my defences leads to a more open dialogue.*

MT: …'It would really help if I could understand at least, I don't know yet if I can do anything about it. You're saying you don't want to feel trapped by me'. *(An image of a chrysalis comes to me)*

S: 'It's any attention, it's not just you'. *Again she is trying to protect me, and I assume herself, from the risk of negative consequences* *if she tells me. This is another example of 'drip-feeding' (Sinason, 2008: 84), testing to see how I receive her.*

MT: 'You're stuck and I'm stumped right now … So any kind of therapy … is a minefield …'

S: 'I know you watch me like a hawk, and my uncle watched me too so that the other men got what they paid for …'. *I wonder briefly if she is getting what she pays me for, and then bracket the thought for now. Is my 'stewardship' of her 'arousal' (Taylor, 2014: 180) based on hypervigilance on my part? And then I downplay it …*

MT: 'I can see that my intention to keep an eye on you goes to hell in what this feels like for you'.

S: 'That, and when you ask questions it feels like you pin me down … *(tears)* There's nowhere to hide'. *It is an enormous risk for her to tell me this.*

MT: 'Oh, that must feel just terrible for you, I can imagine' *(feeling shock, tearful, breathing slowly into my spine)* … 'Thank you, you just handed me a gift … I want to say how sorry I am, I want to take care of my part in this'. *Although I am uncomfortable and a bit lost with this information, I am grateful that we can finally address the co-creation of an enduringly oppressive situation, a traumatic re-enactment.*

S: *Silent – I check her breathing. Pause.*

MT: 'How is this landing with you?'

S: 'Fine'.

MT: 'Hmm, I'm fine too, in that I can take care of my uncomfortable feelings, and I'm not falling apart …'

S: 'I think sometimes I come in triggered, like today, and that makes it worse'.

MT: 'I don't know what to do about this – I think you're giving me a good lesson in understanding how you feel trapped – like I can't win'.

S: *Relief on her face, eye contact for the first time.* 'That's what it's like for me'

While this session felt like a big shift and a relief to me, three days later I receive a text message from Stephanie, telling me that she has taken some pills because things are getting worse. Could we have a telephone conversation before the next session? I suggest a time for a 15-minute phone call the following day, which she accepts. She is angry and feels that I don't care. We talk about the child part that feels abandoned when she can't see me. I remind her that I will see her next week at the usual time. Until the next session I feel a despair, anxious that I can _anything right for her (fear, shame, helplessness). The more I give the more she seems to need. And I recognize the pattern of collapse away from sessions, influenced by her unsteady relationship with her wife who has rheumatoid arthritis, and for whom Stephanie is a carer. When we meet, she has a headache, tells me she hasn't slept. I feel as though she wants to pull me in, to rescue her. 'Help me, but don't you dare come near ...' My breathing is tight and I feel restless; I want to pull away. I can't find the right distance and feel disconnected and disinterested. The cries of the wounded child feel too much to bear. I worry that my attention is doing more harm than good._

The kind of therapeutic backlash we see happening here is very familiar: a step forward is followed in short order by two steps backwards. I am aware of being in a co-created field characterized by loops of fear and seduction. The contact we made during the session could have felt like a seduction to the abused child in this woman, while she in turn seduces me into trying to rescue her (Davies and Frawley, 1992: 29). I am inclined to agree with Davies and Frawley's proposition that:

> The relationship has, in essence, become an addiction for the patient, who must receive larger and larger infusions of compensation to be satisfied. As with any addiction, each dose stimulates an inevitable demand for more, and ultimately the demands can simply not be met. (1992: 27)

Nothing I can offer to her dissociated self can compensate for the abuse and betrayal that she 'knows to be true'. It is a state embedded in her relational history and therefore is not amenable to change; I am doomed to fail.

The presence of the abusers is also keenly felt in the dissociative enactment. The feeling of being pinned down does not start here, much though that it feels as though it does. The fear is a mongrel fear, belonging first to the abusers, so unable to regulate their impulses that they passed the dysregulation on (see Chapter 3).

The over-reach model

A natural compensatory move in the face of trauma is to over-extend ourselves, by means of sometimes incremental shifts in our capacity to bear the trauma and the suffering of the other, or in taking an excess of responsibility. As with all trauma responses, over-reach is concerned with survival. We go beyond the person we are working with and limit their space to come forward. In over-reach, there is an incremental lessening of our capacity to bear the suffering of the other. Most therapists will recognize the feeling of being 'bent out of shape' at times in their work.

Dropping in

I have a strong awareness of an area in the small of my back, where I tighten a fraction when I begin to be bent out of shape, as if preparing to lift up from my seat. Checking in with myself regularly in sessions, and particularly with this area, serves as an early warning signal, allowing me to make a choice to lean further in or to drop back into my seat. Take a moment to check in with your somatic experience. What would be your first sign that you are beginning to be bent out of shape? How could you tell? And how might you use this early warning? Maybe you have a voice in your head that argues with this.

Roubal suggests that therapists tend to become polarized against the depressed experience of the people he works with:

> A kind of mobilizing potential ... starts coursing through me kind of automatically. The gloomier the person is, the more fiercely I mobilize myself. This works also vice versa. The more mobilized the therapist becomes, the gloomier the client is. (2019a: 78)

the more I solve, the more the solution is concealed ?

The same process can be observed within the traumatized and dissociated relational field. In either situation, the mobilization of the therapist supplies energy to fill the void, which is equally energetically resisted. Furthermore, Alpert argues that an 'excessive tilt toward the other can create an alienation from the self, and that this alienation from the self can actually limit our capacity to know the other' (2016: 153). While the most seasoned therapist is vulnerable to 'tilt' too far, there is a developmental consideration here for newer therapists and their supervisors.

In my earlier book, I proposed that the four components of trauma experience outlined above each have their polarities (Taylor, 2014). We can move from fear to safety; from helplessness to autonomy (or agency); from disconnection to contact; and from shame to acceptance. This provides a map of sorts for the therapeutic journey. Each polarity has a position within the window of tolerance, requiring sufficient regulation and distance from the traumatic experience. The therapist, in their relationship to trauma, has the same therapeutic potentialities, but when they stand in as compensatory moves they can be excessive. The over-reach model (Figure 7.1) illustrates how this bypassing of the window of tolerance might look. We see here how safety can become an excess of certainty; autonomy or agency translates into power; contact becomes identification; and acceptance becomes ego. These are extensions of the original polarities. All are defensive reactions in the face of trauma, and will typically move therapists 'into their heads' and away from embodied experience in the present.

Figure 7.1 The over-reach model

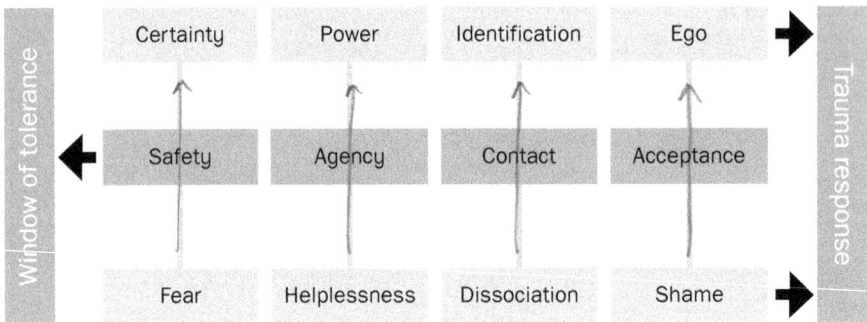

<handwritten>(*) interesting model, in face of these
I move upwards ("over-reach", kead, ch.)</handwritten>

Certainty

Adopting a position of over-certainty can be an energetic shift as a response to the fear of the unknown. It is useful here to acknowledge some specific fears related to working with traumatized people. Therapists have reported the following to me:

- Fear of retraumatizing
- Fear of being unable to contain
- Fear of being 'contaminated'
- Fear of facing evil
- Fear of being unable to take care of yourself
- Fear of being naive to the impact of trauma until it's too late
- Fear of having inadequate skills or experience
- Fear of letting the other person down, over-responsibility
- Fear of feeling lost (losing)

> **Dropping in**
>
> Which of these fears, if any, do you recognize? As you read this list, what do you notice happening in your body? Is this a familiar sensation? Read through this again, more slowly this time, and note what happens to your energy, and whether it feels better or worse. Do you soften or tighten; feel clearer or more fuzzy; stiller or more agitated; do you shift awareness away from your body, or something else? Experiment for a few minutes with exaggerating the effect, and then alternating with coming back to a neutral position.

We might manage personal uncertainty by adhering more strongly to cultural values and norms or our implicit biases. 'After being primed to think about their own personal uncertainty, people become more rigid and closed-minded' (Anderson et al., 2019). Thus we might tell ourselves that a certain technique has always been effective with this person in the past and 'should' be now. Here we make a subtle shift away from the subjectivity of the person we are with, and fail to respond from a more creative position in the moment. We can get into struggles about the 'rightness' of our position, and the impact of this may be to create a sense of deficit in the person we are with, possibly 'invited' as a re-enactment of an existing deficit. Some kinds of certainty are founded on theory or orientation (see also Chapter 4). We need to rest our work in more than one theory of change or theory of personality, in order not to become pulled into a binary position, and we must *always* seek to fit the person to the theory rather than the other way round. Stephanie implicitly insists that I sit up and listen without pre-judging the situation.

Power

Trauma almost by definition includes the experience of a relational power imbalance. Inescapable threat results in a sense of helplessness which is disorganizing. Gantt considers that suffering is in itself a state of powerlessness (2000: 11). It is therefore inevitable that power issues in one form or another will be present as part of the therapeutic endeavour. I referred to structural power within the mental health professions in Chapter 4; here we look at inherent relational power. This includes gross abuses of power by therapists, which, I wish did not need iterating, must *never* be considered as acceptable by therapists of integrity. I intend more particularly to focus on the everyday power of simply being in relationship.

Regardless of our theoretical orientation, it is not comfortable to examine the power that we hold, especially as far as vulnerable and traumatized people are concerned. However, I am inclined to agree with Totton, who asserts that *ignoring inherent power is itself a use of that power* (2009: 18), especially where we might over-extend our presence to reach out to a dissociated, shamed, or helpless other. Chidiac and Denham-Vaughan (2020: 27) regard the operation of power as an organizer of the implicit relational and contextual field, which is predicated on privilege. To be powerless is to lack resources (Chapter 2), whereas to hold power is to have access to resources. In Chapter 6, I situated the therapist's resources as an ethic of good practice, and thus we can regard power as an ethic. It is important therefore to distinguish between 'power-over' and 'power-with'; ultimately, some of each will be present. For example, the therapist holds power-over the person who comes to see them by setting fees, environment, and times. Power-over also has a potentially more subtle negative aspect, whereby the mis-timing of an intervention, the positioning of expertise, directing the pace of the session, the withdrawal of presence, or assumptions about shared social values may all be received as oppressive. It is in our power to make figural someone's pain, which causes them to suffer, and equally to avoid or deny their pain. Here are some of the differences between power-over and power-with:

doing these now?

Power-over	Power-with
• Imposition	• Invitation
• Directing attention	• Checking for understanding
• Changing the pace of a session	• Giving choices
• Adhering to modality regarding expressive style or body work	• Negotiation and collaboration
• Taking expert position	• Following the person we are with; 'tight therapeutic sequencing' (Polster, 1991)
• Timing of interventions	• Pacing; allowing emerging themes
• Assuming agreement about what is going on	• Enquiring how an intervention 'lands' with someone
• Assuming shared understanding of how therapy works	• Making provisional statements
• Recalibrating presence defensively	• Sharing some embodied responses
• Staying with pain for too long or avoiding it	• Working on your own relationship to power

How we use or misuse our personal power will depend on our attachment style and enduring relational themes. Precisely *how* we offer choices about which figure to follow will arguably preference those of interest to us. Your strong point might be in hanging in and being tenacious, though you may be less comfortable at dealing with contempt, for example.

Chapter 8 will examine some of the power-with processes in more detail.

Dropping in

What comes to mind when you consider your power as a therapist? How do you hold or resist it in your body? Do you consider power to be a bad thing, or something that you can utilize with awareness? How might you use your power to move people in or out of presence?

According to Levinas (see Chapter 5), we owe everything to the suffering Other. Where they have nothing, the attention and understanding we offer is profoundly powerful. To know someone is an act of power, because we have had to mobilize resources to bear upon the situation. Our leverage of resources *becomes* our power (Chidiac and Denham-Vaughan, 2020). Whether this is received as power-over or power-with is an enquiry that begs to be explored in dialogue. Calling attention to how we are met by the Other opens the space for a joining together as power-with.

Totton (2009: 16) contends that very few human differences can be neutral with regards to power, which can lead to disagreements about what is happening in the room. In this instance, whose preferences will adapt to meet the other's? (Totton, 2009: 18). Conscious awareness of the power dynamic in the moment requires recalibrating to a position of relative neutrality on the part of the therapist. Such a struggle with perceptions may itself be therapeutic if it is held dialogically and from a spirit of power-with. However, where the therapist compensates too readily, the over-reach may lead to a power-over position.

Identification

It is commonly understood that we end up working with the people we need. Being in any relationship can show us our own wounds. It won't be a surprise, therefore, when I tell you that I have tended to attract people with complex and sometimes very toxic relationships to their own mothers, following my story in Chapter 6. Working with a traumatized individual stirs memories of our own relational traumas, and in Trickster-fashion this can readily show up as parallel process in the work. I gave an example of this in Chapter 5, when describing my response to Luke. Subtle identification with the other person can lead to impatience or confusion, where something – an approach, an intervention, or a technique – that you found helpful in your own therapy doesn't have the same effect when you offer it in good faith. Another form of identification may come when something you have been taught or advised to try by your supervisor biases you in the counter direction: 'I don't think I would like that so I won't do it'.

> **Dropping in**
> Call to mind a time when you might have over-reached through identification. Drop into your body with curiosity and notice whether you feel pulled or pushed, softened or contracted, or something else?

Ego

Closely linked to power, as helplessness is to shame (Taylor, 2014: 117), ego can become an agentic organizing factor in trauma therapy. Shame is a marker of oppression. Preservation of the self is an automatic survival response, no less for us therapists than for the people who come to see us. When continuity of self is threatened, shame takes hold and becomes an inherent risk within the therapeutic relationship. In the compensatory over-reach we may seek to be likeable, look knowledgeable, self-aware, or make smart and pithy interventions, especially when struggling to understand (Lichtenberg, 2004: 238). We reach out to make contact and meet in the other the shame of being seen or found out. This may lead to defensive reactions of attack, retaliation, contempt, rejection, or denial. My Gestalt training taught me to prize contact and the modality fits my interest in relationship. When my need for contact is not met, I can feel wounded, which is an enduring relational theme of mine: 'After all I've done for you, you treat me so badly'. For me here lie echoes of my mother: 'Look at what you've done'. While I may become fed-up and disinterested, in over-reach mode I try to outwit or outshine this person. The tilt here is less towards the other person than towards my own need to be seen in a good light.

> **Dropping in**
> What happens to your focus and the quality of your thought processes as you get in touch with your experience of moving towards ego? What goes with this – a feeling or a sensation or an energetic shift of some sort?

While none of these aspects of over-reach involve risky or unethical behaviour, they do alter the orientation of our compassion, and therefore our capacity to listen deeply to the other person is subtly impacted. And we may equally under-reach, unable to wriggle free of the primary phenomena of fear, helplessness, disconnection, or shame. This is akin to more frozen states of *hypo*-arousal that keep us in a rigid and ineffective position. In under-reach we cannot escape feeling afraid, helpless, and ashamed. Under-reach is more of a given starting position that we wriggle our way out of via the somewhat more *hyper*-aroused over-reach, bypassing the window of tolerance we 'aim' for. Either way, we stay in unmetabolized trauma defences and require an honest level of self-reflection and supervision. It is noteworthy, too, that these forms of over-reach are largely cognitively based, while under-reach is implicitly somewhat dissociated. In over-extending or under-extending we are more likely to remove ourselves from our embodied experience. How are we going to know the impact of any of these unless we slow the work right down, stay open to dialogue, and enquire?

The edges of relationality

The relational aspects of trauma work are endlessly varied, complex, and fascinating. In my view, trauma is best understood as a process of energetic shifts, sometimes micro-shifts, communicated via changes in arousal of the autonomic nervous system. The energetic communication is relational; Siegel (2012) proposes that communication is an exchange of energy. The work of the trauma therapist is to attune to these shifts in ourselves and in the person we are working with, moment by moment. Such attentive stewardship will be explored in some detail in the next chapter. The people who turn to us for help have rarely had good relational experiences to support their engagement with us, and their energetic communications may not be coherent. While we may

naturally feel shocked or shamed by the brutality and isolation of their enduring relational themes, they too struggle to connect with us and may over-reach
or under-reach. Here I describe some possible relational configurations.

Learning to be super-vigilant for signs of escalating arousal, some people
develop the capacity to read the atmosphere, or to know aspects of our personal lives we have not disclosed as though they are psychic. These people
have learnt to survive by knowing before others can know. They may make
inferences from the information we do share, showing the degree of
thought – and worry – that this disclosure creates in them. For example, when
I took time off after a close family bereavement, one person figured out my
relationship with this relative, including particulars of the funeral, although
none of this was information I had shared. Intrusive though this felt when I was
vulnerable, maybe I shouldn't have been surprised that she found a way into the
details of my life. My absence and loss paralleled her early trauma with her
depressed and drug-dependent mother whose life she needed to monitor endlessly. She was frightened by my temporary unavailability, and ruminated on
what was happening in my life.

There can be a degree of energetic disturbance in trauma work that comes
to possess therapists. The energetic tone the traumatized person carries
through their lives is chaotic and charged. With no possibility of settling the
intense arousal, the trauma overspills into the relational space and beyond. It
can permeate our skin, disturb our sleep, and enter our dreams, hooking into
our own familiar patterns of arousal. Here the face of trauma becomes our
face, the longed-for 'solution' becomes our quest. Therapists may register this
as feeling trapped within the energetic field and want or not to know how to
find the way out of the relationship. As a mirror of the original trauma experience, relived in current time, the relationship feels unending and inescapable.
Occasionally, the disturbed energy may have a malevolent quality, opening a
window into the relational world of the person concerned, and without fore-
warning and experience we get caught. This resonance may last within us far
longer than is comfortable. While my instinct has been to lean towards the distressed cry of the abused child – to over-reach protectively – experience has
taught me that greater clarity comes from leaning back a little, which seems to
create a different energetic boundary where none has existed before. We need
to work from outside of the energetic bubble, rather than from within it. That
'less is more' is a useful truism to bear in mind. This offers a more containing
therapeutic position for both parties, one in which we may be able to meet.

A particular caution arises when we meet dissociation by working too hard,
or feeling too much. The energetic tone of the relational field is not evenly distributed, and it can seem as if we are carrying all the feeling for two people, or
in some cases for an entire family system. Identifying the context together can
alleviate some of the pull into this configuration. Absence is not only in the self/
other dyad and the space between them, it is in the wider situation; by naming
it appropriately, we validate rather than shame the person we are with. However, learning to read the relational space honestly without becoming anxious
is a therapeutic skill that needs to be developed.

A further relational communication we may be sorely challenged to meet is that of self-harm and suicidality. Fisher (undated) compassionately advises us not to pathologize these phenomena, but to understand them as an indication of the unbearable pain an individual may feel. Rather than *causing* pain, there can be a degree of *relief* in harming oneself, or in thinking about doing so, coupled with a release of neurochemicals and natural anaesthetics. Relationally, self-harming behaviours represent a complete loss of hope that anyone can help, coupled often with deep shame. Ultimately, many people who have experienced trauma have learnt not to rely on others, and to retreat to a place of isolated self-reliance. 'I don't believe anyone can ever help me stop binge eating' one woman told me, relaying an implicit message that I wasn't going to become important to her. Fisher comments that among other common mistakes of therapists working with self-harm is that of 'not understanding the need of trauma survivors to rely on their own resources or to avoid relying on others' (undated: 2). Here is the profound disconnection that is a consequence of trauma. Whatever logic lies behind self-harming and suicidal behaviours, I am sometimes profoundly challenged by the particular forms they can take, especially self-mutilation of the face or genitals. The self-loathing that accompanies such attacks on the body reveals splinters of original trauma that I would rather not face, and can be disgusted by in turn. We sit in the presence of the internalized abuser and can end up colluding with it by not dealing with it, which replicates the power-over dynamic of the earlier abuse. This can easily leave therapists feeling ground down, helpless, and uncertain about how to challenge risky behaviour. A fundamental ethic therefore is not to work with trauma without adequate training and supervision.

Limits of a relational approach

Because the experience of life threat increases self-reliance, it also greatly reduces relationality and curiosity. Attachment, founded on enduring relational themes in which love and safety have been compromised, is complicated and frankly dangerous to the people who seek our help. In a similar vein, as in the transcript above, so are attention and care. Sources of potential soothing and regulation are preserved within the individual. Moving from a ground of unformulated experience in which human relationships are objectified, to taking into account one's own subjectivity is in itself a big step. To begin to consider the impact that one has on another requires taking a far more complex position in relation to two subjectivities (Lichtenberg, 2001: 73; see also Chapter 6). It may be a very long time before someone who has experienced any degree of disturbance to relational systems is able to see *anyone* else as other than a threat. In the meantime, the therapist is expected to tolerate being objectified, demeaned, or rejected, which is asking a lot of any of us. Adherence to a relational approach by attending explicitly to the relational field, therefore, has its limits. The safest therapeutic position the therapist can take is, in some situations, one of distance.

" needy "

Shame for having relational needs is certainly a factor here. When survival has been predicated on self-reliance, the need for others, despite being hard-wired, threatens one's identity and can feel like a failure. Asking for help is equated with weakness: 'It's as though my existence depends on doing it on my own – I can't make myself vulnerable', said one person. A common adaptation to trauma involves making oneself seem invisible. To see, therefore, that we have an impact on another human being is painful. For some, the pain of con-trast arises, in which the novelty of the warm attention offered by the therapist evokes the pain of what has been absent or neglected in the past (Casement, 1990: 106). Being unable to differentiate between qualities of pain and their meaning means that any pain is generalized as 'bad' and to be avoided. We will have a look at differentiating the nature of pain in the next chapter. Co-created regulation requires surrender, letting go of control, and trust. The energetic shift needed to reach towards another rather than withdraw into one-self must not be underestimated, especially if that withdrawal has involved a dissociative cut-off from contact functions. There are, therefore, costs associated both with reaching out and with not doing so. For some seriously traumatized individuals, it is not realistic to engage in therapy and their recovery will be limited.

★ I am repaired to need, but this is of course dangerous if I have been let down !

Limits of capacity

The energetic force of trauma is felt on a visceral level, taking us to our limits at times. I have said earlier (Chapter 6) that our responsibility to the suffering face of the traumatized person has to be in balance with our capacity. What I mean by capacity is not something fixed but an aggregate of personal, professional, somatic, and spiritual resources, in need of constant revision. There are countless things that affect our capacity: training, knowledge, experience, situation, relationships, health, for example. Not all of these are subject to our control, but a relative balance between several different domains is necessary to support effective and safe practice.

It is a concern that relatively few training courses prepare people adequately, if at all, to work with trauma, whether their own or that of others. We can sit through an entire master's programme and not know that we have trauma responses. They are not spotted in us and we escape exposure, as I noted in the last chapter. Trauma is regarded as a specialist subject, when the reality is that most trainee counsellors and therapists start their clinical practice in placements which offer low-cost or free sessions to people with sexual abuse histories, or substance abuse difficulties. Similarly, we are usually not taught to question the limitations of our approach or experience, or to take our vulnerabilities seriously enough. From the outset, we may be plunged into the world of trauma in one guise or another, without real preparation for what we encounter.

An inherent property of trauma is to reduce our thinking capacity, and having theoretical frameworks to fall back on supports a re-engagement of cognitive function. Training, knowledge, personal therapy, and good supervision can serve us well by grounding us in the present, and as experience builds so does our own window of tolerance. Learning how to assess for trauma is key to mitigating some of the pitfalls of trauma therapy, as is knowing when and how to refer someone onwards. I consider these to be part and parcel of an ethical sensibility. Even if we have established expertise, we need to consider in each instance whether we are able and willing to use it at this time. A fundamental premise, therefore, is that we cannot get away from doing our own work, both professionally and personally. Developing the reflective capacity required for this is an undertaking that cannot be underestimated, and we turn to this in the next chapter.

Part 3

Ecological Perspectives

Trickster story: Waking up

Trickster happened to look in the water and much to his surprise he saw many plums there. He surveyed them very carefully and then he dived down into the water to get some. But only small stones did he bring back in his hands. Again he dived into the water. But this time he knocked himself unconscious against a rock at the bottom. After a while he floated up and gradually came to. He was lying on the water, flat on his back, when he came to and, as he opened his eyes, there on the top of the bank he saw many plums. What he had seen in the water was only a reflection. Then he realized what he had done. 'Oh, my, what a stupid fellow I must be! I should have recognized this. Here I have caused myself a great deal of pain.'

– Lewis Hyde, 2008: 55

8 The shared mindful field

We have questioned earlier how we meet the intense pain of trauma, and the personal and environmental factors that can get in the way. The degree of self-care and compassion for our own wounds that I have advocated earlier provides a great support not only to live more engaged lives but to build capacity to be present to the suffering of the Other. Here we come to consider how one part of the field influences another, the therapist shaping the experiential world of those we work with, and opening the possibility of something beyond. In this chapter, the three elements of Self, Other, and Situation (Chapter 2) come together, united by the concept of ethical presence instead of being torn apart by dissociated absence.

The term 'the shared mindful field' derives from Harris (2011), and I believe it to be an important concept in working with trauma. In contrast to the dissociated absence so typical of trauma, which has been explored in depth (Chapter 5), mindful awareness of the here-and-now forms a counterpoint which holds the potential for recreating the relational boundary and moving through the trauma together. The shared mindful field denotes a particular quality of authentic open attention in which the self of the therapist becomes instrumental in shaping the relational field. This shows how crucial an intervention it is to support and develop the capacity for personal presence. The inner presence of the therapist is conveyed mostly non-verbally, through prosody of voice and embodiment. *Being, in this sense, is doing.* Furthermore, the shared mindful field begins to offer the possibility of mutuality. Embedded in it is the notion that our therapeutic presence becomes an invitation to the people we work with to enter into a more present state within.

We saw in Chapter 2 that Gestalt theory suggests that the meeting between individuals, or between an individual and the environment, takes place at the 'contact boundary'. It is a point at which contact becomes possible, in which intentionality translates into a new experiential reality. By contact we do not privilege any particular form of contact, because we cannot *not* be in contact at every moment with some aspect of the total field represented by the SOS model (Denham-Vaughan and Chidiac, 2013). Rather, *how we make contact* becomes the focus of a Gestalt description, already suggested by Lichtenberg's (2001) four corners of contact, adapted in Chapter 6 as the hexagram of contact. We are interested in how we respond to the Other, who is equally responsive within the responsive field. This opens a transition from I–It to I–Thou relating:

> The recognition of significant and empathic others is the means by which we become able to experience ourselves as subjects, while at the same time learning to recognize the subjectivity of others ... the capacity for mutual recognition ... allows for the flexibility in moving between subjective and objective perspectives. (Shaw, 2014: 9)

Juliet Denham positions authenticity as a clear requirement of this depth of contact (2006:18), which I understand as an ethical position of embracing our vulnerability. As such, it becomes a potent leveller of the relational field.

Hannah

Hannah is struggling to reconcile contradictory aspects of herself; she finds them unacceptable because they confuse people who don't know who she is. She wants always to be good. This a belief she has trouble letting go of, reinforced constantly by a voice in her head which chips in with comments about what she 'should' do to be worthy of attention. I comment that by trying to be someone who is always good, she makes it harder to be known. Next, Hannah wonders how she can be authentic if she can't put other facets of herself into words, how will anyone ever know her and meet her if she can't explain herself? Is she going to be condemned to a life of loneliness? She seems not so much to be telling me as musing out loud, left alone in the moment.

Hannah feels ungrounded and unsettled and we shift attention for a while to an image of a favourite tree in her garden, looking at its roots and the texture of the bark, enquiring about the season. She finds it difficult to stay with and gets irritated with me for the process; she says she wants the ground and can't find it in her body. She becomes very still in her upper body and I sense simultaneously some activation in my stomach. I don't know where this is going to go, and name this to myself as a small anxiety that I have lost contact with Hannah. My breathing stills, not stopping but feeling constricted. As I notice this, I recognize that I have lost my own embodied sense of ground a little, and refocus my breathing and attend to my lower back and pelvis. As I drop into this anchor point, Hannah comments that I seem to be working hard. I tell her that I had wanted to adjust myself a little so that I could stay with her, and that in this moment I feel open and clear. Hannah sighs and tears come to her eyes, saying that she feels less afraid. I nod slightly, and quietly acknowledge this: 'I know'. Moment by moment, I have been tracking Hannah's energetic shifts in my own body, and recalibrating my own presence accordingly. This is a process, consistent with the methodology of phenomenological tracking, which supports the presence that Chidiac and Denham-Vaughan describe as 'energetic availability and fluid responsiveness' (2007: 10).

Dropping in

The first step in building the capacity to be present is choosing – using the left brain – to direct our attention inward. We ground ourselves by noticing points of contact between ourselves and what is outside: noticing our feet on the ground, sensing the bones that we are sitting on, being aware of the back of the chair against our back. Then we ask ourselves, What am I experiencing right now? What am I sensing in my body – aches, pains, nothing much? Am I hot, cold? Am I comfortable or uncomfortable in the way that I am sitting right now? What am I thinking? What am I feeling? (Westland, 2015: 79).

Shifts of consciousness

One of the tasks in establishing a shared mindful field is to redirect attention to a wider frame. A familiar characteristic of traumatized people – and therapists – is that they constrict their focus to a vigilance for potential threat, and it is helpful, as it were, to widen the aperture. 'The kind of attention we bring to bear on the world changes the nature of the world we attend to' (McGilchrist, 2009: 28). In Chapter 5 we looked at two perspectives which relate to a necessary shift in consciousness in working with trauma, which we drop into more deeply here. First , a segment from Laub and Auerhahn:

> The knowledge of trauma is fiercely defended against, for it can be a *momentous, threatening, cognitive and affective task*, involving an unjaundiced appraisal of events and our own injuries, failures, conflicts and losses. (1993: 288, emphasis added)

As I read this, one implication is that we need to learn to adjust our mindset, among other things, in order to create a shift of perspective. Secondly, and in similar vein, Parlett writes:

> All of us are part of this phenomenon of identifying and alienating [which subtly reduces the personhood of the other]. *It takes an enormous shift in consciousness to transcend this dynamic, to step outside it, to recognise it, and to avoid being caught in it.* (2015: 124, emphasis added)

These writers are alerting us to the rigour and commitment to self that this work requires. This a move towards the restructuring of the ground of our being; when we learn to do this, 'straight away, the trauma figure enlarges to one of "trauma *and* ..."' (Taylor, 2014: 52, original emphasis). We do this for our own healing and in service of those we work with. It is imperative that we are compassionate with ourselves over the long time that it takes a more mindful awareness to awaken in us.

The tendency to generalize experience after trauma often leads to a loss of differentiation, and a phenomenological enquiry invites a more nuanced perception. In this way, if someone makes a statement such as, 'I hurt all over', it might cause me to offer this: 'I wonder if you could check inside to see if there is some small part where it is less intense?' This in turn may produce an unexpected awareness: 'I feel the hurt mostly in my solar plexus, and least in my feet', which points to attending to the feet in order to support the distress held in the solar plexus. We start with an enquiry into what is potentially possible. How might such an expansion support our presence? It requires a considerable shift in consciousness to notice that life still goes on in the face of trauma, and we will explore this further in Chapter 10.

Westland suggests that there are three basic positions we may adopt: a panoramic view, a 'short rein', and a 'long rein'. She says: 'We can energetically hold clients in different ways, keeping them either on a short rein or a long rein or something in between … We can let the reel unwind or keep it more tightly held, but all the while keep hold of the reel of thread' (2015: 92). We can think of these three positions in relationship to the SOS model. Working with short rein is dialogically and experientially close, akin to the Self, while long rein is more spacious and inclusive, akin to the Other, and the panoramic position can be aligned with a perspective of the Situation.

Meeting difference

Practising the ethic of self-care (Chapter 6) puts therapists in a position to respond cleanly to the summons of the Other, without blurring the boundaries. In essence, a relational approach to therapy is concerned with meeting difference. However, sometimes the experience of difference contains a threat which links this discussion to trauma. Meeting difference involves appreciating the uniqueness of another's experience and knowing it is not our own. This may appear to hold a contradiction in terms of the shared mindful field. We share in the sense of recognizing and resonating with one another within the relational field, but not in the sense of knowing what it is like to be that person or to make the same meaning out of their existence. The challenge, though, is to be able to meet difference without maintaining or creating a split.

The ethic of self-care also means that we gravitate towards a position of 'power-with' as opposed to 'power-over' (Chapter 7). Aspects of power-with are popularly understood as 'empowerment', which carries a more individualistic flavour than the relatedness we are proposing. Power-with invites us to foster a number of important qualities: curiosity, dialogue, awareness, creativity, vitality, presence, humility, and vulnerability. With awareness of our patterns of defendedness, we do not back off from staying with the process – tracking and attending to shifts in energy or self-state as they emerge, and in a spirit of creative indifference, we remain open and welcoming of what comes next. This is a more horizontal position than the hierarchical power-over structure. This is facilitative of connection to networks, which is 'the central metaphor for the ecological paradigm' (Capra and Luisi, 2014: 14).

> **Dropping in**
>
> The most important thing you can do to unravel your own personal, historical, and intergenerational trauma around privilege, power, and bias is to notice what your body does in the presence of an unfamiliar body: black, disabled, older, 'other', 'not-me'.
>
> Bring to mind an image of someone whose physicality is 'different' to yours, and pay attention to your body as you do so:
>
> - What do you experience in your body?
> - Where and how is it constricting?
> - Where and how is it released and open?
> - Does it sense a threat?
> - What emotions, images, or impulses arise?
> - Is any sense of danger a reflexive response, or is the threat potentially real?
> - Ask yourself, 'If this body was like mine, how would I experience it right now?'
>
> This *daily* practice is not intended to create trust, but to practise discernment as you would with any stranger. Eventually, your brain will stop seeing unfamiliar bodies as foreign, and start seeing them as human beings (adapted from Menakem, 2017: loc 3972).
>
> You may also be interested in trying an extension of the loving kindness meditation offered in Chapter 6. With this difficult person in mind, repeat to yourself the following statements: 'May you be kind to yourself in this moment; may you accept this moment exactly as it is; may you accept yourself in this moment exactly as you are; and may your compassion bring healing and growth'.

These powerful practices may have raised some questions for you about *how* to move into a more receptive state with regards to some sort of perceived 'differences'. Our capacity to meet difference is deeply embodied, and we talk here also of our embodied presence to meet the traumatized body. The significance of this is that we respond as defensively to difference as we do to those who are traumatized. In Chapter 6, we looked at Germer's five-stage model for developing self-compassion (2009: 28). I believe this is equally valuable here, primarily because when we are more compassionate towards our own wounds, we will naturally become more compassionate towards others. An 'intrapersonal' process strengthens our 'interpersonal' capacity (see Chapter 1). In addition, with the intention of meeting a more challenging 'Otherness' which contains some implicit threat such as trauma, we can deliberately apply the same model effectively. To reiterate, then, the steps are as follows:

1. *Aversion*: the Other is someone from whom we avert our eyes. Their suffering is too hard to bear, or we alienate ourselves making it difficult to approach safely.

2. *Curiosity*: we begin to turn towards this person with interest, and formulate some questions to help us understand. Curiosity loosens the rigidity or fixed Gestalts of trauma. We move from contraction to expansion, and come into a more aware relationship with them. In letting go of some of our defensiveness, we have to trust our ability to stay with the process. Because we are now in a better position to choose, this step builds ground for relationship.

3. *Tolerance*: we suspend judgement and safely endure being in their presence and become less guarded. We can breathe in the other and respect increases. We begin to listen more deeply. However, it is important to stress that *the capacity or resilience to endure endless pain is neither the purpose nor the end goal* of this process. I will say more about this later in the chapter. A more enriched and vital engagement with the world is where this work beckons. This is comparable to sustainability, which goes further in the next two stages.

4. *Allowing*: we can open further to the Other, without seeking to change them. Spontaneity together is possible, a more fluid responsiveness, allowing access to a range of self-states. This is a powerful position which requires courage, and creates some distance from suffering.

5. *Friendship*: we actively welcome the engagement, which becomes mutual and growthful.

It is possible to map these stages onto the Gestalt 'cycle of experience' (see Appendix A and, for example, Taylor, 2014: 42), in which we might roughly pair aversion with sensation; curiosity with mobilization; tolerance with action; allowing with contact; and friendship with acceptance. This is not necessarily a linear process, and just as with the cycle of experience, there may be some recursive sticking points. Some of these stages are a natural process of making any relationship, of which we might not be aware. The adaptability of this model makes it a useful tool for mapping the process and progress of therapy. Whether we move through these stages quickly and with ease or struggle over time is relatively unimportant; the honest intention to loosen familiar patterns of resistance represents a shift in orientation.

Developing curiosity

Curiosity can be seen as an effective therapeutic tool to keep dialogue alive. Rooted in conscientious self-reflection, curiosity emerges relationally out of the imaginative space that we call empathy or inclusion, in which 'speculation about the self in relation to other, attunement to the other's experience, identification of personal risks and threats, and development and testing of options and outcomes can occur' (Carroll and Shaw, 2013: 155).

Assumptions and bias take a back seat in a more open and curious space, allowing for a provisional understanding to come into focus. An element of surprise can come through offering deep curiosity, as the people we work with come to consider themselves differently in response. The

Other attracts our fascination, which changes us in the contact: 'How interesting, I would never have seen it like that'– the selfhood of both is created and honoured, in the moment, at the contact boundary. 'To attempt to see a phenomenon in its wholeness, relationally speaking, requires us to open to multiple perspectives and to experience the contact boundary as a prism, rich and full and deep of meaning and possibility' (Timberlake, 2005: 196).

A good starting point is one that is not pathologizing, as I suggested in Chapter 1. I regularly ask the people who come to see me about the best moment of the past week, or what is going well in their lives, and they usually tell me about small growth points, or resources that they have dismissed or downplayed. Here is grist for the therapeutic mill, that provides a counter-force to the gravitational pull of the black hole of trauma (Chapter 2). Identifying a strength that is under-developed is something I tend to linger with, enquiring further into the felt sense, to lend more weight to the novel and increase the possibility of integration on the bodily level. A sense of coherence gathers around the mutual appreciation of strength. This challenges a rigid identification with the all-suffering, never-ending perception that many traumatized people hold. Unless we are able to maintain an even curiosity and welcome it in those we work with, how 'do people learn what is safe and what is not safe, what is inside and what is outside, what should be resisted and what can safely be taken in?' (van der Kolk, 2014: 127).

It is obvious that every new person requires that we learn how they need to be met, which in turn calls into question our willingness to respond fluidly and energetically. This necessitates that we enter a state in which we drop assumptions and have awareness of our own biases, not just at the outset, but in every shifting, emergent moment. The wisdom of the beginner's mind (see also Chapter 4) asks that we no longer know what we think we know in order to meet the person afresh. Knowledge does not impart wisdom. It is not so much that we don't know but that we don't know *if* we know: 'Would you teach me how this works for you?' I cannot be the expert on anyone else's way of being other than – possibly – my own. This can be summed up as having both courage and compassion, dealing with my fear, allowing myself to reflect in deepening ways and beginning to think systemically, as well as individually, 'staying with my feelings, even when painful, being curious rather than evaluative, knowing what I need to let go of, keeping the context and its many challenges in mind' (Carroll and Shaw, 2013: 190).

Tolerating uncertainty

Confusion and conflict are hallmarks of traumatic experience, mediated by the dynamic presence of the Trickster. As we saw in Chapter 5, we operate often in the territory of the unknown and the unknowable: 'We enter a state of disjunction and implicitly we raise questions: What do I do now? What does this mean? What is that smell? That sound? And so on. There is a sense of unknowing' (Carroll and Shaw, 2013: 273). This can feel unsafe and the tendency can therefore be to pull into the polarized over-reach of certainty (Chapter 7). Creative adaptations to trauma arise *because* the certainties of life are at least temporarily disrupted, and safety is to some degree predicated on restoring a sense of control and predictability. To be uncertain involves a degree of helplessness. The line between living with unpredictability and tolerating uncertainty is a fine one. It is natural to seek to make order – and meaning – out of chaos, where a more unifying position is to recognize and stay with both.

> By remaining alert in the center, we can acquire a creative ability of seeing both sides of an occurrence and [of] completing an incomplete half. By avoiding a one-sided outlook, we gain a much deeper insight to the structure and function of the organism. (Perls, 1969: 14–15)

Notice that the alertness Perls advocates has much in common with the shifts in consciousness described above.

Friedlander's (1918) concept of 'creative indifference' offers a useful framework, in which an individual, whether traumatized or not, is supported to determine their own path to growth and healing – or not. Importantly, from this therapeutic position we do not hold expectations or have an outcome in mind; we eschew a power-over position. The therapist is not invested in the future life of the Other, but simply trusts in the shared meeting at this time. According to Geller and Greenberg exploratory therapies such as Gestalt rest upon a high need to trust in the process and in the moment as a guide to the unfolding of clients' experience. There are moments when it is unclear what will emerge, and the skill of following the moment and tolerating uncertainty and the unknown is highly important (2012: 12).

We experience a non-linearity in letting go of certainty. This is particularly challenging when we are faced with the intensity of suffering when working with trauma, and requires courage. Trust has to be placed firmly both in creating the conditions that can permit change and in the understanding that given those conditions the nervous system will organize around well-being. When I understood many years ago that I do not have the wisdom or the authority to determine the right path for another person, my anxiety dropped, I became more open to possibilities, and I felt less burdened by responsibility for the consequences (see Chapter 6). According to Stevenson, '*Being* is the creative indifference that dissolves the polarity between doing and not doing, acting and waiting' (2004: 2, emphasis added). This then becomes the necessary ground of contact (2004: 4).

We remain lost without discovering some points of reference. Grounding ourselves into our embodied anchors provides a degree of certainty in the ongoingness of being that supports the development of uncertainty, and the capacity to stay with it for a longer duration. This is the reference point from which we may be able to respond in a more vital and fluid manner: 'Wicked problems exist in a dynamic and largely uncertain environment, which creates a need … [for] the flexibility to respond to unimagined and perhaps unimaginable contingencies' (Stevenson, 2004: 12).

Under the right conditions, this place of ignorance and unknowing is often the point of transformation, the creative space Gestalt theorists define as the fertile void (Perls, 1969). From here we can enter into dialogue in which provisional and shared understandings may emerge. Attentive and responsive in the moment, I check time and again in a session: 'I might not be right but …'; 'I wonder if this fits …?'; 'This is my word – what word would you use to make it your own?'; 'Could I just check with you if I have understood'; 'Tell me if I am wrong …'. As Siegel says:

> We don't know where an interaction will take us and we cannot control its outcome. Resonance immerses us in the unknown and brings us face to face with uncertainty … Ironically, sometimes the most powerful statements we can make are an authentic 'I don't know' or 'I'm not sure'. (2010: 56)

Reflections on presence

The need to stay in dialogue has been explicit in the above discussion. Dialogue is one of the pillars of Gestalt theory and is based on four interwoven principles: presence, open communication, confirmation, and inclusion (Buber, [1923] 1958). 'Mostly, people who are distressed want us to be with them. They want to feel that we "understand" because we feel our version of it too. We communicate this to them in our way of being with them (right brain to right brain)' (Westland, 2015: 78).

Our right brain to right brain 'way of being with them' is another way of thinking about presence. Presence is not necessarily a verbal communication, indeed it may be more powerful without words. We convey our presence through gaze, an open receptive attention, active curiosity, and grounded centredness, as suggested in the opening lines of Chapter 1. And as Westland implies, presence in the therapy setting is bi-directional. Geller and Greenberg concur:

> We see presence as a reciprocal process that enhances the quality of each person's presence and deepens the connection to create a relational presence … Clients' presence can be activated by therapists' presence through both being deeply met by the therapist as well as by intersubjective sharing. (2012: 61)

Since presence is predicated on a sense of safety (Siegel, 2010: 21), it is contingent also upon the therapist's own inner sense of safety. This is the territory of dyadic or even mutual regulation, which I have addressed at some length elsewhere (Taylor, 2014: 207ff.). Because regulation is a central organizing principle of the dynamics of relational therapy, I will take this opportunity to revisit this. Founded in the early Gestalt concept of organismic self-regulation (Perls et al., [1951] 1998), I have touched already on the idea that given optimal conditions the human organism can recover. However, the potentially isolating and non-contextual nature of self-regulation was overlooked by our founders. In Chapter 7, I spoke of the adjustment that has taken place from the concept of transference to that of co-transference. A similar shift has taken place in our formulation of the concept of regulation, from the focus on the individual to the interaction at the contact boundary, of which regulation is one possible exchange.

Research into relational dynamics has taken two directions. The first is an exploration of mother–infant communication, usually extrapolated by relational analysts and intersubjectivity theorists to be a prototype for the interactions between therapists and the people they work with. Tronick (1998) and Beebe and Lachman (2002) are prominent in making significant contributions to this field of study. The second area of research is into the field of interpersonal neurobiology (see Appendix B), the findings of which seem to support the felt experience within the therapy context. Some key figures in this domain are Siegel (2012), Porges (2017), and Schore (2003). Carroll observes that we can include more than one person in the process of self-regulation:

> The two-person system is a dynamic balancing act, with the level of feeling often fluctuating as the interaction between client and therapist is managed both implicitly (through self-regulation and interactive regulation) and explicitly (as far as these processes are the subject of verbal exploration). (2009: 103)

When considering presence, we are talking of an energetic resonance, or vibration, which Denham-Vaughan compares to the rapid vibrations of a hummingbird, adding: 'I am highly aware of my physical sensations and particularly of my breathing and heartbeat. My attention is shifting rapidly from myself to the other, and to the felt sense of the nature of the embodied relationship emerging between us' (in Chidiac and Denham-Vaughan, 2007: 15). There is thus an energetic quality, which 'is more than [unidirectional] attunement … it means allowing the client's energetic communications to reverberate within us' (Taylor, 2014: 205). Porges explains the mechanism for this:

> This ability to feel another's feelings is based on our neurophysiology. We can detect and interpret how another person feels, because the nerves that control the striated muscles of the face and head are linked in the brainstem to the myelinated smart vagus. We functionally wear our heart on our face. (2017: 133)

The resonant attunement of presence requires that the therapist, in the first instance, uses their self as an instrument, 'the intended application of self to the resonance of the environment' (Chidiac and Denham-Vaughan, 2007: 16). Presence is shared when I implicitly and in awareness include my own experience and vulnerability and can remain in relationship to those of the Other.

While presence 'cannot be rehearsed … it must be planned for, in so far as one musters all one's resources prior to setting out on a trip' (Chidiac and Denham-Vaughan, 2007: 11). We build our resources in order to sustain this challenging way of being, the foundational ethic of self-care (Chapter 6) coming once again to the fore.

> The cultivation and deepening of presence, for both novice and seasoned therapists, demand that therapists have a high level of self-care, self-awareness, and self-compassion … Presence also demands that we work through unfinished business issues that keep us stuck. (Geller and Greenberg, 2012: 11)

These writers carried out research into therapeutic presence: 'Therapists in our study also noted that attention to their self-care and personal well-being improved their presence and ultimately improved their effectiveness as therapists' (2012: 10). If we wish to be effective and ethical therapists, we simply cannot dodge this.

Dropping in

If you are physically able to, I invite you to do this practice standing preferably without shoes, feet hip-width apart, tail tucked in a little, knees unlocked. If you need to sit, try to position yourself forward in the seat. First, find a sense of contact with the ground or the chair under you. Now slowly see if you can get a sense of your spine, each vertebra stacked from the bottom up, each on top of the one below. It may help to lengthen your spine a fraction.

An extension of this is to imagine your backbone as a flag pole, and then begin to swing your arms around your body, as though they are the flag wrapping around in a wind. All the while, keep a sense of your backbone. Try to gather a gentle rhythm with this, bending your knees as you swing your arms, and perhaps coordinate your movements with your breath. Gradually slow the movement right down until you come to a stop.

Because the communication of presence is largely non-verbal, it follows that it is deeply embodied. In order to be present, someone will convey an attitude of stillness and stability, as if their 'centre of gravity was steady' and 'what is thrown at them, won't throw them'. This involves being impacted enough, but not too impacted or overwhelmed (Chidiac and Denham-Vaughan, 2007: 10). This is consistent with the thinking of Geller and Greenberg, who see physical presence as one of several levels of presence, adding that psychological, emotional, and transpersonal levels are also embedded in relational therapeutic presence (2012: 139). Our bodies carry our groundedness (see Chapter 9).

> Centeredness is an expression of personal integration, a unity of body and mind. Centeredness carries the paradox of detachment and involvement; we

need to be open and detached first in order to experience the fullness of the other. (Geller and Greenberg, 2012: 22)

Siegel understands the integrative potential of presence: 'What presence may essentially be is the ability to create an integrated state of being *that becomes a trait in our lives* … [when] a system becomes integrated, it is the most flexible, adaptive, coherent, energized, and stable' (2010: 31, emphasis added). It is my contention that the body is the great integrator, and thus that the embodied aspect of presence is critical.

Mindfulness and trauma

The essential purpose of bringing mindfulness into trauma therapy is to safely access the body which we inhabit. I am reminded here of Kepner's (2002) observation that dissociation is a flight from embodied life, and we seek to guide people home. The solidity and groundedness of presence has a felt sense of relationship to gravity and the earth beneath our feet that supports us, which we will explore in Chapter 9. A simple definition of mindfulness is 'awareness of the present moment', consistent with foundational Gestalt principles. There is a 'just notice', allowing quality to mindful explorations, without judgement.

There are several approaches to mindfulness, some based in thousand-year-old Eastern spirituality:

- *Formal meditation*: spending a period of time in open attention, which can lead practitioners into an expanded awareness.
- *Guided meditation*: common to both established and contemporary practices, such as Vipassana Insight meditation, Mindfulness-Based Stress Reduction and Headspace, is the use of guided meditation, typically a whole body-scan. This is a process in which attention is directed progressively to each part of the body in turn, a letting go into the ground and leading to a deeper sense of ease and well-being. Because we don't linger on anything, a sense of continuity and flow can be possible.
- *Focused meditation*: here a single focus is chosen, for example: following the breath; a candle or other object; a phrase, sound, or loving-kindness practice which is repeated; a photograph of a special place or a loved one. This kind of focus may arise spontaneously, such as when our attention is caught by the feel of the breeze against our face.
- *Informal meditation*: bringing attention to aspects of everyday life – mindfully brushing teeth, washing dishes, walking, or taking conscious deep breaths when stopped at a red traffic light (Nhat Hanh, 2011). I suggest that this has much in common with the integrated state that is referenced in Siegel, above, as a 'trait in our lives' (2010: 31).

In all but formal meditation, there is judgement about the choiceful direction of attention, which I suggest gives sufficient anchoring in the present to safely create some experiential distance. This choice of focus is different from an evaluative judgement, and it is essential to understand that mindfulness is not about trying to 'achieve' a particular state, but to simply notice what arises moment by moment. I now agree that we need to be more nuanced about the application of mindfulness.

Since I first wrote about the benefits of mindfulness for traumatized people (Taylor, 2014: 84), clinical experience has taught me a more cautious position. I no longer advise people to seek mindfulness 'training' outside of therapy, because these courses are rarely tailored to or sensitive to the needs of people who tend to dissociate. Britten is one of several writers who express concern about the risk of mindfulness taking people further into dissociative states: 'Mindful-ness shares some neurobiological correlates with dissociation, including high parasympathetic tone' (2019: 160). For people who are chronically hypo-aroused, in an out-of-body state, it can be more difficult to achieve a switch from a first- to a more detached third-person perspective. 'Given this overlap with dissociation, how does one ensure that mindfulness produces the optimal level of psychological distance that "steps back" far enough but not too far?' (2019: 160). My proposition is that we learn together by trial and error, informed first and foremost by solid personal experience.

Dropping in

Close your eyes for a moment or drop and soften your gaze if you feel more comfortable. Check inside for awareness of your current sensations, including your breathing, becoming present to yourself in this moment. Now ask yourself what presence means to you.

What aspects of your own bodily experience let you know when you are fully present? What feelings or bodily experiences accompany presence?

What does it feel like to be fully present with another human being? What did it feel like? How did it affect your relationship in the moment with that person?

What does it feel like to be fully in the moment with someone you work with? How might your experience of presence with someone in your personal life differ from that with someone in your professional life (adapted from Geller and Greenberg, 2012: 38)

The regulatory benefit of mindfulness practice is underscored by Badenoch: 'Often in the teaching of mindfulness, there may be an unseen co-regulatory process at work because of a teacher whose ongoing presence multiplies the effectiveness of the practice itself' (2018: 184). I note here that the therapist stands in for the 'teacher'. What we do understand is the benefit in modulating arousal when we take a witnessing position. 'When we allow ourselves to rest in experiences of calm, centeredness, acceptance, immersion, and equanimity, we are increasing the possibility that these experiences will become "neurological imprints"' (Geller and Greenberg, 2012: 163).

To support this line of thinking, research is showing that practising a form of breath awareness or meditation 'adds billions of synaptic connections and thus a measurable thickening of brain tissue in the regions that deal with attention and sensory awareness' (Geller and Greenberg, 2012: 162). The non-judgemental observing in mindfulness also reduces reactivity to intense somatic and emotional states as well as to neutral states without seeking to change them: 'This includes developing more capacity to be present for intense and highly charged emotion, physical discomfort, or pain, as we stay with what is here right now' (Gold and Zahm, 2018: 202). A further important benefit of a mindfulness approach is that by 'staying with' subjective phenomenology, the continuity of experience, broken by traumatic events, can be restored.

It is, however, critical to be wary of encouraging increased tolerance of difficult, abusive, or oppressive situations, as indicated earlier. Clearly no one should feel under any kind of duress to do so, or be left feeling that it is because of weakness that they cannot. That would be tantamount to individual victim-blaming and distorts the relational reality of the situation. Luisa's story in Chapter 3 is a case in point.

What is meant by the concept of tolerance and resilience is an expanded appreciation of multiple dimensions of a vital and engaged life, *including* our deepest and most authentic pain, in the absence of fear. Menakem distinguishes between what he calls 'clean and dirty' pain. By clean pain he means, 'pain that mends and can build your capacity for growth ... only by walking into our pain and discomfort – experiencing it, moving through it – can we grow. Clean pain hurts like hell' (2017: loc 584). Because the body is able to feel fully, the pain can be metabolized and it has the quality of flow. Dirty pain, by contrast, 'is the pain of avoidance, blame and denial. When people respond from their most wounded parts, become cruel or violent, or physically or emotionally run away, they experience dirty pain. They also create more of it for themselves and others' (2017: loc 595). There is a self-perpetuating, inescapable, stuck quality to this kind of pain. I find the terms 'clean' and 'dirty' to be somewhat pejorative, and suggest we might replace them, therefore, with the more phenomenologically descriptive 'fluid' and 'stuck' pain, while preserving the essence of this valuable concept.

David

David had served in Afghanistan, where he was caught with a close friend and fellow squaddie, John, in a roadside explosion. Thrown to the ground in the blast, David was badly bruised, but John was killed instantly. David's most vivid memory was of lying with his face in the dirt, while some local youths shouted angrily, 'Americans, Americans', as the dust settled. When he returned to base camp after the explosion, David was medically checked, and then his commanding officer spoke a few words of commiseration and told him to fill in an incident report. David said that he finished his tour on auto-pilot, and he had not fared well after he left the army. His marriage broke up, he was drinking heavily, and found himself on the wrong side of the justice system. His brother helped him to access therapy.

We had learned through experimentation with some objects in my room that David didn't like soft contact. Firmer contact provided him with clarity where a softer relational contact confused him. I commented that one way we were different was in expressing these preferences, and David nodded and changed the subject. I adjusted my presence, bringing both more energy and a bit more distance into the session. Guilt dominated David's entire life: 'It should have been me, I've let him down, I should have watched more carefully, if only I'd been driving instead of John, I wish I'd shouted back at those kids that we were British, I should have stood up to my officer'. This was the ruminative narrative that preoccupied him, along with white knuckles, a tight, barrelled chest, and pursed mouth. When the feeling got too much to bear, he drank, and got into fights, or committed criminal damage. He had broken his hand after smashing a car. David recognized that his guilt wasn't rational, but he just couldn't look at it.

In this session, I guide David a little deeper: 'When you used those words "I should have …" just now, did you notice if you felt better or worse?' 'Worse, much worse' he replies. 'What is telling you that?' I ask, inviting his curiosity. 'I dunno … I suppose my heart started banging, and my head feels, well, just kind of fizzing … I can't think'. I somehow sense that David is moving towards tolerating more than he has previously, and I don't know how much more he can bear. I am aware of my heartbeat, and steady myself by taking some deeper, audible breaths. 'It's confusing, isn't it, when you know one thing and feel the opposite' I reply. 'Too right' David says, 'It's doing my bloody head in', and he bangs his fist onto the arm of the chair. 'Oh, be careful not to hurt yourself, David … what happened there?' David swallows hard and touches his chest, silently. I say, 'There's a lot going on, how about taking a few deep breaths with me? … just see if you can tell whether your in-breath or out-breath settles you more?' We are staying with the process as it unfolds. 'Out-breath, I think' David responds. 'If it helps, try and make your out-breath a little longer than your in-breath, see what you notice'. Using breath in this way supports a more parasympathetic or ventral vagal state (see Appendix B). David needs some support if he is to move through this.

'I feel like I've got a big rock in my chest, like it's going to explode' David tells me. 'Interesting word …' I say quietly. David looks a bit awkward and replies, 'Well, a volcano, maybe. If I stop feeling guilty I'm scared what might happen'. David is shifting from 'stuck' pain to 'fluid' pain. *Of course* he is terrified of another explosion. The energy in the room increases. I feel like a limpet clinging on to the seat of my chair as a huge wave approaches. At the same time, I gather myself into my upper body, to match the rising energy in the room. I say, 'This might be a bit of an odd thought David, but I can't help wondering if that is what happens when you get drunk, that you erupt, and that it never seems to stop. You get hurt, one way or another. Does that fit at all for you or not?' He looks away, swallows again, gripping the arms of the chair. His eyes water, he gathers his breath, and a loud primal bellow washes over him, 'Christ, it hurts so much, I could kill those kids, I could fucking kill my officer, how could they, how could they do it?' David's attention now seems to be fixed on his right hand. 'Your hand, David … are you remembering something?'

I ask. 'Blood', he replies, his voice low and strained. I feel a thud in my chest, a ripple of shock courses through me. I breathe and re-ground myself. 'I tried to help him, I tried ... there was nothing I could do ... nothing ...'. I enquire gently, 'How did you feel, trying and not being able to help?' 'Panic, absolute bloody panic ... shock, I suppose you'd call it'. 'Yes' I say, affirming him. Softer now, he goes on: 'He was my best mate, everything going for him, lovely wife, lovely kids, great guy ... I miss him, I miss him, I miss him so much. I always will'. He's quieter, tears running down his face, his body seeming more centred. We sit for a while in near silence, acknowledging David's feelings and his expression of them. 'You know, I never cried when John died, just sort of hardened myself. I guess that needed to come out', David smiles.

Therapeutic skill set

To achieve the apparent ease of mindful presence is exacting and paradoxically complex. Chidiac and Denham-Vaughan observe that becoming 'a Gestalt therapist is a demanding and challenging path. We would argue that no other form of therapy asks for such rigorous *awareness* of process combined with such vigilant attention to *use* of self as process in order to provide the optimal environmental support for the client' (2007: 18, original emphasis). A number of therapeutic attributes are associated with creating a shared mindful field. For the most part they are self-explanatory, but I think it is important to summarize them here:

- The *'power-with'* stance horizontalizes the relationship, allowing therapists to de-centre from their own ego.
- *Non-defensiveness*: not needing to use interventions that protect the therapist (Roubal, 2019). This is one of the most important strengths to cultivate.
- *Humility*: not taking an expert position; not knowing; accepting that the therapist may never be enough.
- *Authenticity*: finding the right balance between the therapist role and the true self.
- *Courage*: facing the unknown, the horror, the terror.
- *Groundedness*: skills that can be accessed readily.
- *Naming*: being unafraid to bring a hidden aspect, or something obvious, into the therapy when appropriate.
- *Trust in the process*: knowing from within our own experience that what emerges will be in the service of well-being.
- *Vulnerability*: accepting personal and professional limitations.
- The *willingness to interrupt*, to put the brakes on, to assert one's place in the dialogue.
- *Asking for support*: colleagues, supervisor, and personal therapists all have a part to play.

- *Shuttling*: moving attention between different aspects of the field.
- *Humanity*: recognizing with compassion the commonality of human suffering.
- *Decolonization*: rigorously questioning and challenging our own embodied cultural norms, perceptions, prejudices, and attitudes, as well as challenging those of others. We return to this idea in Chapter 10.

A widening space

The weekly therapy session lasts for just 50 minutes or an hour. Sometimes we are led to believe that this is the one hour of the week that people live for – an opportunity to work on our hubris! I suggested in Chapter 6 that we need to create a lifestyle that supports us to be present in this hour – and the next – and the same is true for the people who come to see us. The work of therapy needs to spill over into the rest of the week. An ecological rather than an ego-logical perspective opens us to a vast range of possibilities. Then the boundaries between inside and outside may be less defined, and we can use that to good effect. I have a variety of regular embodied mindful practices which make up my resonant and responsive personal and therapeutic field. I asked Alex if he could identify a better moment in his week. He replied, 'Yes, I suppose it was when I watched the sunset from the train'. I enquired what it meant to him to see that, and he told me, 'It gave me a sense of something larger'. I had seen the same sunset, and we shared a moment remembering it. The experience of grace (Denham-Vaughan, 2005) opens us to bigger contexts, in which we can let go, stay curious, and ultimately transcend. Geller and Greenberg quote Rogers: 'Our relationship transcends itself and becomes a part of something larger. Profound growth and healing and energy are present' (2012: 27).

Dropping in

Try a very simple exploration. Make a note of a meal you have eaten today. List the main ingredients, and then go back and trace, as far as you are able to, the origins of each one. What is the source of the grains, the dairy products, the meat or fish, the plant base, the tea or coffee? Reflect on the relationship of what you have eaten to the parent soil, the people who cultivated it, the sun and rain, and how that has now become part of you (adapted from Olsen, 2002: 161).

In an ecological process, my presence is reinforced and deepened by yours and vice versa. A sense of mutual and reciprocal influence between us is the foundation for thinking about interconnectedness on a wider scale. We go on to explore these bigger ideas in the final two chapters.

9 The well-grounded therapist

This chapter is a revision of an article co-authored with Vienna Duff.[1] In bringing in a different voice, the message we convey is about mutual care and respect. We position this chapter in relation to some theory and background, and later provide examples of our work together. The chapter references some of the themes that are presented throughout the rest of the book, and provides an introduction to the final chapter.

Situating the work

> Caring for myself is not self-indulgence, it is self-preservation and that is an act of political warfare.
>
> – Audre Lorde, 2017: 130

There are many textures and properties of the relational field in trauma work that are so embedded that they go underground (Chapter 2). The cumulative effect of these may well be greater than the sum of its parts, an aggregate more perceptible, paradoxically, by increasing fragmentation and absence. Concerned about the impact of this on therapists and other practitioners, we have collaborated on presenting a series of experiential residential workshops, restorative in style and inviting a deep reconnection with the natural world. Two things followed on from these workshops: a looser enquiry of the effect on participants over time, and an active phenomenological curiosity about *how* the natural world improves a sense of grounding. We describe both below.

We base our work on five core assumptions, drawing on ideas presented earlier. Our fundamental premise is the recognition of the profound sense of disconnection that accompanies complex trauma and other catastrophic disturbances of the contact boundary. We think primarily of relational trauma, in which the survival of the self without support is overwhelmed. Trauma of this nature annihilates a sense of context for the individual affected. Herman speaks of the existential crisis arising from the destruction of 'the victim's fundamental assumptions about the safety of the world, the positive value of the self and the meaningful order of creation … that sustain life' (1992: 51–52). Through the therapeutic relationship these dimensions also impact the therapist. We suggest that this has a particular relevance for practitioners working with complex issues such as trauma, or in challenging environments (see Denham-Vaughan and Glenholmes, 2019) and position our work as an important influence – among others – on the relational field.

A second premise is that we are all traumatized to a greater or lesser extent, and that low level trauma buzzes around us constantly. Taussig has said that we can 'understand our reality as a chronic state of emergency, as a Nervous System' (2004: 270). Coupled with this, our own life-stories shape the relational therapeutic field. A whole-field view includes our personal wounds and concerns (Adams, 2014). Trauma, being so hard to contain, spills out into organizations and into our own lives and work (Chapters 3 and 6), the constant interchange of trauma, like a hot potato being passed around.

Our third premise is that working with trauma will change us as therapists. Pearlman and Saakvitne (1995: 279) remind us of the personal investment therapists make, involving inevitable gains and losses. Implicit in the therapeutic contract is that we open ourselves to feel threatened, devalued, objectified, ignored, and hated (Davis and Frawley, cited in Pearlman and Saakvitne, 1995: 24). We meet people who test us, reject us, drip feed us appalling stories, who try to possess us, to hold us captive to their suffering whilst also navigating a journey of recovery. It is not an overstatement that such a potent traumatized field puts us at psychological and physical risk. Consistent with Gestalt principles of co-creation, Gartner (2017: 7) coins the term 'countertrauma' in acknowledgement of our response. However, the countertrauma that resonates within us can be problematic to identify, partly because the therapist will also inevitably become caught in the process of dissociation (Bromberg, [1998] 2001, 2006, 2011; Taylor, 2014: 225). Paradoxically, a co-created *absence* gets in the way more often than we recognize.

The concerns that are compelling in this area of work are those most resonant of trauma. They stir personal stories within us. Our fourth premise is, therefore, concerned with *how* trauma calls to the self of the therapist, or shuts him or her out. Our own enduring relational themes (Jacobs, 2017) are summoned in the therapeutic endeavour. Dissociation, by definition, is an absence rather than a presence (Taylor, 2014: 129), thus what we might cut off from is clinically relevant. '[Much] of the survivor's reaction and experience will be both theoretically and experientially groundless' (Kepner, 1995: 94), and we suggest that the same is inevitably true for the therapist to a degree. Calling attention to a wider range of resources, increasing the field of choice, becomes a major intervention and influence on the therapeutic field (see also Chapters 6 and 7).

Finally, we are mindful of how sensitive traumatized people are to their therapist's capacity to bear with them, so often communicated on an implicit embodied level outside of awareness. As a defence, they have learnt to read others for clues as to their safety, and to moderate the levels of arousal of their caretakers. Kepner suggests that 'our own body process is an intrinsic part of the transaction with the client' (2003: 11); a primary transaction is the level of arousal between us.

These five premises underpin our overall argument that failure to attend to all aspects of the field perpetuates splits and disconnection. We are mindful of the irony that this chapter focuses only on one view of the whole other-than human field, in which we can acknowledge trauma too. How therapists situate themselves in relation to the whole field – our way of being in the whole world – will resonate with the people we work with and therefore becomes a vitally important aspect to be attended to. A core argument, laid out in Chapter 6, is that *the people we work with pay us primarily to take care of ourselves*. This preserves our capacity to remain present to multiple aspects of the field, within an expanded window of tolerance which is continually resourced and updated (Taylor, 2014: 195–196). The commandment that Levinas (1985) sees in the face of the suffering there is also a reflection of our own face. The act of self-preservation through self-care becomes political in the service of the people. Therefore, there is an ethic in which therapists' and supervisors' responsibility for shaping the relational field becomes both necessary and paramount (see Chapter 5). To respond to this, we devised a series of immersive workshops to increase awareness of the effects of grounding contact with the natural world, experienced in the presence of others.

Mapping new territory

Our proposition is that the existential experience of those moments in which the restorative and regenerative qualities of the natural world become available to us is essential. This occurs through embodied awareness of our relationship with the natural world. Without exploitation, we consider nature's propensity to support healing, not as a resource but as a *relationship*. This is not to dismiss other properties of the whole other-than-human field, but to focus our thoughts through this particular lens. We recognize that the total field encompasses 'the overall human habitat' and agree that 'sensory and bodily engagement' is richer for greater contact with and awareness of our relationship with all aspects of life on Earth (Parlett, 2015: 135). By fully embracing interdependence (see Chapter 10), our relationship with nature is enhanced. This mutual contact is consistent with core Gestalt principles of field theory and Buber's dialogic attitude ([1923] 1958). The style of this chapter and our approach demonstrates these processes.

We have drawn on a vast and complex interplay of influences for this work about self-care, both personal and theoretical, and attempt here to tease them out. First, the work is situated within basic Gestalt theoretical frameworks. In particular, the relationship between the things that catch our attention or express our most immediate needs (figures of interest) are seen against a more complex ground (see Appendix A and also Taylor, 2014: 41). In Gestalt therapy, increasing attention is being paid to the structure of the ground (e.g. Chidiac et al., 2017; Stawman, 2011; Taylor, 2014; Wheeler, [1991] 1998). The relationship between figure and ground is a dynamic one, not linear or hierarchical, and reflects a quality of emergent process. We are aware that an ungrounded figure may take us in damaging directions (Taylor, 2014: 44–45). We find support also in experiments in awareness where we are invited to notice that which had *not* first caught our attention (Stevens, 1971: 10). This invites an intention to consider new figures.

A consideration when working with trauma is to know what we are looking for. Here we turn to contemporary trauma theory to help us make sense of the processes operating on the field, such as the situational processes outlined in Chapter 2. Many such processes are subtle symbolizations of implicit learning and creative adjustments. Therefore, much of our attunement in trauma work is to the embodied rather than the spoken; it is also fragmented and disorganized. A key learning is that recovery needs to take place in circumstances that are different from those in which the trauma took place, and that inherent in the therapy there are significant dangers of re-enactment of traumatizing relational conditions (Taylor, 2014).

The new field of ecotherapy is also of relevance to us, which in turn rests on other multi-layered grounds. McGreeney (2016), Totton (2011), Rust (2011), and Marshall (2016), for example, move from a body psychotherapy background into ecotherapy. Other writers voice a concern for conservation, activism, and traditional indigenous healing. Among these are Chalquist (2010), Plotkin (2003), and Mackinnon (2012). Another genre of nature writing appeals to a new relationship and dialogue with the natural world (e.g. Abram, 1997, 2010; Snyder, 1990), while others (e.g. Dillard, 1974; Macfarlane, 2007; Thoreau, [1854] 1973) are more evocative in their approach. All this stands on a rich engagement with the pastoral by poets and artists from the eighteenth century onwards, emerging into direct use of the land, sometimes involving the body as instrument, by contemporary artists such as Goldsworthy (Reidelsheimer, 2001), Long (2018), and Drury (1998). The natural world invites generative responses.

From this background, we wish to highlight the contributions of a few individuals. In his fine paper on Gestalt ecopsychology (2015), Will Adams argues that healing can be bi-directional and mutual, and we wholeheartedly echo the sentiments he expresses. However, whilst like Adams our thinking is inspired by Levinas, for the purposes of this approach we hear the commandment of the Other coming from the consulting room first, rather than from the natural world. In accepting Adams' concept of dissociation between body and nature, in this instance we apply this specifically to the area of trauma work (see Taylor, 2014: 129–131). Rachel and Stephen Kaplan made a major contribution to the study of environmental psychology in the 1980s, conducting a number of research projects into the interaction between the human and other-than-human (Kaplan and Kaplan, 1989). They did not anticipate some of their findings, such as the prevalence of mystical experience in the natural world, or the difficulty in expressing and quantifying results. Some of their conclusions are discussed below. Ana Mendieta was a Cuban performance artist whose work focused on the dialogue between her own body in relation to the Earth, often developing themes of presence/absence, belonging, and inherent cycles from a feminist perspective. Underpinning our workshops has been the influence of Olsen, and her remarkable contribution *Body and Earth* (2002). This book is difficult to categorize because it offers a sophisticated integration of highly diverse concepts; the experience it brings captures the essence of our thinking and writing.

From theoretical grounding we move now to the experiential. We are likely to have ways of grounding ourselves before we greet our clients, and may seek in turn to ground them. Finding ground is a fundamental first process, enabling us to engage. Quite simply, we meet the Earth through our bodies. According to Merleau-Ponty (Todres, 2007), embodied experience must always be considered alongside being and knowing. Geller and Greenberg place this embodied concept as the 'first major subcategory of presence' (2012: 110; see also Chapter 8), and consider spending time in nature as an element of preparing for deepening presence in *daily life* (2012: 74). They define grounding as 'being present in the moment, in the body, with a sense of inner integration and inner steadiness in self' (2012: 213). For us, grounding is the precursor to the practice of inclusion (see Chapter 6). Although we can think of ground in other terms, such as relational, conceptual, sexual, or spiritual (Anagnostopoulou, 2015: 686), grounding in our sense invariably refers primarily to the body and its relationship to gravity.

Grounding, gravity, and bonding take us closer to the Earth. Grounding relates to 'our contact with the body, the Earth, nature, other human beings, family, culture, country, God' (Anagnostopoulou, 2015: 686). This association between grounding and contact will be of prime interest to Gestalt therapists. But as Belz-Knöferl suggests, we need first to find and to sustain this ground for ourselves: 'Therapists who do not know both grounding dimensions [of somatic resonance and necessary distance] within themselves, and who do not know how to balance them in a specific situation, will have difficulties working successfully with this concept' (2015: 680). Grounding offers up a more flexible and present response to trauma. And yet, as Marcus (1980) points out, it is possible to be over-grounded as well as under-grounded. However, in all ways, in trauma work it is wise to consider what is needed and multiply it.

Dropping in

How do you attend to grounding yourself before and after sessions? Do you find something to focus on in your room, take some deep breaths, use movement to orient yourself in the present, re-read supervision notes? Here is a simple practice.

Stand with your shoes off, your feet hip-width apart. Bring all of your attention to the contact between the soles of your feet and the floor or ground. Allow yourself to drop into the contact, noticing perhaps which parts of your feet receive most weight, whether the left and right foot are different, and noticing without judgement where you may resist this yielding into the ground. What is the ground offering you? Can you allow yourself to receive it? Imagine the boundary between the soles of your feet and the floor to become less distinct, as though your feet are extending roots into the Earth. What difference does this make? Breathe into this experience.

And then ask yourself how you might extend this sense of ground to be what you live from, rather than something you drop into from time to time?

The bodily adjustments that accompany grounding may include a release of tension, a slowing of heart rate and of breathing, and greater perceptual acuity. There is a sense of greater safety and opening, while a sense of belonging and connection can also be expected. The process of grounding is therefore both physiological and psychological (Anagnostopoulou, 2015: 686). Boadella (1987: 94) offers the opinion that we need also to find our sense of inner ground, such as the stability of our spine, the regularity of heart beat, our inner rhythms. These bring different pairings of internal and external. By connecting to ground we integrate some of the dichotomies of human experience, and may experience a degree of interconnection with the other-than-human world. The immediacy of physiological grounding opens us to numerous other grounds of being.

We can also develop this notion of the mutually influencing field beyond the therapeutic relationship and into ever expanding fields. Numerous writers attest to the fact that human beings are but one part of a larger system, *all parts having equal value* (see Abram, 1997, 2010; Chalquist, 2010; Plotkin, 2003; Snyder, 1990; Totton, 2011). Olsen spells this out: the substances that create the human body are the essential materials of the planet: 'Cells are the structural building blocks of all living beings' (2002: 26); the composition of bone is similar to that of marble (2002: 95); and she compares soil to the skin of the Earth (2002: 105).

Snow: After the storm

Putting the relationship between humans and the natural world into words is difficult. On the first pass, I (MT) went straight into my head and got stuck. As Kaplan and Kaplan recognize, 'it is hard to justify the role nature plays in rational terms' (1989: 1).

> I needed to go back to the raw experiential data (Abram, 1997: 48). Putting my conceptual self in my back pocket, so to speak, a new question for the land arose: 'How does the natural world want me to write about this?' Being the first day of a week off in early March, I get in the car and head north, about 50 miles to the east coast. Even being on the open road makes a difference. The sense of getting away from it all is one of four key aspects of restorative environments identified by Kaplan and Kaplan (1989: 176). They point out that where we are going to is as important as where we are escaping from. There is blue sky for the first time in a week, and a sense of freedom and openness. Slowing down behind a lorry, I put my daily life behind me for a while, and enjoy the drive. Right now it's not just about finding a way to write; I have an old trauma playing on my mind, which takes time to settle even as I get away.
>
> And then comes the first glimpse of the sea. I arrive at a beach I have never visited before, but without reference to a map I know how to do this; there's nowhere else to go. I've been doing this all my life; perhaps I'm tapping into some ancestral wisdom? At any rate, this offers a degree of recognition and familiarity at the start of my exploration. I'm about to enter a dialogue, based

on phenomenological enquiry, about how to meet and learn from 'other' – other-than-human. Crossing the dunes I notice a brief moment of being on a threshold (Denham-Vaughan, 2010), an anticipation before I drop down onto the beach. And then I pause, and scan the horizon, the lie of the land and the sea. I smell the breeze, cool and directional. I let it in on my breath, deeply, quietly, without anxiety about this contact. My lungs seem to double in volume with each breath; I notice the expansion between my shoulder blades. The second element Kaplan and Kaplan (1989: 189) identify is that of extent. Here we appreciate the scanning and scope that the non-human world offers us, the imagination, and the mystery. This notion includes also perception, spatial awareness, an appreciation of the organization of the features, and a sense of safety. 'To achieve the feeling of extent it is necessary to have interrelatedness of the immediately perceived elements, so that they constitute a portion of some larger whole. Thus there must be sufficient connectedness to make it possible to build a mental map' (Kaplan and Kaplan, 1989: 189). This sits comfortably with a Gestalt sensibility towards organization of perception, contact, and unified field.

My limbs adjust instantly to the texture of the firm sand, sinking just a little to each step, amplifying the contact, catching my attention. My heart rate slows in sync with my pace, natural, comfortable. I feel fluid in my legs even as they make clear firm contact in the sand. I call to mind Olsen's (2002: 172–174) taxonomy of seven integrated and integrative fluid systems in the body and their associated movements. What fluid sense is this, I wonder? Deliberate in a mindful, aware way, not ponderous, simply the beat, beat, beat of my heart, the flow of my blood, corresponding in turn to lymph, synovial, and interstitial fluids. Olsen explains: 'Because fluids are the transportation system of the body, integrating various parts, most movements reflect a blend of fluid states, comparable to the interconnected rhythms of water in the world around us' (2002: 175). I am aware of the different ways water and land meet in this place.

I relish the ease of being here, where I can take in more, feel more receptive. I feel roamy; not following any defined path I wander wherever my curiosity takes me in this vast expanse, and my mind roams too. I'm aware that my curiosity is guided by my limbs and senses, my animal self, rather than by conscious intent. The need to explore is a pervasive human need (Kaplan and Kaplan, 1989: 51), perhaps based partly on an instinctive need to establish a sense of safety, but also more creatively in terms of the search for novelty and growth.

I let go of my personal trauma as I walk; out here it seems less important as I let the natural world do its work in me. I sit for a while and make some gestural marks in my sketchbook, my eye and hand following edges, shapes, textures, blending and smudging. Words only begin to form as I speak some 'notes' into my voice recorder, which later give shape to this piece. My senses, my perceptions become more acute as I wait, attune, and listen to what comes without words. Sounds carry differently, there's much activity in the stillness around me. Here I notice the glint and textures of sunlight on water, the shapes and contours that the many channels of water cut across the beach, the sound of the waves, the offshore windfarm, tracks in the sand, the behaviour of gulls. I am equally caught by the 'big picture' and the small details; a macro and micro perspective that colours some of the best writing in the genre (see, for example, Dillard, 1974 or Olsen, 2002). This attentional range supports and reflects my endeavours in the therapy room, where I might be working with the precise detail of phenomenological experience while simultaneously holding multiple other perspectives: individual, relational, historical, and collective.

Discussion

Fascination (Messer Diehl, 2009: 170), or soft fascination as Kaplan and Kaplan (1989: 169) call it, refers to the quality of attention the natural world evokes in us: 'Soft fascination … permits a more reflective mode' (Kaplan and Kaplan, 1989: 191). They suggest that this may have something to do with cognitive clarity, a redirection of attention that corresponds to the window of tolerance (Siegel, 1999: 253; Taylor, 2014: 63). Although there are potentially competing figures for my soft fascination, there is time and space for enough of them to emerge, and I can regulate myself accordingly. 'There is less conflict between what one wants to do and what needs to be done and less that seems arbitrary or irrelevant' (Kaplan and Kaplan, 1989: 139). The arising sense of simplicity and ability to make choices in the ordering of experience is important for a number of reasons. These involve taking a number of small and related steps.

A sense of well-being and improved self-esteem are almost universal consequences of spending time in agreeable and hospitable natural surroundings. 'Previously frozen self-constructs can start to thaw, and the possibility of transformation and greater authenticity naturally arises … our journey into wilderness becomes a journey into the unconscious' (Kerr and Key, cited in Totton, 2011: 168). This describes an integrative process giving rise to a sense of wholeness. Such organismic self-regulation is considered by Totton as 'an expression of the situational Gestalt' (2011: 83), intimately arising as co-creative. Totton cites Gibson, who claims that any theory of perceiver and the perceived as two separate entities is dualistic, and that we can think more holistically of the field as 'co-perceiving' (Totton, 2011: 83). This is echoed also by Olsen (2002: 60), and expanded upon by Taylor (2014: 188).

Relationships with the other-than-human are sometimes described as involving a dialogue. Perhaps being in solitude we are able to listen and engage at this implicit level of communication, appreciating an 'inter-being dialogue [that] is the recognition of the other as the all' (Conn and Conn, 2009: 115). 'Otherness' becomes less threatening as we acknowledge that 'the phenomenal field contains many *other* bodies, other forms that move and gesture in a fashion similar to our own (Snyder, 1990: 37). A sense of reciprocity is therefore possible, since the 'exterior landscape and its creatures are an inseparable part of the interior landscape, the landscape of the spirit and the heart' (Totton, 2011: 165). Snyder takes us a step further: 'The sum of a field's forces becomes what we call very loosely the "spirit of place". To know the spirit of a place is to realize that you are part of a part and that the whole is made of parts, each of which is whole' (1990: 41). This sense of being part of a greater whole can be healing in itself, bringing a new perspective on the place of suffering in an enduring cosmos. Closely aligned to these experiences is the sense of wonder and awe inspired by the natural world. Kaplan and Kaplan (1989: 196) see interconnectedness as a spiritual dimension of the natural environment. In addition, 'the quest for tranquillity, peace, satisfactions and silence resonates with what in religious contexts might be considered serenity' (1989: 146).

Putting all this together we can see that the experience of nature is deeply integrative and offers a profound opportunity to resolve some of the inherent splits and disconnections that are inherent in trauma processes. This seems to happen because of the physiological regulation that is first and quickly possible in the natural world – create the conditions for regulation to take place and then the body knows how to heal itself (Taylor, 2014: 31). This requires safe reclaiming of embodied process and a loosening of rigid patterns, supporting spontaneity and choice in the here-and-now.

Narrative continued ...

And then the flow of my attention is arrested. There's been a trauma here. Just three days ago, the British Isles were in the grip of the worst blizzards for some years. There's still lots of snow on the roadsides and in the dunes, although the thaw has come quickly in the last 24 hours. The blizzards would have made landfall hereabouts, barrelling across the North Sea from Eastern Europe, causing much mischief and loss of life. The human loss numbered about ten; at my feet on a stretch of shoreline lie many hundreds of other casualties: crabs, wrasse, sea urchins, sea-suns, starfish. From a unified field perspective (Parlett, 1991), taking into account our finely tuned ecosystem and a recognition of interdependence this loss is significant. An animistic view might call them brother crab, sister starfish. I've never seen such a sight; it is terrible, grotesque, smelly. The boundary between sea and land has been breached and things are not in their rightful place. Dislocated. Out of context. I imagine a monster wave flinging these creatures onto land, a car crash of an event. I learn later that the sea temperature dropped by three degrees during the storms, tolerance levels for these creatures exceeded, comparable to relational trauma. Some commentators considered this to be an effect of climate change, the human imprint on the natural world gone to extremes. Termed 'trans-species psychology', we can understand the other-than-human world as capable of experiencing 'PTSD' (Bradshaw, 2009: 158). Our relationship with this world is indeed complex.

I slow right down, heaving shocked and sorrowful breaths now. It is an emotional sickness that rises in me. Slightly dazed, I try to comprehend. This has something to do with me, my life, and my work, though I don't at first know what it is. I can only feel this. I discover later that I share more than 50 per cent of my DNA with starfish. I am transfixed for some time before I step

away, back into the wider expanse, seeing the 100 yards or so of devasta-
tion at the tide line in relation to the vast and broad expanse of the shore. It
is only as I find this distance that I notice the context and can begin to inte-
grate the experience. I first realise that I have seen a glimpse of an underwa-
ter world not normally visible to me. I consider the gulls, and how they
survived the storms, a bigger sense that life carries on, in awe of their resil-
ience. Taking all this in, I sense a reorganization between my physiological
and psychological responses. Becoming both observer and active partici-
pant, the land moves in me and I in it. As parts of co-created, nested, and
interdependent fields, our relationship with the non-human world is always
reciprocal (Totton, 2009: 159). I have come to listen and to let the land speak
to me. As witness to this catastrophe of human origin, I don't know who is the
therapist now.

The questions I have of the land and the sea and all that live thereon or
therein become more insistent. How does life move through you? What has
it cost you to survive? What do you draw on as resources? How do you nav-
igate forces that you are part of and yet are bigger than you? I might ask
the same questions of someone I see in therapy, a supervisee, or indeed
colleague.

Rain: A conversation

After the storms came spring; as an integral part of our collaborative work and
writing, Vienna (VD) and I met and talked. We walked along a canal, sometimes
in silence, sometimes stopping to explore a particular point or be in contact
with the landscape. The key themes are reflected in the conversation below.

As we set off, it was raining lightly.

MT: *I have been thinking about my experience on the beach and what has*
emerged for me is that one of the most important aspects about this
work for therapists is hope.

VD: *As I listen to you, I hear the birds... the sound of bird song connects*
everything as I feel connected to the woods in Belarus.[2] My trip was a
lived experience of seeing hope in nature and feeling hope in people;
regeneration, reconnection ... a process of dying and coming forth. The
woods have become a place of healing and growth, not just of horror.
During the commemorative ceremony I could hear the birds just as we
can hear these here today, so what we are talking about today was hap-
pening there in nature ... is this what people do too, connect with hope
and heal?

MT: *As though healing one part of the field so the rest of it can regenerate?*

VD: *Hope! We each do (or don't do) even one small thing, it contributes to*
wider change processes ... we are interconnected.

MT: *I think without that kind of connection the relational ground has an absence of ethical care.*

Our attention is then caught by a new sight, the colour and form of some fallen trees. We consider the trauma to the tree and the new tree which has regenerated. We make connections to other examples … when a forest burns it will regenerate, the burning of stubble after the straw has been harvested, bushfires where the fire stimulates the release of seeds from certain plants. In an ecological system, trauma and regeneration are meshed.

Miriam then notices some pussy willow. We reflect on the relationships between buds and leaves and the growth of new branches as we trace growth up one stem in the hedgerow to the tip. We wonder at the way in which trees and other plants communicate. Widening our perspective from Earth and what grows from it, we note the residue of flood water.

MT: *What's this got to do with body? Water is ancient and its history is within our bodies. I love that! Fluids are vital to all life processes: the human body, plants, animals, trees, and Earth. It plays a central part in life and regeneration, connecting across millennia.*

VD: *By making what was ground figural, shifting in and out of focus as we look at this landscape, this conversation is sharpening my awareness of integrated relationships with nature and how 'respect' for difference is an ingredient in symbiosis within an ecosystem, co-creation in human relationships and in therapeutic work.*

Our discussion turns to an ethic of care being a political and systemic responsibility. The rain has stopped, we pause and enjoy the moment.

VD: *I see it all the time, that therapists' endeavours to take responsibility for staying well nourished are not supported by others. A therapist's well-being, their sustainability, often isn't foreground until it becomes 'a problem', and then it is generally 'given' to the therapist to rectify. So, the 'I' repeatedly regenerates the self. If I do this in isolation, as is often the imperative, a fragmented rather than unitary field is maintained. I wonder if, for some, the need for continual personal and professional self-care is potentially shaming? If becoming depleted is shameful? In contrast, recognizing and accepting our vulnerability within the work that we do, which I think is exactly what we are putting forward, is honouring of the self of both the therapist and the good intentions. This seems a more vital approach and this process of regeneration, of death and destruction on small or larger scales, is what we have observed and connected with today. It is an integral part of the habitat of the natural world.*

MT: *I am just thinking about language … Inhabiting myself, my body, the Earth; I in-habit, and therefore, I come to myself. So do I come into a* *different relationship with the physical world, which emerges freshly, when I in-habit my body? Environmentally and theoretically this provides a means through which the therapist/supervisor can experience their still point – be mindful and present.*

VD: *Do you mean finding a still point with support of, and in the gaze of, the 'Other'? When the natural world becomes present and we become open to the relational artistry of this process?*

MT: *Yes, I do; the still point of responsiveness that opens up physiological regulation. So, whose conversation is this? – today this is us together, we are thinking about Gestalt theory, ecotherapy, and dialogue within the natural world and community.*

VD: *We are embodying theory as we walk and as we write …*

[stops and points]

VD: *The spider's web has just come into my focus – it is delicately robust – see the contact with air through its movement in the breeze but it's also interconnected and connected to its surrounds – attached, some holes and flexing within its limits … within its limits of tolerance. Seeing this web I am connecting with Land Art and my first experience of seeing Andy Goldsworthy 'live' as it were.[3] A vast curtain, made only of horse chestnut twigs, held together with thorns, stretched across the gallery … visually showing interconnectedness … it was so delicate, balanced, breath-taking … Movement in one part of the whole created movement in another. Each web is amazing; both help me to make sense of this process of contact at the boundary.*

We are approaching the last stretch of canal and summarize the range of topics touched on in the conversation. Our main focus has been on the power of relational contact with human, place, and the natural environment in specific landscapes: the history of this canal and how waterways are part of the anatomy of this country just as fluids are rivers within our bodies. We have also ranged between attention to Belarus, Paris, Australian bushfires, and European refugee camps. We stop for a while looking at trees along a high bank. The interconnected root system is exposed and, looking across the water and up into the branches and canopy of the trees, this system is mirrored – for squirrels, a natural corridor.

Sun: Grounding the self

In the previous three sections, we have been describing our rationale. We noticed that many people we work with and teach turn to the natural world to feel safe and connected; we drew also on personal experience. Interested in the embodied properties of the relational field outlined above and elsewhere in the book, and with a deeply embedded relationship with the land, MT approached VD to collaborate on developing this work. Together, we developed a range of CPD opportunities, from a two-hour workshop to a four-day residential 'retreat', under the title 'The Well-Grounded Therapist'. Each one invites participants into an intrinsically embodied dialogue with nature, them-selves, and with each other. We create opportunities to experience self-in-relationship within a specific place and co-participating with the natural world.

Whatever the workshop format, content and processes are underpinned by Gestalt principles: contact, experimentation, embodied presence and awareness, dialogue, mirroring and witnessing: '*Extending* [presence] involves a process whereby therapists actively extend their boundary out to the other and to their surroundings' (Geller and Greenberg, 2012: 39, original emphasis). These workshops offer support for self-regulation as well as enquiry about the responsiveness of the whole field. Slowing down, we invite attention to the unfolding processes of contact/exchange between inner and outer landscapes. We do this through awareness of breath, appreciation of food grown on the land, and physical movement indoors and out. We provide time for individual contemplation, paired reflection, and contact as a whole group. This requires a softening of the boundary between self and other, noted elsewhere and also in Appendix A.

The immediate environment and wider landscape in which we situate each workshop provide context, to which participants are introduced through the geology, geography, and history of human interaction with the land and then extend through their own excursions in relation to place. Relationship with the wider field is also integrated through the cardinal directions (north, east, south, and west) and with the four elements of life. In Western culture these are earth, fire, water, and air, and their interrelationships are woven throughout the workshop. These spatial and elemental orientations frame our contact with the land. We offer experiments and enquiries as we shift between indoor and outdoor spaces, working on and with the land and exploring stillness as well as movement. Present moment awareness is enhanced through experiments which invite embodied contact. We explore the four sets of sensory receptors in the human body (Olsen, 2002), which are: the special senses of sight, sound, smell, taste, and touch; interoceptors (located in organs which monitor the inner workings of the body); exteroceptors (skin and connective tissues which monitor the outer environment); and proprioceptors (in joints, ligaments, tendons, muscles, and the inner ear, which register movement, balance, and the body's position in space and in relation to self). Key interests of identification and alienation – where I end and you begin – are implicit in our work.

To give you a feel for this, here are four examples to illustrate the immersive experiential, right-brain nature of the work, rather than left-brain conceptual thinking. We identify both what we do and the reasons for inviting participation in these practices.

Storytelling

> … we are made of the same minerals that comprise the soil.
> – Andrea Olsen, 2002: 106

Storytelling integrates many dimensions of experience (Olsen, 2002). Stories engage the limbic brain linking interest, emotion, and memory (Taylor, 2014) and have the capacity to stimulate right-brain activity (Pernicano, 2014). Through guided ritual, participants tell, receive, and re-tell stories of the soil or Earth material they have brought with them from their own part of the country or world. First, we invite participants to tell stories and then exchange their soil/Earth material. They change partners and repeat this process. These meetings employ all senses as well as support interpersonal connections. Human skin touches the Earth's skin. The constituent elements of soil are explored with eyes. Temperature, colour, texture, and smell are all explored. Both story and soil are entrusted to 'the other' and become part of a larger process of witnessing and transformation within the group. The outside has been brought inside. Making contact with Earth, we build ground as community.

Dropping in

Find a handful of soil from a garden, park, or other open space near you. Spend some time feeling it, smelling it, looking at it, and imagining the story that it tells. Who might you tell this story to: a partner, a child, a dog?

Conversing

> … the earth's surface is about 71% water, roughly the same percentage as fluids in the human body.
> – Andrea Olsen, 2002: 179

Maintaining connection with the rhythm of 'inside–outside', through awareness of breath (air) the group go to the nearby river, gathering elderflower blossoms as we walk. The five special senses plus exteroceptors and proprioceptors are all engaged. Plants and flowers who have grown through a combination of air, Earth, and water, and the warmth and light provided by the Sun (fire) line the lane and cover the water meadow. The group explores the presence of water through curiosity about how the river makes contact with land: high mud banks, a low pebble beach, trees and grasses that line the banks and the life within the river. Some enter … water on skin.

Our collective enquiry is about water and fluids. We experience the river herself, not a concern with what she might offer us, and this alone invites a shift in perspective and the potential for finding a still-point. On one occasion in this location, the natural world responded by inviting us to linger on and watch a large colony of swans repeatedly, and in formation, ride the flow of this ancient, life-sustaining river.

Expressing

Interconnectedness is clearly represented in our relationship to air.
– Andrea Olsen, 2002: 124

The group work outside in small groups. They are invited to create a short, written expression of one of the four elements. They do this together and by giving a voice to the element in question. To encourage immediacy, the process of creation is done in the style of the game of 'Consequences'. (Each participant contributing one line at a time without being able to see the line written by the previous person.) They are finished when they feel finished and present what they have created to the rest of the group in any way they choose. Developed through an implicit level of communication, these pieces consistently show remarkable coherence.

Earth	*Air*
I am earth, the rain, streams, oceans All water is mine to give and to fill all creatures with the 7 streams coursing through their bodies Do you know my ways, my lines and caves? If you did would you speak of me to those who don't know?	Air provides the lift beneath my wings I am everywhere I am a warm embrace Air brings scents to lift my soul and soothe my mind Breathe me in – I am air
(extract – Participants 2016)	(extract – Participants 2018)

Seeing and being seen

Perception is the basis for connection.
– Andrea Olsen, 2002: 59

This experiment involves being outside and allowing a creature or other-than-living object to become our focus. We have adapted it in several different forms from the work of Olsen (2002). Participants are invited to give open attention to their creature or object, immersing themselves in whatever occurs as it occurs; then, to allow this object or creature to witness them reciprocally, opening themselves to the gaze of the other. For instance,

A small bird landed in a hedge to my left. My energy stayed with her as we witnessed each other. I wondered briefly what else she had seen and how she saw me. I returned my attention fully to the bird. I was not judged and did not judge; self-consciousness melted, my body relaxed. We saw …

This experiment is offered as a translation of Buber's I–Thou attitude, opening ourselves to a dialogic relationship with the other-than-human-world. Staying present in the presence of 'other' is experienced in the moment: 'if I have both will and grace, that in considering the tree I become bound up in relation to it. The tree is now no longer an *It*' (Buber, [1923] 1958: 20).

Dropping in

Find an object, preferably from the natural world, that is small enough to hold in your hand. Close your eyes and spend a little while playing with it, feeling its texture, weight, and temperature against different areas of your skin. Does your object have a smell? What sounds can it make? What do you imagine it would taste like?

Now place the object a little way in front of you, on the floor or table. Use a hand to 'draw' the space between you and your object, the ground you share. Rest your attention in that space between you, not on the content of what you see. Speak to your object: 'When I see you, I feel …, I receive …'. What does your object say/offer in return?

Discussion

What may emerge for participants is, of course, not for facilitators to say. Our intention is simply to invite and support the development of awareness, contact, and co-perception within the total field. This allows participants to experience the triangular relationship that is a distinctive element of nature-informed therapy (Berger, 2016), which can be compared to the elements of the SOS model (see Chapter 2). As facilitators, we build and hold ground; vary pace and form of contact; offer opportunities to shape new interests and needs; offer flexible spaces and opportunities to withdraw; digest and support the balance (or rebalancing) of self-regulatory systems, akin to the optimal zone of arousal proposed by the window of tolerance model (see Appendix A).

On arrival, some participants have described feeling utterly depleted by their work and/or personal or professional field conditions. Some participants come with curiosity about working with the land and venturing outside of the therapy or supervisor's room. Others are aware of reducing levels of energy – may already be mindfully engaged in a journey of recovery and restoration or are sustaining themselves. During and after different workshops, we invited and received some reflections which illuminate the potential in this work. We listened, with curiosity, to what emerged from experimenting and regulating within the 'nature triad'.

I am traumatized by my work. I treat myself like a machine, which means I also treat my clients like machines. If I don't take nourishing myself seriously, I will have to stop working.

I saw my client tonight and there was a very different energetic tone to our session ... we did some good work at greater depth than we've achieved before, and I can't help but think this weekend contributed significantly to that.

I experienced the [recording of] earth sounds[4] in a very powerful way ... it was like nothing I'd ever heard before; an audio gravity, holding and grounding the whole workshop. Calming, nourishing, and strengthening me for many hours afterwards.

As part of agreed, on-going contact in 2016, some months later we enquired whether and how participants felt they had integrated anything into their practice/life:

What emerged from the workshop for me was how much trauma material I was carrying around with me and feeling in my body. I left behind my 'over-responsibility' and I would say that I am trusting more in the whole and the shared task of healing and supporting.

One of the ways I think my horizons were extended over the weekend was to start to include the human community in this 'earth' grouping, and indeed, to allow myself to feel safe and welcome in a human group. That really struck me ... There's something about feeling truly grounded in the earth that's highly congruent and nourishing for me in work with death and grief.

Conclusion: Call and response

It is now mid-summer. We set out to explore the ways that Gestalt theory and practice frame and inform the workshops we developed, and to illustrate the potential benefit of working in relationship with others and the natural environment. Our conclusion from this work is that changes we make in relation to the unified field have the potential to support and sustain a reorganization of self. Based on five premises about the impacts and processes involved in working with trauma or in traumatized, traumatizing contexts, we have put forward our view that the natural world has much to offer the therapist or supervisor about regeneration and the ethic of self-care.

During the workshops, stories emerged of culture, attachment, and belonging associated with a strong sense of place, coming in alongside a sense of loss, stuckness, disconnection, and absence, similar in essence to the Prologue with which this book opens. The rhythm of the rise and fall of these stories felt easy, with a quality evocative of storytelling, oral history, and folk song. Resonant of the questions that came 'after the storm', deep, existential themes emerged from connecting with the total field: 'How does the land sustain my living?', 'What happens to me when I die?', 'How do I connect?', 'How does life regenerate?' Rejoinders are a form of call and response in dialogue with our elemental context. A profound acknowledgment of hope, interconnectedness, and trust in regeneration has been expressed during and beyond the workshops. Movement from depletion towards energetic nourishment and holding of one's ground are hallmarks of the generative qualities of this work: reconfiguring from a position of surfeit rather than of deficit. We will take some of these ideas forwards in the next chapter.

We position a re-engagement with the natural world as an intervention in the relational therapeutic field, and anticipate enduring effects. For us, the intersubjective field includes relationships within the total field. 'The experience with the environment changes us quickly and quietly. By and large it is not a process to which words are attached. Nor are people aware of how radically affected they are by the way they see the world' (Kaplan and Kaplan, 1989: 35).

There is a reciprocal process in the implicit realm of contact: first the traumatic resonance which replays in subtle ways, and second the implicit response which, through our engagement with the natural world, may offer a different capacity to be present and bear witness. The deeper we can go with ourselves, the deeper the therapy will go; the more connected we feel, the stronger the contact between ourselves and the people we work with; the more we open ourselves to wider perspectives, the more the therapy will open; the more integrated we become, the greater the possibility of the people we are with becoming integrated. This is consistent with the proposition central to Chapter 6, in which the self of the therapist is a key instrument in the service of the traumatized Other. Supervisors and therapists alike need sustenance for their capacity to offer an expanded window of tolerance. The degree to which we can contain trauma and reorganize it in our own being, the more this will become true for the Other.

Many factors appear to influence the restorative experience of the natural world. These include belonging, contact, context, curiosity, continuity of experience, waiting, hope, openness, soft fascination, presence, coherence, embodiment, integration, perspective, and regulation.

Notes

1   The original article first appeared in the *British Gestalt Journal* (2018, Volume 27 (2): 18–29) and is reproduced here with permission. I am grateful both to the journal and Vienna.

2   In May 2017, Vienna visited Blagowschtschina Woods, near Maly Trostinec in Belarus, as part of a commemorative trip for the murder of her great-aunt and

many tens of thousands, possibly over a hundred thousand, Jewish people from the country now known as Belarus and transported from all over Europe. These mass murders in the woods near Minsk took place as part of the Final Solution by the Third Reich.

3   Yorkshire Sculpture Park (2007). Andy Goldsworthy at Yorkshire Sculpture Park [Exhibition], 31 March 2007 to 6 January 2008.

4   As part of one group activity we played a recording of the sounds made in the Earth 5 miles below the surface.

10 Vital connections

The image of the mobius strip offered in Chapter 1 is a metaphor for the journey this book has taken so far – an infinite loop that widens, and narrows, crossing over from internal to external (Figure 10.1). Along the way we have explored some deep existential questions about the nature of trauma, the world we live in, and ourselves as therapists. The relationship between all of these is indeed complex, and provides the basis for a paradigm shift towards understanding trauma as an ecological process. To recap, there are three reasons why this is so critical to our understanding. First, we need to account for the complexity of trauma in the wider ecological field. Secondly, the experience of disconnection or dislocation as a core existential experience of trauma came under scrutiny in Chapter 2. In this sense, ecological refers to the whole network of relationships that is severed in traumatic experience and needs compassionate and humane restoration. Lastly, the natural world is increasingly appreciated for its contribution to well-being, and it is important to bring this to the fore, as suggested in the previous chapter. This both positions trauma as an ecological experience and therefore an ecological perspective as being central to an understanding of trauma. This guides us towards consideration of the widest aspect of the field from a fresh perspective.

Figure 10.1 Contextual mobius strip

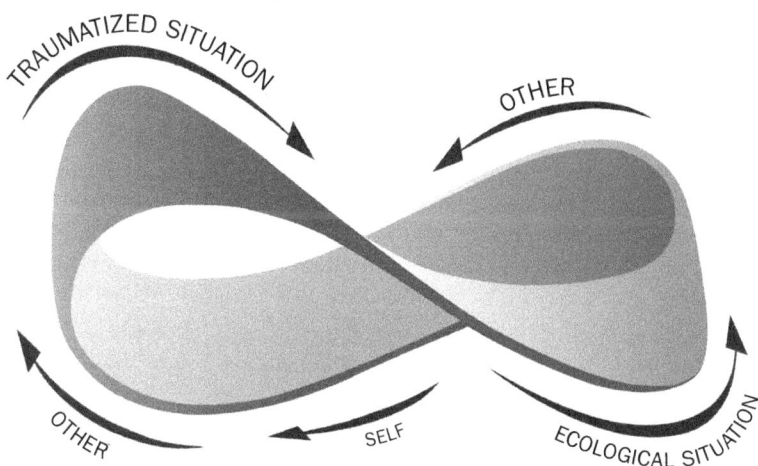

Multilarities and complexity

As stated elsewhere in the book, an instinctive response to trauma is to narrow focus and gravitate towards experiential extremities. However, to adhere to a deficit discourse creates a rupture. This is how we come to take polarized positions. Binaries are inherent properties of polarities, without middle ground. Because it draws on Eastern philosophy, Gestalt theory offers a less reductive way forward. Gestalt theory posits that every figure that captures our attention can only be shaped in relation to its opposite: the shadow is meaningless without the Sun (see, for example, Taylor, 2014: 47). A number of binaries are woven into this book, both implicitly and explicitly, including:

- Power/vulnerability
- Privilege/oppression
- Fear/survival
- Dissociation/presence
- Alienation/identification
- Knowing/not knowing
- Violence/ethics
- Mind/body
- Nature/culture
- Reductionism/complexity
- Individualism/collectivism
- Indifference/compassion
- Being/doing

Many of these binaries can be easily observed once we understand what we are looking at (Descola, 2013: 31). Although it is tempting to imagine that the resolution of these binaries is the solution, this, too, is reductive. When we agree to live in a fragmentary way or a make the compromise of a limited version of ourselves, we suffer.

> Every reduction – by systematizing, classifying, pointing, even describing – is, for Levinas, violence, a violation, a form of murder. (We easily understand the outraged response even today to refugee quotas, and to rigid distinctions between migrants and refugees. These can evoke selections.) (Orange, 2017: 113)

It is incongruent to try to apply reductive models to aspects of the field that are wide. A good starting point is always to be able to see the opposing polarity because it helps open up the frame and evokes curiosity. However, Gestalt theory offers the notion of the continuum between opposing poles, a rather linear proposition, but one that nonetheless leans towards a more differentiated prospect. 'In actuality, we soon begin to realize that all polarities are multilarities, multiple opposites that are interpolating into a higher, creatively indifferent meaning' (Stevenson, 2004: 2).

Even my favoured framework for trauma, the window of tolerance model, contains polarities of hyper- and hypo-arousal, but it is within the 'window' itself that possibilities begin to emerge. Because the window of tolerance is not simply a comfortable resting place (Taylor, 2014: 67) but a vital space in which we can, without fear, live out our most intense feelings, it is a model of the whole containing the parts. Ataria refers to 'the *unity of multiplicity*, the ability to live in harmony with all that is inside oneself, to live in peace with the divided world' (2017: 157, emphasis added). In other words, we come to the concept of complexity which is a core feature of the organization of ecological systems; ecology is multi-faceted, non-binary, complex, and integrated.

Complexity theory, sometimes known as 'nonlinear systems theory' or 'dynamical systems theory', provides a way of organizing and making meaning of intricate, interwoven, and interdependent processes. In this, the parallels with the natural world become clear, because adaptation and growth throughout the material and biological world are similar. This, we have seen, is true for trauma-organized systems, from individual to family to group to society, and vice versa. A new paradigm is non-hierarchical, and radically reorganizes power dynamics. The oft-cited 'butterfly effect' is a further property of complex non-linear systems, in which 'small changes may have dramatic effects because they may be amplified repeatedly by self-reinforcing feedback' (Capra and Luisi, 2014: 106). Trauma responses, without intervention, become self-reinforcing because they are stuck in a self-referencing dissociated absent loop. It can take a small change in the direction of ethical presence to change the pattern of feedback.

Perhaps unsurprisingly, with their less linear and binary understanding, early Gestalt theorists were influential in the development of complexity theory (Capra and Luisi, 2014: 66), leading to the key concept which states that 'the whole is greater than the sum of the parts'. What does surprise me, though, is that these ideas are taken up by others outside Gestalt who are interested principally in systems theory, anthropology, and ecology. Abram (1997), Descola (2013), and Capra and Luisi (2014) are examples. These writers lean towards the theory of phenomenology to further their understanding of the subjective organization of parts relative to one another. (See Appendix A for more explanation of this concept.) To give a taste of how phenomenology relates to domains other than therapy, this is what Husserl offers: 'The encompassing earth … provides the most immediate, bodily awareness of space, from which all later *conceptions* of space are derived' (Husserl, in Abram, 1997: 34, original emphasis).

I have argued before that the degree of differentiation offered by the phenomenological approach serves to promote integration (Taylor, 2014: 76). This is because unformulated experience is fundamentally undifferentiated and therefore cannot be assimilated. According to Descola, and I agree, phenomenology is the path to the resolution of dichotomies: 'It favors describing the interlacing of the experience of the social and physical worlds while remaining as free as possible from the objectivist filters that hinder its immediate apprehension as a familiar environment' (2013: 64).

We move from 'either/or' to 'both/and' and thence to 'all'. Parlett introduced the concept of the unitary field, saying: 'Arguably, overcoming self-world dualism or the split between parts of the unitary field is one of Gestalt therapy's most radical contributions' (2011: 54). It is, however, not realistic to imagine that we can fully resolve binaries. The question that remains is this: *How do we hold polarities within our wholeness?*

An ecological SOS

Let us take a loop back to the beginning. Historically, Gestalt therapy has struggled with the notion of field. 'In the beginning is field' says Wolfort (2000: 77), an incongruous attempt to represent the totality by leaning towards the dominant Judeo-Christian Western tradition. What is missing from this is a non-Western, multi-faith, and indigenous cosmology, even where many other creation stories would align with the sentiment. Bednarek, in her 2018 article asks, 'How wide is the field?', arguing for a more radical and inclusive perspective: 'My four-year training focused entirely on the dyadic relationship. Sociopolitical issues were not part of what was deemed to be a relevant focus for the aspiring psychotherapist. They were understood to be part of the field but this part was hardly ever made figural' (2018: 9).

As suggested in Chapter 8, a separation of 'inside the therapy room or hour' and 'outside' it persists. As I observed in Chapter 2, the new understanding of the total Situation represented by the SOS model is a somewhat larger concept than 'field' as it is usually applied. Nevertheless, here we are interested in the traumatic underpinnings of the cultural, historical, and literal ground that shapes us. Because arguments are not necessarily linear, I want to pick up a defining polarity that has taken centre-stage at several points in this book: power and vulnerability. Consistent with a fractal view, we have seen how power operates at multiple levels to create the binaries of trauma: 'Contexts nest, one within the other, and some also collide' (Jacobs, 2004: 42).

It can be argued that the original SOS model presented in Chapter 2 lends itself more to an understanding of structure than of process. I attempted to resolve this by identifying a number of unifying processes for all parts of the model. Among them is power, nesting itself within contexts that enable it. This link between context and power is clearly positioned by Chidiac and Denham-Vaughan in their 2020 reconceptualization of the SOS model. This takes us a further step towards understanding complexity, for *structure* and *process* are two properties of complex systems. A third property is *organization*, or the configuration of relationships between the parts. Taken together, these three properties are 'different but inseparable perspectives on the phenomenon of life' (Capra and Luisi, 2014: 302). As suggested above, Gestalt therapists take an interest in the organization of wholes and the patterns revealed in them. It so happens that Chidiac and Denham-Vaughan (2020: 24) consider

Figure 10.2 Power as moderator of the whole emergent field

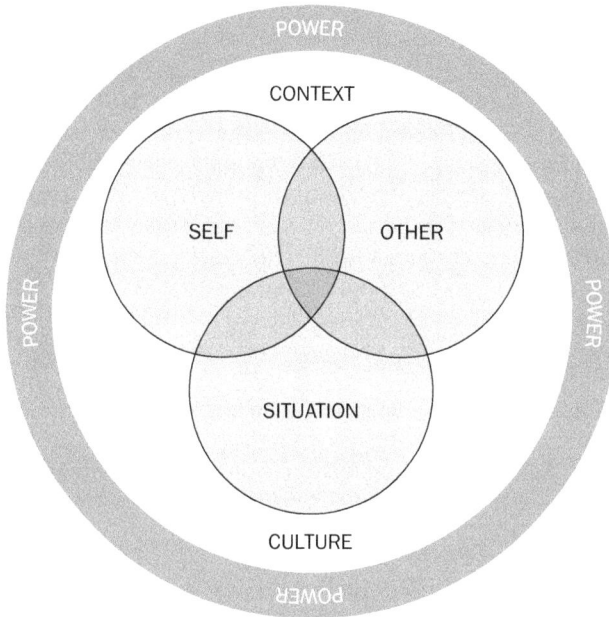

power to be a moderator of the whole emergent field, as shown in Figure 10.2. In other words, it is an organizing property, for better or for worse.

This is in line with my thinking about the two domains of power-over and power-with, discussed at various places in the book. I think it is important to also think about the polarities of these, which I describe below as 'structural vulnerability' and 'existential vulnerability'. I choose 'vulnerability' in preference to 'oppression' because I think the latter is confusing. The word 'oppression' can correspond to either side of the equation; the situation of being oppressed and the act of the oppressor – both verb and noun. While power certainly creates an experience of oppression, Lichtenberg (2004: 239) also ties vulnerability with the process of power, seeing it as the disowned part of the oppressor. Situational vulnerability is the state of being on the receiving end of oppressive forces which are disadvantageous or discriminatory. This relates to concepts of intersectionality (Chapter 3) and habitus (Chapter 2). It is possible to recognize how the effects of situational vulnerability may be cumulative and leave us open to further exploitation. For example, someone who is poor also has reduced access to resources or to opportunity, and may suffer ill-health as a result. Existential vulnerability, on the other hand, simply relates to the condition of being human, an unavoidable and even necessary adjunct to the messy flow of life: we get hurt, hurt others, make mistakes, accumulate losses and regrets, grow old. Both forms of vulnerability are relational. To be situationally vulnerable creates a trauma bond with the oppressive structures on which life depends; it is survival based. Existential vulnerability, on the other hand, keeps us connected to the life force that unites us.

Extending this thinking to the domain of ethical presence, Chidiac and Denham-Vaughan write: 'Presence implies a certain intentional flow which … *Our personal access to this state of presence is a reflection of our state of privilege* in that moment and is therefore often mediated by a set of implicit power relationships operating in our favour' (2020: 27, emphasis added). I think there is an ethic implied also in Siegel's comment that, 'Being present in our lives enables us to be present for our planet' (2010: 2), because our responsibility to the other-than-human is part of our responsibility to ourselves. Conversely, being present to the planet allows us to be more present to ourselves. Inevitably, power sits at the intersecting boundaries of the entire network of relationships that is our ecosystem; it is a relational phenomenon (Chidiac and Denham-Vaughan, 2020: 24).

Abram observes that:

> The life-world … is not a private, but a collective, dimension – the common field of our lives and the other lives with which ours are entwined … our experience of this field is always relative to our situation within it … [it] is thus peripherally present in any thought or activity we undertake. (1997: 40)

The three pillars of Gestalt – phenomenology, dialogue, and field – operating within each domain of the SOS model, come together in this construct. None is separate, all are intertwined. The relevance of this is captured by Totton, who understands that when we grasp the limitless nature of the field, the work of therapy changes from something we might feel we have control over to something we can simply be curious about: 'Like everything else in the world, a therapy relationship is one detail of a huge collective process extending far in space and time, an open system in dependent co-arising with everything else' (2011: 188).

This leaves us with some questions about the nature of the total situation. If it is more than the sum of its parts, can we say it is undifferentiated, or highly differentiated? Or, in the spirit of the Trickster, can it be both? Since we can only differentiate what can be observed and yet so much of the world we live in is yet to be explored, an incongruence emerges. Is the total situation, like the seeming balance in the SOS model, an idealized proposition, or is it simply something ineffable that defies description? If we think in terms of global complexity, the total situation is in constant and emergent flux.

Complexity theory suggests that there is a tipping point in any system, and contemporary concerns about climate emergency recognize this. Orange is not alone in recognizing the psychological threat: 'The climate crisis … traumatizes … forces us to revalue our past and to doubt our future. Not only will any future differ from the past in ways we would not have foreseen, it will differ in ways no one could possibly want' (2017: 17). The gathering interest in ecotherapy and conferences such as 'Small Earth' run primarily for psychotherapists and which I attended in the autumn of 2018, demonstrate the concern and the potential momentum that is present in this profession. I think also in more creative and right-brain ways about including qualities of imagination, spirit, awe, and intuition into the mix. This is a transcendent context without which, according to

Figure 10.3 The interconnected field

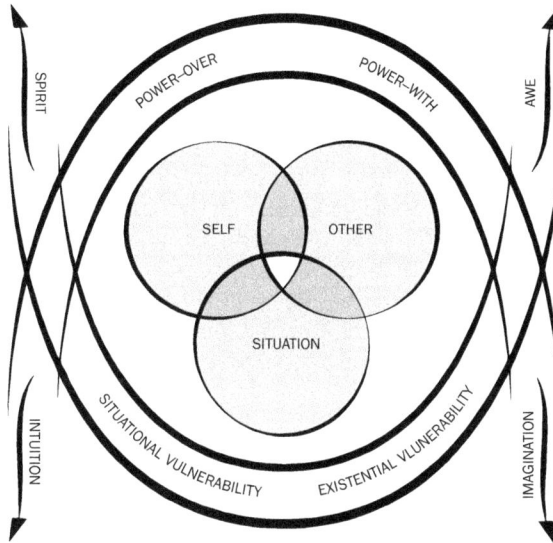

Kepner, 'It seems difficult if not impossible for the survivor to complete the cycle of healing' (1995: 133). Figure 10.3 brings all these ideas together.

Liz

Liz had been stalked by a participant in an HIV project she managed in South America. The charity she worked for did not take any action because the man in question was considered to be vulnerable. She was asked to sign a non-disclosure agreement as she negotiated a forced redundancy, and she returned to her native UK. Feeling unsafe, she changed her social media profiles so she could not be traced. After a series of house moves she came into therapy. Loss of meaning, purpose, and roots left Liz in crisis. In many ways, her lack of ground was literal as well as embodied, and it seemed appropriate to go out together into an open space. As we walked, Liz told me of a visit to her parents at the weekend and how delighted she was to see a tree that she had played on as a child, and I referred to it as her 'home tree'. Later, we stopped in the shade and talked about how alone she felt. I suggested she find something in the immediate environment that she could use for support. She stood by a small tree with her back against it, and I supported her to fully describe what it felt like. I then asked if she had a sense of what the tree might say to her. 'Come home' was her spontaneous reply, tears running down her face. On our way back to my consulting room, we reflected on the meaning of the support and ground offered by her two home trees, and Liz commented that being able to see the trees around her had given her some distance from the rawness of her grief.

Reconnecting

Loss of context – in other words, dislocation or dissociation – is a primary experience for traumatized people. It underpins an ecological, relational approach, and, it turns out, has huge implications for our life on this planet. In Chapter 2, I referred to Woodbury's (2019) premise that disconnection is part cause of climate trauma. This accords with my premise of breakdown at the contact boundary and discussion of disconnection in that chapter as a situational process. In his ground-breaking paper, Woodbury begins at a very local level, suggesting that the aggregate of individuals' disconnection from the land and from traditional practices, involving entitlement to ownership, to power, and consumption of resources, has resulted in the imminent breakdown of stable and predictable climate. 'The relationship between humans and nature will, in all probability, be the most important question of the present century' (Descola, 2013: 81). I suggest that it *already* is, and that it is an immediate concern for psychotherapists. Living in the age of the Anthropocene, this position has some traction: 'Prioritizing the suffering of human beings returns us to an irreverent and dominating humanism, including views of human exceptionalism, causing the climate crisis' (Orange, 2017: 121). How we reimagine the relationships that can turn this around is our first task. 'There is an urgency to recover stories of connection that affirm popular, ecological healing strategies – which promote more decentralized, equitably distributed agency and dependency' (Ullman and Demaris, 2020: 226).

Dropping in

As I sit at my desk writing, I notice the pebbles and plants on the windowsill and the houses, trees, and grass outside. At the same time, I wonder about the origins and the journey of the trees that will become the paper on which this book will be printed, and which you now hold in your hands. It seems quite extraordinary to me that my fingers tapping against my keyboard today will be connected to you in this way. The simple practice here has something in common with this way of thinking. It is adapted from Mark Fairfield (2018, 2019), and goes as follows:

Take a little time to consider all the people and things that have gone into making the last five minutes of your life possible. Start local, and then see how far your connections extend. That's it. How does your body respond? What emotions arise? What thoughts and images follow? What meaning do you make of this?

While this exercise can be revelatory, we could conclude that the wider field is there for our benefit or consumption. That is a power-over position. This gives rise to some essential questions: What might we give back to the material world, that we also benefit from, and how might we do that? I agree with Adams that using our sensate bodies is a starting point. He notes how 'direct experiential attunement with our embodied (inter)existence can foster attunement with and care for the rest of nature; and how experiential attunement with nature can foster our embodied awareness and health' (2020: 81). A first level of disconnection is with our bodies, and with the traditional wisdom that helped our ancestors literally navigate the world. Abram (2020) observes that reliance on GPS has severed our use of maps, our innate capacity to explore different terrains and orient ourselves as we need. This is beautifully described in a paper about recovering the trust in the stars necessary for seafaring (Baker, 2019).

Photojournalist Sebastião Salgardo spent his career recording some of the most harrowing examples of the human condition, and retired to his native Brazil where he planted a million trees on his ancestral land (Wenders, 2014). I repeatedly observe how we turn spontaneously to the natural world for sanctuary, and in doing so can recreate ourselves. Establishing a felt sense of inner safety is fundamental to all trauma therapy, and has been described as bringing a sense of belonging and oneness. After carrying out a safe place visualization (Taylor, 2014: 103), one woman told me: 'I *am* the butterfly I see, I *am* the blade of grass'. Our survival instinct drives us towards being whole:

> We long to connect with an other – be it word, skin, food, or air – in order to become ourselves. In this experience, we are not separated from the world, but deeply incorporated into it: feeling parts of the whole. (Weber, [2014] 2017: xiv)

The centrality of this is captured by Totton: 'I believe that this "longing", this deep spiritual connection with the more-than-human world, is a central human trait which is suppressed and alienated by much of Western society' (2011: 176).

The spirit of this longing is illustrated by the proliferation in recent years of popular books, podcasts, and programmes which connect the natural world with well-being. There is scholarly support for why this re-engagement heals us. Kaplan and Kaplan, referenced in the previous chapter, were some of the early researchers into the phenomena of our contact with nature. Interest is growing in working with therapeutic animals (see, for example, Lac, 2017), which offer a safer relationship than a human–human one for some people. The benefits go beyond the psychological; our physiology also changes in contact with the natural world. Haluza, Schönbauer, and Cervinka (2014) reported alterations in brain activity, immune system function, cardiovascular rate, and the endocrine system. They focused primarily on the experience of forest bathing, or 'Shinrin-Yoku', popularized in Japan. Studies into Shinrin-Yoku showed that 'beneficial physiological effects of natural environments were often already detectable before experimental exposure, concluding that physiological parameters might adapt promptly when people anticipate contact with natural outdoor environments' (2014: 5457). Simply tuning into the rhythms of the natural world, the sounds of a stream, or the movement of leaves in a breeze can be deeply regulating. We instinctively turn to the natural environment in one form or another to help regulate us. However, caution must be taken about adopting a romanticized view of the natural world, which can also be dangerous, frightening, barren, impenetrable.

Just as awareness of the body in the here-and-now can provide a sense of continuity of experience, so can contact with the wider, natural environment. It may be deeply reassuring to appreciate how a mountain has endured the ravages of human history, and that our bodies are intimately connected, being composed of matter that exists in the Earth and water. Our planet's surface is about 71 per cent water, roughly the same percentage as the fluids in the human body. Furthermore, 'Earth's water is more than 3.8 billion years old … the total amount of water in the earth's system has changed very little since then' (Olsen, 2002: 179). From this we can infer, astonishingly, that much of the water in your body at any moment is over three billion years old.

The natural world reveals a myriad of similar connections, from microorganisms, to the interactions between plant and animal life, and the shaping of rivers and land. The concept of interdependence has been around for a long time, but like the parameters of field theory, has not fully 'landed' in terms of its implications for us as human beings who share the planet with others. When we privilege human life over those of others, we fall back into a binary trauma process. Some will go so far as to see *all* matter as animate. Some writers surprise by suggesting that we think 'like a mountain' (Weber, [2014] 2017: 21) or ask 'What it is like to be a funghi' (Sheldrake, 2020: 3). An experimental Gestalt way of working with dreams might be to suggest that we 'speak' from the position of any element in the dream, because each element is a creative symbolic expression of ourself. If I dream of a mountain, I speak as a mountain and might learn something from it.

Interdependence: Reimagining relationships

The success of a dyadic therapeutic relationship depends on the working alliance – the degree of mutuality and reciprocity of attunement that permits co-regulation. 'The important aspect is really the ability to reciprocally interact, to reciprocally regulate each other's physiological state, and basically create relationships to enable individuals to feel safe' (Porges, 2017: 99). The regulating checks and balances between entities is a feature of the feedback loop that characterizes ecosystems:

> 'The social system is an organization like the individual, that is bound together by a system of communication, [having] dynamics in which circular processes of a feedback nature play an important role' (Wiener, in Capra and Luisi, 2014: 91).

Systems thinking takes us inevitably into the concept of interdependence. This idea has, in principle, been around for hundreds of years, but we struggle to integrate it, perhaps because it challenges the boundaries of our sense of self. The air I inhale is 'not me', but when I exhale, has that air now become 'me'?

The study of inter-species dependence is fascinating and mind-blowing. Let's take a simple example, one of infinite possibilities, from the natural world. Indigenous peoples of the Americas have for thousands of years grown three crops together: squash, beans, and maize. These are known as the Three Sisters, grown because of their mutually beneficial properties. By co-regulation through the sharing of light, water, and soil nutrients, each thrives because of the different needs and patterns of organization of the other two: 'There are layers and layers of reciprocity … between the bean and the bacterium, the bean and the corn, the corn and the squash, and, ultimately, with the people' (Wall Kimmerer, [2013] 2020: 134).

We can take this a step further: 'Occasionally – once or twice in a lifetime if you are lucky – you encounter an idea so powerful in its implications that it unsettles the ground you walk on' (Macfarlane, 2019: 87). The powerful idea Macfarlane refers to is the so-called 'wood-wide-web', an underground social network. This is of profound importance for the survival of our species and others, and teaches us a lesson, if we will listen and learn from it. The wood-wide-web consists of a network of hyphae – the fibres of mycorrhizal fungi that connect species of plants and trees together. More than that, they have been found to be the means of 'communication' between species, for example, by moving resources from a healthy tree to a sick one (Macfarlane, 2019: 90). This system seems to be facilitated by older, 'well-connected' trees, which form a hub or node in the network, analogous to Google or Amazon. This means that less connected or more specialized (i.e. individual or isolated) trees can connect with others through partnerships with more abundant species of mycorrhizal fungi (Sheldrake, 2020: 189).

If this is not astonishing enough, Sheldrake asks whether this exchange of resources can be understood as a form of altruistic behaviour (Chapter 6), involving costs to the donor and benefits to the recipient. He has an answer for this: 'If a plant's surplus carbon passes into a mycorrhizal network where it is enjoyed by many as a "public good", the charge of altruism can be avoided because no-one – whether donor or receiver – has incurred a cost' (2020: 176).

What inferences for the psychotherapy of trauma can we make from this? How might we establish well-connected 'hubs' for mutual benefit? Some parallels can be made with our understanding of neural networks and neuroplasticity (2020: 191). Social and interpersonal networks operate in similar ways to forests and plants, with uneven distribution of resources and social capital (Chapter 2). Power and privilege come back to the fore, in terms of reciprocal and interdependent benefit; I refer here to power-over.

> The ideal structure for exerting this kind of power is not the hierarchy but the network, the central metaphor of the ecological paradigm. In a social network, people are empowered by being connected to the network. Power as empowerment means facilitating this connectedness. (Capra and Luisi, 2014: 14)

As things stand, our understanding of non-linear interdependence is that much is not yet known and maybe much is not knowable. We can conclude though, that this is 'a *Gestalt field ethic*, … because without a vibrant, nurtured field of caring, there is no place for me to stand and flourish and grow' (Wheeler, 2004a: 303, original emphasis).

Vital presence

The need for sustainable survival is a driving force in all trauma and in all ecological systems; life depends upon it. However, the disconnection that we meet in traumatized people may be so profound that the sense of life is all but sucked out of them. A further binary that we cannot avoid, therefore, exists between the life force of ethical presence and the symbolic death of dissociated absence. Indifference leads to indifference to life, love of life as a polarity. The tension between the two is a space holder at the boundary of the black hole and the rest of the world.

> The trauma that many experience early in childhood is a catastrophe of broken reciprocity. It is ecological because it impairs our capacity for connection, which is the basis for all … The tragedy begins when we pay no attention to our own aliveness. (Weber, [2014] 2017: 141)

The work begins with small moments of success, with curiosity and wonder. Like Weber, O'Shea considers this kind of sensuous embodied engagement with life to 'expand our definition of the erotic to include experience beyond the sexual' (2020: 130). I would like to take this moment to bring my own story up to date.

Miriam Part 3: The buck stops here – a work in progress

Two important things happened in the 18 months after I was raped: my mother died suddenly and I gave birth to my first child. Free to be the mother I chose to be, without criticism, I made a conscious decision that I would make sure my children knew they were loved. And they do. In seeking not to replicate the hurts of my own upbringing, I was mostly, but not entirely, successful. I knew clearly how *not* to be a mother, but had to improvise the rest, seeking out friendships with older role models. Being a mother was hard at first. While I looked to the future that I was creating for my children and for myself, during their early years I was simultaneously dealing with my past. To be frank, there were moments when I barely held any of it together. My deepest grief was, inevitably, for the mother I never had. Drawn eventually to a therapy group for incest survivors, I found recognition, healing, and could begin to feel the pain I needed to feel. The group was exhilarating and raw, and there I discovered the potential therapist in me. Part of the healing was knowing intuitively that one child I needed to love was myself. It was at that time, 30 years ago, that I changed my name, the best gift I could have given myself. Miriam means 'longed for, desired, and wanted child'; 'YES!' I thought, 'I'll be one of those!' I needed to begin to define myself and not fit into the constraints and expectations that had shaped me. Easier said than done, of course, though my intention still carries me through periods of forgetting and getting lost.

The knowledge I gained through training, significant personal therapy, and the relationships I formed on different ground have been nothing short of transformative. To the extent that I have suffered, I have inversely reclaimed a passion for life. I sometimes wonder if I embody the deeply misdirected vitality that was in my mother, and the endless curiosity of my father. These are legacies I am grateful for. Slowing down, to the level of sensation, through meditation and my deep connection with the natural world, has created a space in which I can be more self-reflective and bear more of the hard stuff, in me and in the world around me. Personal and professional development, body, mind, and spirit all grew hand in hand. My most creative moments of writing have consistently occurred when doing the simplest things – breathing in large vistas, watching insects crawl up a tree trunk, or chopping vegetables for soup.

For too many years I thought that the world owed me something – justice, redress, putting things to rights. I became the cause of my own suffering by holding out, impossibly, for a better childhood, for redemption that no one could give me. I learned in time to let go of that sense of deep unfairness and entitlement that locked me into a shame-prone position. Importantly, my once harsh inner-critic became quiet. I came to acknowledge that the people who hurt me were deeply troubled in their own right, which does not in any way absolve or stop the original hurt, but gets the situation into perspective. All I ever did wrong was to be small and vulnerable. My sense now is that I have been tasked with processing some of the wounds of previous generations. I do this on their behalf and for the future; my first book was dedicated to them all. Looking back, I consider myself to be incredibly lucky. As I approach my twilight years, I think I have had a pretty good life. Trauma is simply a part of a bigger whole.

As I began to write this book, I had a nasty accident, a brush with my mortality and the survival of my leg. It put my writing project on hold for some months, and involved surgery, serious infection, and lengthy rehabilitation. Despite all the personal work I have done and the knowledge I have gained, my body simply did what very shocked bodies do. I cut off: from my embodied self (this can't be happening to me); from my vitality; from my ability to soothe myself; from my routines; from my engagement with my community; from my orientation to my land. I revisited disconnection in real time. I moved tentatively back into the world as someone with a temporary disability, feeling shrunken and unsafe. I was quick to recognize that aspects of this new trauma had 'got stuck' in my system, so I returned to body-based therapy for a while. There, tuning in with my therapist, I found pockets of earlier traumas locked unsurprisingly into my damaged knee. Finding a more spontaneous voice I protested loudly! My physical injury made my life history visible. The scars on my knee hold several histories, and I can live with that.

> **Dropping in**
>
> List some simple things that you feel grateful for. Place your hand on your heart, and as you bring each thing to mind, slowly breathe into your heart and hand. What changes, if any, do you notice as you do this?

There is a tension for all of us between the need to change and grow and the need to establish continuity. We need a brave vision of change that goes beyond recovery, from sustainability to growth. This is not the economic growth of consumption that has a colonial backdrop. What I mean here is the growth that comes as a result of nurture and connection with our life force that moves us from stuckness to fluid responsiveness. Germer's five-stage model for developing self-compassion provides a possible template. The friendship we can foster with each aspect of the SOS model, and the key question referred to in Chapter 6, have the potential for profound healing. Halifax refers to 'a tenet of systems theory: living systems that break down can reorganize at a higher and more robust level – if they learn from the breakdown experience' (2018: 5). This is not an idealized notion of post-traumatic growth, but one possible outcome among others.

Trickster revisited

In 2014, I ventured into a Wilderness Experience in eastern California with the School of Lost Borders, absorbing the deep listening practices of the Paiute people. In their tradition, the east is understood to be the direction of the Trickster, associated with the crossing of boundaries into different states of awareness. In 2016, I made the decision to move to the area of the east of England known as the Fens. This is an area about thirty miles across; a liminal territory with indistinct boundaries between vast open skies and endless flat landscapes, where distances feel immeasurable and points of reference are fewer. It's a land of mists and water, as well as of generous fertility. There are strange stories about the Fens, of appearances and disappearances in the bog and the mists. I can have a sense of losing my edges here, both open to expansive possibilities and at the same time uncertain, on edge, and disorientated. As this landscape reveals itself to me, it makes its home in me as I do in it, and I have a sense of coming home to somewhere I have always known. It is, in the words of ní Dochartaigh, one of those 'places that holds us tight and that lets us see a way out – a way back *in*' (2021: 228, original emphasis). Because it holds up a mirror to different parts of me, this land grounds me and makes the Trickster knowable and therefore less threatening. According to Jung, the process of rendering the Trickster motif harmless takes an extremely long time (1972: para. 475). The landscape reflects back my inner landscape. 'Excluding any part of the larger landscape of our lives reduces the territory of our understanding' (Halifax, 2018: 2), and therefore, I contend, to our capacity to be present.

The Trickster is an agent of change, a spirit who subverts our habitual ways of being. One of the Trickster's preoccupations, as it were, seems to be to move pain around the world. Occupying a liminal space, the Trickster becomes an intermediary between worlds, or in other worlds, between the different elements of the SOS model. The Trickster has an honesty which holds up a mirror to our collective wounds, and opens the door to healing. When I name an uncomfortable truth or turn something on its head and see it differently, I recognize some Trickster intelligence in myself; maybe there are potential Trickster qualities in all of us. The Trickster awakens our curiosity: Do I really see what I think I see? How do I explain this? Trickster properties are complex: 'across time and space [they] seem often to be the beings that remind people about mulitversality' (Barker and Iantaffi, 2019: 210). I question whether I learn more from within the Trickster intelligence or from outside it, and conclude that it may be some of both. Note, though, how the Trickster has been largely silent in these last chapters, seemingly because we have awakened. Like trauma, like interdependence, the Trickster can never be fully understood, which is its paradoxical unifying quality. The Trickster contains a mystery, which crosses from the material phenomenal reality to the immaterial noumenal reality – that undefinable, boundary-less-ness which cannot be known. The closer I come, the better I understand that this being becomes both adversary and ally.

Decolonization

We are a traumatized species living in social structures that are vested in maintaining the traumatizing status quo. There is an immense amount of unprocessed trauma at large in the world. Peace activist and Nobel Prize nominee Scilla Elworthy (2014) writes not of the shift of consciousness, as in Chapter 8, but of the *leap* of consciousness needed to support the notion of a unitary field. It is going to take a radically different approach to bring about change; the deep ecological perspective for which I speak is such a paradigm shift. Deep ecology raises profound existential questions about cruelty and the human condition, about suffering and hope, and about our place within complex ecological systems: 'The essence of deep ecology is to ask deeper questions' (Naess, in Capra and Luisi, 2014: 13). This approach to trauma bridges the age-old question about the role of psychotherapists and our responsibility to be in the world (Tropianskia, 2020). Like anyone else, therapists are inextricably embedded in structures that oppress, therefore the ethical work we need to undertake has to be both personal and political. As ever, we start local and trust that the ripples will move outwards.

What then, is the work of decolonizing ourselves, our profession, and the structures of the societies we inhabit? How do we use our often crippling discomfort about our privilege as a means to move forward? What part might trauma therapy take in transforming oppressive systems? Aligning with many of the ideas in this book, according to Elworthy, among the tasks that we might consider are:

- the skill of listening
- the ability to nurture and to include
- the choice to exercise 'power with' rather than 'power over'
- the attention to intuition and the creative imagination the makes for great art and invention
- the ability to stand in the shoes of another person
- the practice of dialogue with our inner world
- the compassion and stamina to look after those who are weak or in need
- reverence for the sacredness of creation and of our bodies. (2014: 36)

We must find some understanding and compassion for the ways in which we agree to participate in oppressive systems. Above all else, we need to work on our own relationship to trauma. It is, after all, the body which holds the score (van der Kolk, 2014), and all good trauma work starts there, from reclaiming our senses. The 'dropping in' reflections and experiments I have offered throughout the book have similarities to Johnson's (2018b: 115) cycle of critical learning for embodied social justice. These can be summarized as: embodied experience – prior or novel; embodied reflection; embodied meaning; and embodied experimentation – we try something new as a result. The forward direction in this is a necessary translation of inner process into action. In order to metabolize trauma we need to shift from passive to active embodied defences (Taylor, 2014: 100). One way of looking at this is as decolonization of the nervous system – when conditions are supportive. Herman (1992: 207) believes that a part of recovery from trauma is to become engaged in some form of cause.

In order to make sense of the patterns of organization that we see mirrored for us in the human and other-than-human world, we need to learn to listen deeply. By that I mean listening with our whole body receptive, and in open attention. Deep listening is not ego-centric but eco-centric, and *means that we are willing to be changed by what we discover*. Bednarek offers this challenge: 'What if our primary human need is not to attend meticulously to our own interests or our emotional wounds, but rather to live our flawed and imperfect human lives in deep connection with all that we encounter in the world?' (in press).

In Australia I met an Aboriginal elder of the Yuin people, Uncle Max Dulmunmun Harrison (see https://www.youtube.com/watch?v=aiqQUrLgniQ). He advised that we must 'See the Earth, hear the Earth, feel the Earth' (PACFA Conference, 2019). Uncle Max was searching for the land on which his family had been massacred, certain that the land would tell him when he found the right place. His mission was to honour both the trauma to his people and the trauma to the land itself, and in that recognition, find healing. The trauma he spoke of is the structural one of colonization, which is ongoing. When we intend to restore safety, it is crucial to remember that safety goes hand in hand with privilege, often but not always white privilege. It would be incongruous for Uncle Max to enjoy the privilege of safety while his people and his land continue to suffer. An inner sense of safety is predicated first and foremost upon external structures operating for the benefit for all.

I am left with some questions about how the profession of psychotherapy continues to play into some of the difficult dynamics we seek to resolve. As the concept of trauma finds its place in our collective psyches and in our consulting rooms, it can be used and abused by professionals and lay people alike. Are there traditional and indigenous healing practices that we disregard and which we might incorporate in our work? What stance do we take in our increasingly binary world, on the complex issue of understanding and meeting difference? How can we face up to unsustainable levels of consumption or to the carbon footprint associated with our practice? (Orange, 2017: 89). How do we reposition the important healing potential of our rich diversities of psychotherapeutic practice in an over-medicalized and pathologizing field? How, too, do we face the challenge of continuing to meet ever-increasing demands within an under-resourced field? Could we foresee a more ecological approach to the delivery of mental health services? (Denham-Vaughan and Chidiac, 2013: 103). Could the principles of the PTMF (Chapter 4) be applied to all areas of the SOS model, embodying mutual connection and regulation? This might include attention to physical environment, process, and relationships. How might we start on a local level with this? What values do we want to impart at all intersections of the ecological social systems we inhabit? Perhaps we need to repurpose some old connections in order to seek new solutions. As Wheeler says: 'So many conclusions are possible. Which ones are key, if we want to avoid yet another repetition of these horrors on a world scale?' (2004b: 328).

To paraphrase McGarvey, the great theme of life turns out not to be trauma. He tells us:

> Today, I realise that the most practical way of transforming my community is to first transform myself ... you are no use to any family, community, cause or movement unless you are first able to manage, maintain and operate the machinery of your own life. (2017: 202)

There is no place for a Messiah here. If psychotherapy is the art of having difficult conversations, we need to take them outside the therapy room and have those conversations with partners, friends, children, and grandchildren – conversations about the wounds societies inflict on minorities, conversations about the imperative to take care. When we love ourselves we are able to love others more wholly, and to fall in love again with the natural world.

> We need to relearn the fundamentals that once were natural ... literally remembering what planet we're on. Can we quiet our nerves for a time, to look deep inside our own humanity? ... For we're not dead yet, and the world is still alive to sensitive human touch, so long as we extend it. (Murphy, [2013] 2016: 131)

Epilogue: 2020 vision

I have worked for some time with the main ideas I have written about in the preceding pages, but they only came together in book form in the summer of 2019. As soon as the proposal was submitted to my publishers for review, I began work on Chapter 2, only to be interrupted in short order by my accident. I resumed writing that chapter in earnest in January 2020, and completed it in late March, just as the world was going into lockdown in the wake of escalating coronavirus cases. It simply had not occurred to me before then to consider pandemics under the umbrella of collective traumas; they were out of most of our consciousnesses. This pandemic was followed by the murders of Breonna Taylor and George Floyd and the many Black Lives Matter protests against police brutality and slavery. We have also seen a devastating explosion destroying Beirut, and political turmoil in Belarus. Even as I write, an outbreak of unrest is unfolding in Armenia and Azerbaijan. If that were not enough, we have witnessed major floods and wildfires across different continents. Large tracts of eastern Australia and the western United States have been decimated by fire. Floods in India and Nepal killed hundreds during July, and in southern China over 4 million people were evacuated from their homes because of flood risk in August (Guo et al., 2020). A locust invasion has decimated crops over large tracts of east Africa, affecting the livelihoods of some of the poorest farmers in the world. We are witness to fire, flood, plague, and pestilence on a truly Biblical scale. In terms of trauma, 2020 has so far gone on giving and giving.

My thinking about collective trauma thus proved to be only slightly ahead of the curve of rapidly evolving global events. Some of them have landed on my desk, so to speak, while I have been writing, requiring an urgent response. And it still goes on. I cannot offer a definitive overview on any of this, and others are equally engaged with trying to reframe some of the psychological impact. It is difficult to gain perspective when you are in the middle of something, and rather like the processing of trauma, it can only be handled in bite-sized pieces. I will limit my comments to the themes covered in this book. Given the speed of change, what I say here may not be relevant next year, or even next month, but it would be incongruous *not* to address it at this moment in time. The first question, one that affects us all, is whether the Covid-19 pandemic can been understood as a collective trauma. Without much doubt, life may never be the same again, and we have lived with fear of a virus beyond our understanding or control.

The impact of Covid-19 on our relationships, our lifestyles, and our being-in-the world has been far-reaching. We have become wary of strangers and for some, afraid for a variety of reasons of leaving our homes. Unable to see loved ones or to socialize as normal, we have felt very isolated and disconnected. Those whose coping strategies are to be busy or to rely on others have felt the wheels come off. The virus alone has shown up the fault lines in our society. In the UK and elsewhere, there has been a sense of there being one rule for the elite few and another rule for everybody else. Panic buying, especially in the early stages of the pandemic, created a scarcity of resources. The privileges of having a safe home, access to green spaces, or a job with a guaranteed income have stood in sharp contrast to those who do not have them. Here are a number of hallmarks of trauma as described in this book – overwhelm, fear, privilege, scarcity of resources, and disconnection.

In the UK, use of foodbanks has increased, as has the risk of domestic violence, child sexual abuse, and the predicted mental health problems. Domestic privilege needs to be held up to the light of global privilege. Note the interest paid in the media of the West to the natural disasters of 'developed' countries, compared to the scant attention paid to such occurrences in 'less developed' parts of the world, mentioned above. We go on ticking the boxes of situational structures shaping our experience.

In briefly reviewing the history of pandemics (Taylor, 2020), I found also some parallels with the Spanish flu of 1918. That pandemic hit the US particularly hard. Coming in the closing months of the First World War, it was difficult to shift focus to attend appropriately to containing the spread of the virus. Governments, it seems, can only deal with one big thing at a time. In the UK, Brexit may have diverted attention from what might otherwise have been a swifter response to Covid-19. Brexit necessitated a speeding up, and the virus a slowing down. That we now have the highest death rate in Europe is sobering. A hundred years ago, conspiracy theories appeared, fuelling fears that the Spanish flu had been created in a laboratory, effectively to be used as a weapon. As I write, QAnon, an online collection of conspiracy theorists, is gaining a large following on social media, and anti-vaxxers and anti-mask protesters are vocal in their opposition to what they perceive as government controls and infringement of their rights.

Alongside this, community spirit and a sense of solidarity have spread faster than the virus. Disasters bring out the very best and the very worst in people, as I witnessed first-hand in the aftermath of the Grenfell Tower inferno in 2017. And yet, there are no memorials to those who perished in the great pandemics of the past, nor is the history spoken about. It seems that the Spanish flu has largely gone to ground, as this current pandemic might. That changes the way we begin to think about it, either as shared history or ground trauma. The risk, with so many events to grapple with, is that most of them will go unprocessed. We could be witnessing ground trauma in the making.

Not one of us has been exempt from the changes wrought by Covid-19. Therapists have also become more vigilant, more fearful, and vulnerable. We live with uncertainty as never before. Feeling assaulted by the fear and worry that everyone was telling me about, my first move as the pandemic broke was to assume that others would feel the same, and I set up a therapists' coronavirus support group, which is ongoing. Some therapists have reported concern for their own well-being expressed more openly than before. Speaking personally, the hardest point came when, early in the pandemic, all my adult children had Covid-19 in the space of a fortnight. I was helpless with care and worry. Our vulnerabilities have been exposed and the lines between professional and personal are less distinct as a result. The pandemic has resulted in a previously inconceivable shift in the way we work and our orientation to the people we work with. In so many ways, this is a watershed moment in history.

We have had to negotiate new spaces to work in with the people we live with, as well as with the people we meet in our professional lives. In no way has this been easy for anyone. It seems that the degree of 'success' we have had depends on a combination of our privileged resources and our closest relationships. We have had to make professional compromises alongside great personal adjustments. The so-called space between us has had to be redefined and reconceived as we have all moved our work online. I have experienced this as an indefinable absence, grieving for the loss of human contact. Where, now, is the person I am working with, how do I locate them and conceptualize the contact boundary? I don't know if I am in their room or they are in mine, or if contact is through the screens in front of us or somewhere 'in the ether'. We enter different personal spaces, sometimes less 'formal', perhaps at their end interrupted by a cat on the keyboard or a family member coming into their room. The therapeutic space is no longer animated by the way someone enters the room and arranges their coat or bag before they take their seat. That loss of vitality has hit many therapists hard. Some people have not been able to engage with the new medium and have chosen to terminate or take a break from therapy, at what cost or recreation of a trauma-based isolation, I wonder? Whether continuing to seek a way to manage or not, we feel a dislocation which might be described as a collective trauma.

For those for whom the new medium of working online does work, the distance may be less triggering, and we might explain this effect as already existing in something larger. It is a holding space until a safer reality becomes possible, which does not mean that the work is provisional. I had previously resisted requests to work online, because it seemed incompatible with a body-centred approach. I am not alone in discovering that this is not necessarily the case, but we have to increase the dialogue to negotiate body work. I tune in no less with my own body than I did before. Under the right conditions, there have been those who have found a sense of safety in the reduced stimulus of lockdown that could never be possible before.

Someone caught near the epicentre of the explosion in Beirut returned home after a few weeks, windows repaired but glass and debris everywhere. She described the simple task of clearing up and washing dishes: 'Life goes on, it felt like I had some agency, there was something I could still do, and I felt the satisfaction of being able to do it. It took a lot of effort, and there is still damage that will always be there, but I felt calmer, one thing at a time. It was like a flower that breaks through a rock in a mountain, there will be a way through this and we will survive'. Unsurprisingly, they are reluctant to return to 'normal'. And for others, increasing danger has been a reality – the difficulty of finding a safe place at home from which to talk has made this very different reality palpable.

We are told to expect an increase in referrals as the world changes. And yet, six months in, I am hearing reports of therapists really feeling the stress of all that they are living with. We are part of a bigger shared humanity and vulnerability. Therapists are overwhelmed by the tragic and the banal, and shock can be numbing. I find large numbers well-nigh impossible to comprehend, and yet my tears flow in the instant of hearing of a personal tragedy. We are being drawn into a new way of imagining ourselves and our work, for now certainly, but possibly for the future. We are all implicated in this as never before, and like many people therapists are making new lifestyle choices. It is timely to take note of the issue of therapist capacity, and what we mean by self-care; there is a palpable urgency to this question now. Some therapists are thinking about cutting back their availability even as demand grows. How we pick up the pieces will be interesting.

One thing that has impressed me during these months has been our extraordinary adaptability. Indeed, generations that have gone before have survived plague, natural disasters, and political upheaval. I have no wish to dismiss the terrible costs, but I begin to wonder also about the concept of collective resilience. As Fassin and Rechtman point out: 'Trauma is both the product of an experience of inhumanity and the proof of the humanity of those who have endured it' (2007: 20). I believe we will survive in some way – so long as we don't destroy the planet. In circular fashion, *there are suggestions that Covid-19 would not have crossed to the human species were it not for the loss of habitats forcing other-than-human species closer to our towns and cities.* Our disconnection from the natural world may well underlie this aspect of the problems we face together. However, the simplicity and slow-down of lockdown has refocused many on the natural world, on their consumption, and on appreciation of the world around them. One of the things that has been a sheer delight and an anchor for me in the last months has been an award-winning weekly podcast by novelist and nature writer Melissa Harrison, called The Stubborn Light of Things. In Episode 27 on 14 September 2020, she lamented to a friend about the broken world in which we live. Her friend replied, 'Yes, the world is sick; we have to care for it as we would a sick child'.

Ely
28 September 2020

Appendix A

The sophistication of Gestalt theory provides a coherent framework for trauma work. The main ideas expressed in this book concern the relationship between the self/individual and the environment/other. The SOS model, which forms an anchor point for the main text (Chapter 2), relates to what are known as the three pillars of Gestalt: phenomenology (Self), dialogue (Other), and field theory (Situation). Just as the SOS model represents a dynamic and indivisible whole, so the three pillars are interconnected.

Gestalt theory does not rest in a concept of a 'core self', but instead considers self to be something fluid, changeable, and emergent. The self exists always in relationship to something, and is formed through successive moments of contact with what can be described as 'not self'. Put simply, we react or respond in different ways to different circumstances, sometimes in fixed or predictable patterns, and sometimes in novel or spontaneous ways. Self is organized in response to the demands of the environment, which includes other people and situations.

From a Gestalt perspective, self is therefore not a 'thing' but a process, in dynamic response to the world around us. A simple definition comes from our founders: self is the system of contacts at any one moment (Perls et al., [1951] 1998: 235). The ability to make good contact is one way Gestalt therapists understand psychological health, as fluid, satisfying, and receptive to novelty to support growth. Self can be understood as a function of the field, that is, as a part of how a larger and indivisible whole operates. Self changes as a function of changes in the field as a whole (Parlett, 2005: 55). Self is that process through which life itself is expressed, and in wholesome process is deeply embodied. However, it is important to stress that we are never in contact with the total field at any one time.

When our expression becomes habitual, we consider that there is less adjustment to the actual, immediate situation, which is often the case for people who have experienced trauma, where their feelings, perceptions, and behaviour are shaped by past events. Stress is one of the things that organizes self, and in extremes can become rigid or chaotic as a result. It is assumed in Gestalt theory that the natural cycle of experience will lead to what is called 'organismic self-regulation'. This honours the wisdom of the body to heal itself, but trauma theory calls this into question to some extent. Organismic self-regulation rests on the idea that regulation – a core interest in trauma work – can happen alone, where in reality it needs the support of others at least initially.

In Gestalt, self emerges in contact with the other at what we call the contact boundary. First, we understand a number of functions that support contact, including voice, sight, hearing, and touch. The boundary can be disturbed in a number of ways, modifying contact. Contact is not a discrete event, it is part of a process of the ebb and flow of life and may be modified in a number of ways. In a healthy process, the cycle of contact begins with the body, arising from sensation, through awareness and mobilization to action and contact. The cycle is completed through a relaxing of focus through satisfaction, assimilation, and withdrawal of energy, dropping into a 'fertile void' before the next cycle arises. Contact is related to the notion of 'figures of interest' described below. When figure formation is problematic, the contact cycle may be truncated, perhaps by skipping over the sensation or assimilation and withdrawal phases. Gestalt therapists take great interest in the contact style of the people they work with; the quality of *how* we meet is by extension a process consideration that is a major strand throughout this book. One of the specific modifications to contact referred to in this volume is that of retroflection – the holding in of energy or expression. This has important implications for understanding reactions to trauma, in which there is a devastating reorganization of the boundary between self and other.

The phenomenological perspective draws on the principle of the experiencing self. It is an existential approach. Experience shapes our perceptions of ourselves in the world, which in turn influence how we organize relationships and make meaning. This process is entirely subjective. Therefore, we cannot make assumptions or draw on prior meanings for other people. The phenomenological method is based on questioning and observation, without ascribing meaning. It is essentially a horizontal method, in which everything is potentially relevant, and prefigures the horizontalism of the relationship. I cannot assume to know your experience better than you, or what something means for you. Phenomenology can be described as being 'experience-near', although there are some limits in this approach when working with trauma wherein some experiential distance may be necessary. As a therapist, I leave that to you. When we turn our interest towards an aspect of experience, there is a sense of movement, or what is described as intentionality. Phenomenology is interested in sensation as the basis of felt experience, which is an entry to embodiment. This is a necessary aspect of lived experience and is often split off following trauma.

A major advantage of the phenomenological approach is that it supports formulation of the unformulated experience of trauma, through which the self can be defined. By being able to give name to aspects of experience, the trauma becomes more knowable, more differentiated. And, as I have argued earlier, differentiation leads to integration which many see as the goal of trauma 'treatment', bringing together the fragmented and incoherent aspects of traumatic experience.

The concept of dialogue, as practised in Gestalt, reaches beyond everyday conversation. Dialogue is what happens at the contact boundary at which we meet. Dialogue is not necessarily spoken, because we can also meet deeply through non-verbal contact. Dialogue incorporates Buber's I–Thou and I–It of relatedness, and we do not necessarily privilege the I–Thou. We simply offer it through our availability. We may or may not meet through awareness, receptiveness, and deep consideration of the Other and their humanity. Buber's four principles of dialogue are presence, confirmation, open communication, and inclusion. Inclusion is similar to but uniquely different from empathy (Chapter 6). It means leaning into the world of the other without losing one's own subjectivity.

The use of the term 'field' in Gestalt is used in reference to different things. The term derives from two sources. First, Gestalt psychology (not the same as Gestalt therapy theory) refers to the perceptual field, an individualistic concept. By this interpretation, there can be no shared field. The second meaning is based in Lewin's field theory, and refers to what is sometimes known as the 'lifespace' of an individual, the terms 'environment' and 'situation' also being used interchangeably with field. Sometimes, the term field is used in a fairly limited way, to refer to the circumstances of a person's life, and this lacks a deeper contextual nuance. According to Lewinian theory, the behaviour of the individual is embedded in a context. For the purposes of this book, the term field refers to the total field: personal, historical, social, cultural, and other-than-human. This is a more ecological frame of reference.

The term 'relational field' crops up often in this book. By this is meant the intersubjective, co-created space between two individuals, explicitly that which is known to either party: personal history, attachment styles, social situation, and roles. But the intersubjective space is also affected by hidden or implicit factors, such as culture, gender, race, or sexuality. These implicit intersections of lived experience are also part of the relational field.

How we organize experience is determined by the relationship between figure and ground. What we choose to pay attention to – what becomes 'foreground' or 'figural' – emerges according to need and interest from a complex ground of almost infinite possibilities. I compare this to the relationship between a wave and the water it comes from, is made of, and recedes into. Gestalt therapy has been criticized as being too figure-bound, and contemporary writers seek to redress this imbalance. Ground can be described as an undifferentiated condition containing aspects of the field, historical and contemporary. It also consists of traces of experience and physiology which provide a context to the perception of the figure. At this moment, for example, my need and interests are organized around writing this book, but when I get tired or hungry, my attention will be drawn to other so-called figures of interest. Like the wave, writing will temporarily recede into the background, still part of the ground but not at that moment figural. In repetitive trauma processes, a fear of threat often organizes the perceptual field, with constant vigilance for its appearance. In stormy waters we need to keep an eye on the next incoming wave, to the exclusion of the water. Other figures therefore are felt as less important, and there can be little sense of ground (see Chapter 9). A concept introduced in Chapter 2 is that of 'ground trauma', in which many elements of trauma become effectively indistinguishable, yet which influence the conditions from which figures emerge.

A notion from Gestalt theory which is fundamental to thinking about trauma is that of polarities. This suggests simply that everything that is present or can be experienced has its opposite, which conceptually defines each and is the relationship between them. Thus, day cannot exist without night, on cold, and so on. These polarities are held in dynamic tension, although times one of the polar opposites becomes eclipsed when a particular one dominates someone's experience. Typically in trauma work, fear dominates and organizes experience without consideration for the need for safety, for example. In more regular psychotherapy language, we can think of polarities as related to splitting. An aspect of experience is disowned and becomes fragmented or dis-integrated. It is often helpful to attend to polarities in order to restore a sense of the whole picture.

A final foundation of Gestalt therapy rests on Beisser's Paradoxical Theory of Change. This states that change occurs not when one tries to be different, but when one is able to be fully who one is. The theory informs and underpins much of the process and relational position of Gestalt therapy. We stay with what is emerging and do not seek to adopt an expert position, or that of an agent of change. While in complete agreement with this notion, I have written elsewhere that there need to be certain conditions in place for this premise to be helpful for people with active trauma-based figures, and have proposed an Integrated Theory of Change, which states that 'Change happens under the *optimal* conditions in which one can be fully oneself' (Taylor, 2014: 36, emphasis added). This is consistent with the notion of relational regulation proposed above and throughout this book.

Appendix B

human brain has great capacity to respond and adapt to changing circum-
ces, but also a tendency to form habits. These two ideas help underpin
at we need to understand about change from a neurobiological perspective.
ease bear in mind that as explained in Chapter 1, the principles of neurosci-
nce are far more important to trauma therapists than the facts. There are a
ew theories based on neuroscience that I fall back on continually. I will give a
simple overview of them here, and link them together.

An overarching principle comes from Hebb's axiom, which states that 'Neurons that fire together wire together'. The more we use a particular neural pathway, the more it will fuse together, like two pieces of wire soldered in heat. This
is comparable to conditioned learning, and we can think of trauma as a set of
learned responses. Fortunately, because of this neuroplasticity, a new set of
responses can be learned, or wired together. When a habitual response falls out
of use, it will become weakened, or 'pruned', as the new pathway is strength-
ened. A further consideration is that any function of the nervous system is a
whole-body function, not simply confined to the brain.

The 'triune brain' is a concept proposed by MacLean in 1990. It is a gross
over-simplification of the complex organ that is the human brain, and is a somewhat controversial idea. This is because it is not anatomically accurate, and
proposes an evolutionary basis which is somewhat questionable. Nevertheless,
the triune brain is a very useful concept for understanding survival and trauma
responses. Although the structures in question are more evenly distributed
throughout the brain than the model suggests, the three areas are as follows.

At the base of the brain is the brain stem, leading to the spinal cord. The
brain stem is an area that looks after core physiological functions such as temperature, blood pressure, respiration, digestion, and states of being alert or
drowsy. When the brain stem is compromised we cannot survive. In an extreme
trauma response the brain stem begins to shut down some of the physiological
functions necessary for life, typically through freeze or collapse states.

Sitting on top of the brain stem is an area known as the limbic system. The
limbic brain is implicated in our survival in a number of ways. It is responsible
for our sensory, emotional, and motor reactions, which means we can deal with
the present conditions. It is said to be the seat of structures controlling our
response to threat and is therefore implicated in trauma. In particular, an
almond-shaped structure called the amygdala acts as a 'lookout' for indications
of threat, triggering an alarm system at the first sign. Importantly, the amygdala does not have the capacity to appraise the degree of threat or to make any
kind of meaning about what is actually happening – it may simply be triggered
at the *perception* of threat. This is an emergency response, which in turn triggers a chain reaction involving other structures, glands, and the secretion of a
cascade of neurochemicals, most particularly cortisol, throughout the body.

Cortisol is a neurochemical specifically implicated in responses to fear, and promotes the fight/flight response while affecting metabolism and immune function. Chronic high levels of cortisol can cause damage to different organs, including the brain, heart, and digestive system. The hippocampus is a structure largely in the limbic brain that seems to be the store of traumatic memory, which has a completely different quality from regular and everyday memory. Traumatic memory is more sensory and visceral, often fragmented without coherent narrative.

Sitting atop the limbic brain, directly under our skull, is the cortex, the sophisticated area that processes information coming in. Planning and making strategies are part of the remit of the cortical brain, upon which survival may depend. However, these functions require cognition and that is a far slower process than the micro-second reactions of the limbic area. And here is a key to understanding: *research has shown that this area of the brain effectively goes 'offline' under extreme threat, and the sub-cortical systems run the show.* This helps to explain the heightened reactivity of a trauma response, and the ineffectiveness of a 'reasoned' intervention.

The autonomic nervous system (ANS) is a part of the central nervous system which serves to regulate and mediate our response to stress. Traditional wisdom holds that there are two branches of the ANS. The sympathetic branch, with fibres that stem from the nerves of the spinal cord, is responsible for activation, or arousal of the body in order to meet stress or threat. The parasympathetic branch has many fibres originating in the brain stem, and mostly operates via the vagus nerve. However, polyvagal theory, a more recent development by Stephen Porges, has profound implications for trauma practice. The theory is based on research into the function of the vagus nerve, which is the tenth cranial nerve. It is also the longest nerve in the body, with a Latin root meaning 'wandering' in common with the word 'vagabond'. The vagus nerve reaches to many areas of the head, throat, and major organs of the torso. Importantly, it is a bi-directional nerve, which means it sends signals in both directions between the brain and the relevant organ.

Polyvagal theory proposes three different branches of the ANS, each representing different degrees of activation, and is considered as a hierarchical process. The vagus nerve affects tiny muscles around our eyes, mouth, in our ears and larynx, influencing the communication of associated emotional expressions. Most specifically, when we feel safe and relaxed, these muscles will be soft and communicate approachability and trustworthiness. This is the *ventral vagal* state, involving the anterior myelinated fibres of the vagus nerve, and is a parasympathetic state of rest. Also known as the *social engagement system*, a ventral vagal tone has much in common with the Gestalt notion of contact functions (see Appendix A). In this state, the vagal brake operates principally to steady heart rhythm. When there is a degree of danger present and the social engagement system is compromised, the vagal brake releases somewhat and a *sympathetic* tone follows to enable active defences of fight and flight. When the degree of danger is such that taking action is impossible, a more extreme parasympathetic response takes over, usually with a freeze or collapse response.

These processes can be clearly observed in the body. This state is the *dorsal vagal* state, mediated by the posterior unmyelinated branch of the vagus nerve.

At risk of generalizing, it can be argued that the modern world induces a chronic low-level activation of the sympathetic branch of the ANS, and an appropriate response is to provide conditions in which a parasympathetic, ventral vagal tone is promoted. To a degree this is true, but there is a caution. The dorsal vagal state is also a parasympathetic response, which, in extreme danger, slows heart rate considerably and shuts down the function of other major organs. This can lead to death. We need just the right amount of parasympathetic activation to feel safe.

Associated with the ANS is the window of tolerance model proposed by Siegel in 1999. This also considers the level of arousal and suggests that there is an *optimal* level, neither too much nor too little, in which strong emotions and pain can be tolerated without overwhelm. This is comparable to a ventral vagal state, which is a resourced state of flexibility. Under stress or threat, the window of tolerance effectively narrows, accompanied by habitual trauma responses and a reduction of choice (see Figure 3.1). The window of tolerance is not a fixed state, but rather 'breathes' as the situation requires. It contracts further in situations of increased perceived threat and releases in relative safety. The state of hyper-arousal corresponds to the activation of the sympathetic branch of the ANS. Hypo-arousal, on the other hand, is a parasympathetic state, at its extreme a threat to life, as the polyvagal theory indicates. The window of tolerance model provides an accessible tool for psycho-education about trauma, and a map for the process of therapy. Briefly, trauma cannot be processed in physiological states similar to those in which the original traumatic experience took place. Only when there is reliable access to an expanded window of tolerance, can the trauma be worked through.

This model is also useful for thinking in terms of interpersonal regulation of affect, and in fact changes our notion of an individual self. In order to feel safe with other people, we need to convey our own ventral vagal state or level of optimal arousal. Figure 6.2 shows how the interaction of a two-person window of tolerance works, and can be applied on increasing scales. Mirror neurons, based in the cortex, are likely the mechanism for picking up on the regulation of another person. These are thought to be specialized neurons that fire a similar way to an action that is being perceived; for example, if we see someone eating an ice cream, we might start to crave an ice cream too. Emotional states are also communicated in this way. It is suggested that the brain makes an image of the mind of another through the firing of mirror neurons. The mirror neuron system is thus thought to be the neural mechanism for intersubjective states.

This leads us to the notion that two minds can join together through a fluid exchange of information and energy between them. This is based often on non-verbal signals, as the social engagement system suggests, and creates small shifts at a sub-cortical level. By turning attention to another, we begin to attune to them and then a resonance builds up, coursing through circuits starting in the thalamus. That resonance then leads to sense of 'feeling felt', and a sense of integration follows. The neurochemical that accompanies states of connection and trust is oxytocin.

References

Abram, D. (1997) *The Spell of the Sensuous*, New York: Vintage.

Abram, D. (2010) *Becoming Animal: An Earthly Cosmology*, New York: First Vintage.

Abram, D. (2020) The ecology of perception: An interview with David Abram [Podcast], *Emergence Magazine*. https://emergencemagazine.org/interview/the-ecology-of-perception/ (accessed 22 April 2021).

Adams, M. (2014) *The Myth of the Untroubled Therapist: Private Life, Professional Practice*, Hove: Routledge.

Adams, W.W. (2015) Healing our dissociation from body and nature: Gestalt, Levinas, and earth's ethical call, *British Gestalt Journal*, 24 (1): 32–38.

Adams, W.W. (2020) Nature-healing-body-healing-nature: Embodied relational Gestalt ecopsychology, in M.C. Clemmens (ed.) *Embodied Relational Gestalt: Theories and Applications*, Abingdon: Routledge.

Alexander, J.C. (2004) Toward a theory of cultural trauma, in J.C. Alexander, R. Eyerman, B. Giesen, N.J. Smelser and P. Sztompka, *Cultural Trauma and Collective Identity*, Berkeley, CA: University of California Press.

Alpert, J. (2016) The witnessing gaze turned inward: My Jewish history and the forgotten other, in D.M. Goodman and E.R. Severson (eds.) *The Ethical Turn: Otherness and Subjectivity in Contemporary Psychoanalysis*, New York: Routledge.

Anagnostopoulou, L. (2015) Vertical grounding: The body in the world and the self in the body, in G. Marlock and H. Weiss (eds.) *The Handbook of Body Psychotherapy and Somatic Psychology*, Berkeley, CA: North Atlantic Books.

Anderson, E.C., Carleton, R.N., Diefenbach, M. and Han, P.K.J. (2019) The relationship between uncertainty and affect, *Frontiers in Psychology*, 10: 2504. https://doi.org/10.3389/fpsyg.2019.02504 (accessed 20 July 2020).

Aron, L. (2016) Mutual vulnerability: An ethic of clinical practice, in D.M. Goodman and E.R. Severson (eds.) *The Ethical Turn: Otherness and Subjectivity in Contemporary Psychoanalysis*, New York: Routledge.

Asheri, S. (2013) Stepping in to the void of dissociation: A therapist and client in search of a meeting place, in J. Yellin and O.B. Epstein (eds.) *Terror Within and Without: Attachment and Disintegration: Clinical Work on the Edge*, London: Karnac Books.

Ataria, Y. (2017) *The Structural Trauma of Western Culture: Toward the End of Humanity*, Cham: Palgrave Macmillan.

Atkinson, J. ([2002] 2018) *Trauma Trails, Recreating Song Lines: The Transgenerational Effects of Trauma in Indigenous Australia*, North Geelong, VIC: Spinifex.

Badenoch, B. (2018) *The Heart of Trauma: Healing the Embodied Brain in the Context of Relationship*, New York: Norton.

Baker, A. (2019) Wave patterns [Essay], *Emergence Magazine*. https://emergencemagazine.org/essay/wave-patterns/ (accessed 22 April 2021).

Barker, M.-J. and Iantaffi, A. (2019) *Life Isn't Binary: On Being Both, Beyond and In-Between*, London: Jessica Kingsley.

Bednarek, S. (2018) How wide is the field? Gestalt therapy, capitalism and the natural world, *British Gestalt Journal*, 27 (2): 8–17.

Bednarek, S. (in press) 'The end of innocence': Reflections on the complex relationship between climate change, mental health and the profession of psychotherapy – who needs to change?, in S. Wright (ed.) *The Change Process in Psychotherapy During Troubling Times*, Abingdon: Routledge.

Beebe, B. and Lachman, F.M. (2002) *Infant Research and Adult Treatment: Co-Constructing Interactions*, Hillsdale, NJ: Analytic Press.

Belz-Knöferl, A. (2015) Horizontal grounding, in G. Marlock and H. Weiss (eds.) *The Handbook of Body Psychotherapy and Somatic Psychology*, Berkeley, CA: North Atlantic Books.

Bennett Leighton, L. (2018) The trauma of oppression: A somatic perspective, in C. Caldwell and L. Bennett Leighton (eds.) *Oppression and the Body: Roots, Resistance and Resolutions*, Berkeley, CA: North Atlantic Books.

Bentovim, A. (2002) Dissociative identity disorder: A developmental perspective, in V. Sinason (ed.) *Attachment Trauma and Multiplicity: Working with Dissociative Identity Disorder*, Hove: Brunner-Routledge.

Berger, R. (2016) Renewed by Nature: Nature therapy as a framework to help people with crises, trauma and loss, in M. Jordan and J. Hind (eds.) *Ecotherapy: Theory, Research and Practice*, London: Palgrave Macmillan.

Bloom, D. (2013) Situated ethics and the ethical world of Gestalt therapy, in G. Francesetti, M. Gecele and J. Roubal (eds.) *Gestalt Therapy in Clinical Practice: From Psychopathology to the Aesthetics of Contact*, Milan: FrancoAngeli.

Bloom, S.L. and Farragher, B. (2013) *Restoring Sanctuary: A New Operating System for Trauma-Informed Systems of Care*, Oxford: Oxford University Press.

Boadella, D. (1987) *Lifestreams: An Introduction to Biosynthesis*, London: Routledge & Kegan Paul.

Bollas, C. (2017) *The Shadow of the Object: Psychoanalysis and the Unthought Known*, London: Free Association Books (Kindle edition).

Boston Change Process Study Group (2010) *Change in Psychotherapy: A Unifying Paradigm*, New York: Norton.

Bradshaw, G.A. (2009) Transformation through science, in L. Buzzell and C. Chalquist (eds.) *Ecotherapy: Healing with Nature in Mind*, San Francisco, CA: Sierra Club Books.

Britten, W. (2019) Can mindfulness be too much of a good thing? The value of a middle way, *Current Opinion in Psychology*, 28: 159–165.

Bromberg, P.M. ([1998] 2001) *Standing in the Spaces: Essays on Clinical Process, Trauma, and Dissociation*, New York: Psychology Press.

Bromberg, P.M. (2006) *Awakening the Dreamer: Clinical Journeys*, Mahwah, NJ: Analytic Press.

Bromberg, P. (2011) *The Shadow of the Tsunami: And the Growth of the Relational Mind*. New York: Routledge.

Buber, M. ([1923] 1958) *I and Thou*, Edinburgh: T. & T. Clark.

Bullmore, E. (2018) *The Inflamed Mind: A Radical Approach to Depression*, London: Short Books.

Caldwell, C. (2018) Body identity development: Who we are and who we become, in C. Caldwell and L. Bennett Leighton (eds.) *Oppression and the Body: Roots, Resistance and Resolutions*, Berkeley, CA: North Atlantic Books.

Caplan, P.J. (1995) *They Say You're Crazy: How the World's Most Powerful Psychiatrists Decide Who's Normal*, New York: Da Capo Press.

Capra, F. and Luisi, P.L. (2014) *The Systems View of Life: A Unifying Vision*, Cambridge: Cambridge University Press.

Carlson, C. and Kolodny, R. (2009) Embodying field theory in how we work with groups and large systems, in D. Ullman and G. Wheeler (eds.) *Co-Creating the Field: Intention and Practice in the Age of Complexity*, Santa Cruz, CA: Gestalt Press.

Carroll, M. and Shaw, E. (2013) *Ethical Maturity in the Helping Professions: Making Difficult Life and Work Decisions*, London: Jessica Kingsley.

Carroll, R. (2009) Self-regulation – an evolving concept at the heart of body psychotherapy, in L. Hartley (ed.) *Contemporary Body Psychotherapy: The Chiron Approach*, London: Routledge.

Casement, P. (1990) *Further Learning from the Patient: The Analytic Space and Process*, London: Routledge.

Chalquist, C. (ed.) (2010) *Rebearths: Conversations with a World Ensouled*, Walnut Creek, CA: World Soul Books.

Chesler, P. ([2005] 2018) *Women and Madness*, Chicago, IL: Lawrence Hill Books.

Chidiac, M.-A. and Denham-Vaughan, S. (2007) The process of presence: Energetic availability and fluid responsiveness, *British Gestalt Journal*, 16 (1): 9–19.

Chidiac, M.-A. and Denham-Vaughan, S. (2020) Gestalt, the good and the concept of ethical presence, *British Gestalt Journal*, 29 (1): 21–29.

Chidiac, M.-A., Denham-Vaughan, S. and Osborne, L. (2017) The relational matrix model of supervision: Context, framing and interconnection, *British Gestalt Journal*, 26 (2): 21–30.

Clemmens, M.C. (2020) Embodied contexts: The forms we create, the forms that create us, in M.C. Clemmens (ed.) *Embodied Relational Gestalt: Theory and Applications*, Santa Cruz, CA: Gestalt Press.

Cohen, S. (2001) *States of Denial: Knowing about Atrocities and Suffering*, Cambridge: Polity.

Cohen, S. (2002) *Folk Devils and Moral Panics*, 3rd edition, London: Routledge.

Conn, L.K. and Conn, S.A. (2009) Opening to the Other, in L. Buzzell and C. Chalquist (eds.) *Ecotherapy: Healing with Nature in Mind*, San Francisco, CA: Sierra Club Books.

Cozolino, L. (2004) *The Making of a Therapist: A Practical Guide for the Inner Journey*, New York: Norton.

Crenshaw, K. (2017) *On Intersectionality: Essential Writings*, New York: The New Press.

Cromby, J., Harper, D. and Reavey, P. (2013) *Psychology, Mental Health and Distress*, London: Palgrave.

Davies, J. (2013) *Cracked: Why Psychiatry Is Doing More Harm than Good*, London: Icon Books.

Davies, J.M. and Frawley, M.G. (1992) Dissociative processes and transference-countertransference paradigms in the psychoanalytically oriented treatment of adult survivors of childhood sexual abuse, *Psychoanalytic Dialogues*, 2 (1): 5–36.

Denham, J. (2006) The trainer's presence in effective Gestalt training, *British Gestalt Journal*, 15 (1): 16–22.

Denham-Vaughan, S. (2005) Will and Grace: An integrative dialectic central to Gestalt psychotherapy, *British Gestalt Journal*, 14 (1): 5–14.

Denham-Vaughan, S. (2010) The liminal space and twelve action practices for gracious living, *British Gestalt Journal*, 19 (2): 34–45.

Denham-Vaughan, S. and Chidiac, M.-A. (2007) The process of presence: Energetic availability and fluid responsiveness, *British Gestalt Journal*, 16 (1): 9–19.

Denham-Vaughan, S. and Chidiac, M.-A. (2013) SOS: A relational orientation towards social inclusion, *Mental Health and Social Inclusion*, 17 (2): 100–107.

Denham-Vaughan, S. and Glenholmes, K. (2019) Flying blind: Encountering trauma in organisations, in M. Spagnuolo-Lobb and F. Meulmeister (eds.) *Gestalt Approaches in Organisations*, Milan: FrancoAngeli.

Descola, P. (2013) *The Ecology of Others*, Chicago, IL: Prickly Paradigm Press.

Desmond, B. (2016) Homophobia endures in our time of changing attitudes: A 'field' perspective, *British Gestalt Journal*, 25 (2): 42–52.

DiAngelo, R. (2018) *White Fragility: Why It's So Hard for White People to Talk About Racism*, Boston, MA: Beacon Press.

Dillard, A. (1974) *Pilgrim at Tinker Creek*, New York: Harper & Row.

Drury, C. (1998) *Silent Spaces*, London: Thames & Hudson.

Duffell, N. (2014) *Wounded Leaders: British Elitism and the Entitlement Illusion, A Psychohistory*, London: Lone Arrow Press.

Eaton, J. and Paterson-Young, C. (2018) *The Little Orange Book: Learning about Abuse from the Voice of the Child*, Burton upon Trent: VictimFocus.

Eddo-Lodge, R. (2018) *Why I'm No Longer Talking to White People About Race*, London: Bloomsbury.

Elworthy, S. (2014) *Pioneering the Possible: Awakened Leadership for a World that Works*, Berkeley, CA: North Atlantic Books.

Epstein, R. (2017) *Attending: Medicine, Mindfulness and Humanity*, New York: Scribner.

Fairfield, M. (2018) Sharing resonance with Mark Fairfield [Podcast], *Healing Justice*. https://healingjustice.podbean.com/e/20-practice-sharing-resonance-with-mark-fairfield/ (accessed 23 March 2018).

Fairfield, M. (2019) Personal communication, 5 November.

Fassin, D. and Rechtman, R. (2007) *The Empire of Trauma: An Inquiry into the Condition of Victimhood*, Princeton NJ: Princeton University Press.

Fellows, E. (2020a) Personal communication, 7 May.

Fellows, E. (2020b) Personal communication, 29 August.

Filer, N. (2019) *The Heartland: Finding and Losing Schizophrenia*, London: Faber & Faber.

Fisher, J. (undated) Self-harm and suicidality [Paper], presented at the *Trauma Center Lecture Series*, Boston, MA. https://janinafisher.com/pdfs/selfharm.pdf (accessed 22 April 2021).

Floen, S.K. and Elkit, A. (2007) Psychiatric diagnosis, trauma and suicidality, *Annals of General Psychiatry*, 6: 12. https://doi.org/10.1186/1744-859X-6-12.

Fox, S. (2019) Psychiatry: A dangerous raft in a sea of despair, in J. Watson (ed.) *Drop the Disorder! Challenging the Culture of Psychiatric Diagnosis*, Ross on Wye: PCCS Books.

Francesetti, G. (2012) Pain and beauty: From the psychopathology to the aesthetics of contact, *British Gestalt Journal*, 21 (2): 4–18.

Francesetti, G. and Roubal, J. (2013) Gestalt therapy approach to depressive experiences, in G. Francesetti, M. Gecele and J. Roubal (eds.) *Gestalt Therapy in Clinical Practice: From Psychopathology to the Aesthetics of Contact*, Milan: FrancoAngeli.

Friedlander, S. (1918) *Schöpeferische Indifferenze*, Munich: Georg Müller.

Fromm, E. ([1956] 2002) *The Sane Society*, London: Routledge Classics.

Fryer, P. and Ruis, J. (2004) What are fractal systems? A brief description of Complex, Adaptive and Emergent Systems (CAES). Eindhoven: Centre for Fractal Design and Consultancy. www.fractal.org/Fractal-Systems.htm (accessed 8 May 2020).

Gantt, E.E. (2000) Levinas, psychotherapy and the ethics of suffering, *Journal of Humanistic Psychology*, 40 (3): 9–28.

Gartner, R. (ed.) (2017) *Trauma and Counter-Trauma, Resilience and Counter Resilience: Insights from Psychoanalysis and Trauma Experts*, Abingdon: Routledge.

Geller, S.M. and Greenberg, L.S. (2012) *Therapeutic Presence: A Mindful Approach to Effective Therapy*, Washington, DC: American Psychological Association.

Germer, C.K. (2009) *The Mindful Path to Self-Compassion: The Transformative Power of Feeling Safe*, New York: Norton.

Ghent, E. (1990) Masochism, submission, surrender: Masochism as a perversion of surrender, *Contemporary Psychoanalysis*, 26 (1): 108–136.

Gill, A.K. and Harrison, K. (2015) Child grooming and sexual exploitation: Are South Asian men the UK media's new folk devils?, *International Journal for Crime, Justice and Social Democracy*, 4 (2): 34–49.

Glendinning, C. (1994) *My Name is Chellis and I'm in Recovery from Western Civilization*, Boston, MA: Shambhala.

Gold, E. and Zahm, S. (2018) *Buddhist Psychology and Gestalt Therapy Integrated: Psychotherapy for the 21st Century*, Portland, OR: Metta Press.

Gonzi, M. (2020) Covid-19: Our response as Gestalt psychotherapists, *British Gestalt Journal*, 29 (1): 3–11.

Goodman, D.M. and Severson, E.R. (eds.) (2016) *The Ethical Turn: Otherness and Subjectivity in Contemporary Psychoanalysis*, Abingdon: Routledge.

Greene, A. (2019) The campaign to make ecocide an international crime: Quixotic quest or moral imperative?, *Fordham Environmental Law Review*, 30 (3): 1–48.

Gretton, D. (2019) *I, You, We, Them – Journeys Beyond Evil: The Desk Killers in History and Today*, London: Heinemann.

Guo, Y., Wu, Y., Wen, B., Huang, W., Ju, K., Gao, Y. et al. (2020) Floods in China, COVID-19, and climate change, *The Lancet: Planetary Health*, 4 (10): E443–E444.

Haidt, J. (2012) *The Righteous Mind: Why Good People Are Divided by Politics and Religion*, London: Penguin.

Halifax J. (2018) *Standing at the Edge: Finding Freedom Where Fear and Courage Meet*, New York: Flatiron Books.

Haluza, D., Schönbauer, R. and Cervinka, R. (2014) Green perspectives for public health: A narrative review on the physiological effects of experiencing outdoor nature, *International Journal of Environmental Research and Public Health*, 11 (5): 5445–5461.

Hamadi, l. (2014) Edward Said and the Literature of Post-Colonialism, in *Proceedings of the 1st Mediterranean Interdisciplinary Forum on Social Sciences and Humanities*, 2: 39–45. MIFS 2014, 23–26 April, Beirut, Lebanon.

Hand, S. (ed.) (1989) *The Levinas Reader*, Malden, MA: Blackwell.

Haney, C., Banks, W.C. and Zimbardo, P.G. (1973) A study of prisoners and guards in a simulated prison, *Naval Research Review*, 30: 4–17.

Harris, N. (2011) Something in the air, *British Gestalt Journal*, 20 (1): 21–28.

Herman, J.L. (1992) *Trauma and Recovery: The Aftermath of Violence – From Domestic Abuse to Political Terror*, London: Basic Books.

Hodgson, D. and Skye, E. (2016) Women desiring women: Reflections on the field, in P. Karian (ed.) *Critical and Experiential: Dimensions in Gender and Sexual Diversity*, Eastleigh: Resonance Publications.

Holroyd, J., Scaife, R. and Stafford, T. (2017) Responsibility for implicit bias, *Philosophy Compass*, 12: e12410. https://philpapers.org/archive/HOLRFI-3.pdf (accessed 22 April 2021).

Hopenwasser, K. (2008) Being in rhythm: Dissociative attunement in therapeutic process, *Journal of Trauma and Dissociation*, 9 (3): 349–367.

Hosemans, D. (2020) Relational Gestalt therapy as a potential therapy of liberation from oppressive social forces, *British Gestalt Journal*, 29 (1): 37–43.

Huang, X. (2019) Understanding Bourdieu: Cultural capital and habitus, *Review of European Studies*, 11 (3): 45–49.

Hyde, L. (2008) *Trickster Makes This World: How Disruptive Imagination Creates Culture*, Edinburgh: Canongate.

Inman, P. (2019) Gap between rich and poor grows alongside rise in UK's total wealth, *The Guardian*, 5 December. www.theguardian.com/news/2019/dec/05/gap-between-rich-and-poor-grows-alongside-rise-in-uks-total-wealth (accessed 22 April 2021).

Irwin, S. (2019) Finding my tribe: A survivor's story, in J. Watson (ed.) *Drop the Disorder! Challenging the Culture of Psychiatric Diagnosis*, Ross on Wye: PCCS Books.

Jacobs, L. (2004) Ethics of context and field: The practices of care, inclusion and openness to dialogue, in R.G. Lee (ed.) *The Values of Connection: A Relational Approach to Ethics*, Cambridge, MA: Gestalt Press.

Jacobs, L. (2005) For Whites only, in T. Levine Bar-Yoseph (ed.) *The Bridge: Dialogues Across Cultures*, New Orleans, LA: Gestalt Institute Press.

Jacobs, L. (2017) Hopes, fears and enduring relational themes, *British Gestalt Journal*, 26 (1): 7–16.

Jin, Y., Wu, Y., Li, H., Zhao, M. and Pan, J. (2017) Definition of fractal topography to essential understanding of scale-invariance, *Scientific Reports*, 7: 46672. https://doi.org/10.1038/srep46672.

Johnson, R. (2018a) Queering/querying the body: Sensation and curiosity in disrupting body norms, in C. Caldwell and L. Bennett Leighton (eds.) *Oppression and the Body: Roots, Resistance and Resolutions*, Berkeley, CA: North Atlantic Books.

Johnson, R. (2018b) *Embodied Social Justice*, Abingdon: Routledge.

Johnstone, L. (2019) Do you still need your psychiatric diagnosis? Critiques and alternatives, in J. Watson (ed.) *Drop the Disorder! Challenging the Culture of Psychiatric Diagnosis*, Ross on Wye: PCCS Books.

Johnstone, L. and Boyle, M. (2018) *The Power Threat Meaning Framework: Towards the identification of patterns in emotional distress, unusual experiences and troubled or troubling behaviour, as an alternative to functional psychiatric diagnosis*, Leicester: British Psychological Society.

Joyce, P. and Sills, C. (2014) *Skills in Gestalt Counselling and Psychotherapy*, 3rd edition, London: Sage.

Jung, C.G. (1972) *Four Archetypes: Mother, Rebirth, Spirit, Trickster*, trans. R.F.C. Hull, London: Routledge & Kegan Paul.

Kaplan, R. and Kaplan, S. (1989) *The Experience of Nature: A Psychological Perspective*, Cambridge: Cambridge University Press.

Karpman, S. (1968) Fairy tales and script drama analysis, *Transactional Analysis Bulletin*, 7 (26): 39–43.

Kennedy, D. (2003) The phenomenal field: The homeground of Gestalt therapy, *British Gestalt Journal*, 12 (2): 76–87.

Kepner, J.I. (1995) *Healing Tasks: Psychotherapy with Adult Survivors of Childhood Abuse*, San Francisco, CA: Jossey-Bass.

Kepner, J. (2002) *Energy and the nervous system in embodied experience*. www.pathwaysforhealing.com/pdfs/Phenom%20of%20NS.pdf (accessed 30 May 2020).

Kepner, J. (2003) The embodied field, *British Gestalt Journal*, 12 (1): 6–14.

Klimecki, O. and Singer, T. (2012) Empathic distress fatigue rather than compassion fatigue? Integrating findings from empathy research in psychology and social neuroscience, in B. Oakley, A. Knafo, G. Madhaven and D. Sloan Wilson (eds.) *Pathological Altruism*, New York: Oxford University Press.

Krysteva, J. (1982) *Powers of Horror: An Essay on Abjection*, New York: Columbia University Press.

Kubesch, A. (2005) In the shadow of the Holocaust, in T. Levine Bar-Yoseph (ed.) *The Bridge: Dialogues Across Cultures*, New Orleans, LA: Gestalt Institute Press.

Lac, V. (2017) *Equine-Facilitated Psychotherapy and Learning: The Human–Equine Relational Development (HERD) Approach*, London: Elsevier.

Laub, D. and Auerhahn, N.C. (1993) Knowing and not knowing massive trauma: Forms of traumatic memory, *International Journal of Psychoanalysis*, 74 (2): 287–302.

Lee, R.G. (2004) Ethics: A Gestalt of values/the values of Gestalt – A next step, in R.G. Lee (ed.) *The Values of Connection: A Relational Approach to Ethics*, Cambridge, MA: Gestalt Press.

Lemov, R. (2011) Brainwashing's avatar: The curious career of Dr. Ewen Cameron, *Grey Room*, 45: 60–87. https://scholar.harvard.edu/files/rlemov/files/lemov-cameron-grey-room2011.pdf.

Levinas, E. (1985) *Ethics and Infinity: Conversations with Phillipe Nemo*, Pittsburgh, PA: Duquesne University Press.

Levine, P. (1997) *Waking the Tiger: Healing Trauma*, Berkeley, CA: North Atlantic Books.

Levine, P. (2010) *In an Unspoken Voice: How the Body Releases Trauma and Restores Goodness*, Berkeley, CA: North Atlantic Books.

Lewin, K. ([1948/1951] 1997) *Resolving Social Conflicts and Field Theory in Social Science*, Washington, DC: American Psychological Association.

Li, M. and Rodin, G. (2012) Altruism and suffering in the context of cancer: Implications of a relational paradigm, in B. Oakley, A. Knafo, G. Madhaven and D. Sloan Wilson (eds.) *Pathological Altruism*, New York: Oxford University Press.

Lichtenberg, P. (2001) The four corners at the intersection of contacting, in J.-M. Robine, (ed.) *Contact and Relationship in a Field Perspective*, Bordeaux: L'Exprimerie.

Lichtenberg, P. (2004) On treating agents of oppression, in R.G. Lee (ed.) *The Values of Connection: A Relational Approach to Ethics*, Cambridge, MA: Gestalt Press.

Long, R. (2018) *Circle to Circle* [Exhibition], Lisson Gallery, London.

Lorde, A. ([1988] 2017) *A Burst of Light and Other Essays*, Mineola, NY: Ixia Press.

Lynch, T. (2019) Working therapeutically with clients with a psychiatric diagnosis, in J. Watson (ed.) *Drop the Disorder! Challenging the Culture of Psychiatric Diagnosis*, Ross on Wye: PCCS Books.

Macfarlane, R. (2007) *The Wild Places*, London: Granta.

Macfarlane, R. (2019) *Underland: A Deep Time Journey*, London: Hamish Hamilton.

Mackenzie-Mavinga, I. (2009) *Black Issues in the Therapeutic Process*, Basingstoke: Palgrave Macmillan.

Mackinnon, C. (2012) *Shamanism and Spirituality in Therapeutic Practice: An Introduction*, London: Singing Dragon.

MacLean, P.D. (1990) *The Triune Brain in Evolution*, New York: Plenum Press.

Marcus, E. (1980) Grounding, resistance and decision-making, *Gestalt Journal*, 3 (1): 112–119.

Marlock, G. and Weiss, H. (eds.) (2015) *The Handbook of Body Psychotherapy and Somatic Psychology*, Berkeley, CA: North Atlantic Books.

Marshall, H. (2016) A vital protocol – embodied-relational depth in nature-based psychotherapy, in M. Jordan and J. Hind (eds.) *Ecotherapy: Theory, Research and Practice*, London: Palgrave Macmillan.

McConville, M. (2005) The gift, in T. Levine Bar-Yoseph (ed.) *The Bridge: Dialogues Across Cultures*, New Orleans, LA: Gestalt Institute Press.

McGarvey, D. (2017) *Poverty Safari: Understanding the Anger of Britain's Underclass*, London: Picador.

McGilchrist, I. (2009) *The Master and His Emissary: The Divided Brain and the Making of the Western World*, London: Yale University Press.

McGreeney, A. (2016) *With Nature in Mind: The Ecotherapy Manual for Mental Health Professionals*, London: Jessica Kingsley.

McIntosh, A. ([2001] 2004) *Soil and Soul: People Versus Corporate Power*, London: Arum Press.

Menakem, R. (2017) *My Grandmother's Hands: Racialized Trauma and the Pathway to Mending our Hearts and Bodies*, Las Vegas, NV: Central Recovery Press [Kindle edition].

Messer Diehl, E.R. (2009) Gardens that heal, in L. Buzzell and C. Chalquist (eds.) *Ecotherapy: Healing with Nature in Mind*, San Francisco, CA: Sierra Club Books.

Meyer, I.H. (2003) Prejudice, social stress, and mental health in lesbian, gay, and bisexual populations: Conceptual issues and research evidence, *Psychology Bulletin*, 129 (5): 674–697.

Milgram, S. (1963) Behavioural study of obedience, *Journal of Abnormal and Social Psychology*, 67 (4): 371–378.

Muller, R.T. (2018) *Trauma and the Struggle to Open Up: From Avoidance to Recovery and Growth*, New York: Norton [Kindle edition].

Murphy, S. ([2013] 2016) The Koan of the Earth, in L. Vaughan-Lee (ed.) *Spiritual Ecology: The Cry of the Earth*, Point Reyes, CA: Golden Sufi Centre.

Neff, K. (2011) *Self-Compassion: Stop Beating Yourself Up and Leave Insecurity Behind*, London: Hodder & Stoughton.

Nepo, M. (2000) *The Book of Awakening: Having the Life You Want by Being Present to the Life You Have*, London: Quercus.

Nhat Hanh, T. (2011) *Peace Is Every Breath: A Practice for Our Busy Lives*, London: Ebury Press.

ní Dochartaigh, K. (2021) *Thin Places*, Edinburgh: Canongate.

O'Connor, L.E., Berry, J.W., Lewis, T.B. and Stiver, D.J. (2012) Empathy-based pathogenic guilt, pathological altruism, and psychopathology, in B. Oakley, A. Knafo, G. Madhaven and D. Sloan Wilson (eds.) *Pathological Altruism*, New York: Oxford University Press.

Ogden, P., Minton, K. and Pain, C. (2006) *Trauma and the Body: A Sensorimotor Approach to Psychotherapy*, New York: Norton.

Olsen, A. (2002) *Body and Earth: An Experiential Guide*, Lebanon, NH: Middlebury College Press.

Oppenheimer, J. (dir.) (2012) *The Act of Killing* [Documentary film], Det Danske Filminstitut.

Orange, D.M. (2011) *The Suffering Stranger: Hermeneutics for Everyday Clinical Practice*, New York: Routledge.

Orange, D.M. (2016a) *Nourishing the Inner Life of Clinicians and Humanitarians: The Ethical Turn in Psychoanalysis*, Abingdon: Routledge.

Orange, D.M. (2016b) Is ethics masochism? Or infinite ethical responsibility and finite human capacity, in D.M. Goodman and E.R. Severson (eds.) *The Ethical Turn: Otherness and Subjectivity in Contemporary Psychoanalysis*, New York: Routledge.

Orange, D.M. (2017) *Climate Crisis, Psychoanalysis and Radical Ethics*, Abingdon: Routledge.

O'Shea, L. (2020) Erotic ground: Always and already there, in M.C. Clemmens (ed.) *Embodied Relational Gestalt: Theories and Applications*, Abingdon: Routledge.

Parlett, M. (1991) Reflections on field theory, *British Gestalt Journal*, 1 (2): 68–91.

Parlett, M. (2005) Contemporary Gestalt therapy: Field theory, in A.L. Woldt and S.M. Toman (eds.) *Gestalt Therapy: History, Theory and Practice*, Thousand Oaks, CA: Sage.

Parlett, M. (2011) Letter to the editor: Fields in practice: A response to Neil Harris and to Francis Taylor, *British Gestalt Journal*, 20 (2): 53–55.

Parlett, M. (2015) *Future Sense: Five Explorations of Whole Intelligence for a World That's Waking Up*, Kibworth Beauchamp: Matador Press.

Pec, O., Bob, P., Simek, J. and Raboch, J. (2018) Dissociative states in borderline personality disorder and their relationship to psychotropic medication, *Journal of Neuropsychiatric Disease and Treatment*, 14: 3253–3257.

Pearlman, L.A. and Saakvitne K.W. (1995) *Trauma and the Therapist: Countertransference and Vicarious Traumatization in Psychotherapy with Incest Survivors*, New York: Norton.

Pearlman, S. (1999) *The Therapist's Emotional Survival: Dealing with the Pain of Exploring Trauma*, Lanham, MA: Rowman & Littlefield.

Perls, F. (1969) *Ego, Hunger, and Aggression*, New York: Random House.

Perls, F., Hefferline, R. and Goodman, P. ([1951] 1998) *Gestalt Therapy: Excitement and Growth in the Human Personality*, London: Souvenir Press.

Pernicano, P. (2014) *Using Trauma-Focused Therapy Stories: Interventions for Therapists, Children and Their Caregivers*, Hove: Routledge.

Pilgrim, D. (2018) *Child Sexual Abuse: Moral Panic or State of Denial?*, Abingdon: Routledge.

Plotkin, B. (2003) *Soulcraft: Crossing in to the Mysteries of Nature and Psyche*, Novato, CA: New World Library.

Polster, E. (1991) Tight therapeutic sequencing, *British Gestalt Journal*, 1 (2): 63–68.

Porges, S.W. (2017) *The Pocket Guide to the Polyvagal Theory: The Transformative Power of Feeling Safe*, New York: Norton.

Read, J. and Magliano, L. (2019) 'Schizophrenia' – the least scientific and most damaging of psychiatric labels, in J. Watson (ed.) *Drop the Disorder! Challenging the Culture of Psychiatric Diagnosis*, Ross on Wye: PCCS Books.

Recuber, T. (2016) From obedience to contagion: Discourses of power in Milgram, Zimbardo and the Facebook experiment, *Research Ethics*, 12 (1): 44–54.

Reidelsheimer, T. (dir.) (2001) *Rivers and Tides: Andy Goldsworthy Working with Time* [DVD], Artificial Eye.

Rhodes, W. and Valencia, C. (2019) Venezuela's healthcare crisis needs emergency attention, *Financial Times*, 8 February. www.ft.com/content/f1d3b414-2af2-11e9-88a4-c32129756dd8 (accessed 22 April 2021).

Ricard, M. (2015) *Altruism: The Science and Psychology of Kindness*, London: Atlantic Books.

Ross, J. and Watling, C. (2017) Use of empathy in psychiatric practice: Constructivist grounded theory study, *BJPsych Open*, 3 (1): 26–33. https://doi.org/10.1192/bjpo.bp.116.004242.

Rotenstreich, N. (1967) Martin Buber and the theory of knowledge, in P.A. Schlipp (ed.) *The Philosophy of Martin Buber*, La Salle, IL: Open Court.

Roubal, J. (2019a) Surrender to hope: The therapist in the depressed situation, in G. Francesetti and T. Griffero (eds.) *Psychopathology and Atmospheres: Neither Inside nor Outside*, Newcastle upon Tyne: Cambridge Scholars Publishing.

Roubal, J. (2019b) Process of change in Gestalt therapy: Three perspectives [Keynote speech], *Gestalt Therapy Now – Vitality, Integrity and Visibility*, UKAGP 2019 Residential Conference, High Wycombe, 27 July.

Rust, M.-J. (2011) Double vision? The Gestalt of our environmental crisis [Lecture], *Marianne Fry Lectures – Psychotherapy Lectures in Bristol*. https://mariannefrylectures.uk/past-lectures/2011-mary-jane-rust-double-vision-the-Gestalt-of-our-environmental-crisis/ (accessed 18 June 2018).

Sachs, A. (2013) Intergenerational transmission of massive trauma, in J. Yellin and O. Badouk Epstein (eds.) *Terror Without and Within: Attachment and Disintegration – Clinical Work on the Edge*, London: Karnac Books.

Sander, L.W. (1977) The regulation of exchange in the infant–caretaker system and some aspects of the context–content relationship, in M. Lewis and L. Rosenblum (eds.) *Interaction, Conversation and the Development of Language*, New York: Wiley.

Scaer, R. (2014) *The Body Bears the Burden: Trauma, Dissociation and Disease*, New York: Routledge.

Schaverien, J. (2004) Boarding school: The trauma of the 'privileged' child, *Journal of Analytical Psychology*, 49 (5): 683–705.

Schore, A. (2003) *Affect Regulation and the Repair of the Self*, New York: Norton.

Schwegler, V. (2017) The disposable nature: The case of ecocide and corporate responsibility, *Amsterdam Law Forum*, 9 (3): 71–99.

Shaw, C. (2019) The language of values, the value of language, in J. Watson (ed.) *Drop the Disorder! Challenging the Culture of Psychiatric Diagnosis*, Ross on Wye: PCCS Books.

Shaw, D. (2014) *Traumatic Narcissism: Relational Systems of Subjugation*, New York: Routledge.

Sheldrake, M. (2020) *Enchanted Life: How Funghi Make Our Worlds, Change Our Minds and Shape Our Futures*, London: Bodley Head.

Siegel, D.J. (1999) *The Developing Mind: How Relationships and the Brain Interact to Shape Who We Are*, New York: Guilford Press.

Siegel, D.J. (2007) *The Mindful Brain: Reflection and Attunement in the Cultivation of Well-Being*, New York: Norton.

Siegel, D.J. (2010) *The Mindful Therapist: A Clinician's Guide to Mindsight and Neural Integration*, New York: Norton.

Siegel, D.J. (2012) *The Pocket Guide to Interpersonal Neurobiology*, New York: Norton.

Simons, A.M.W., Koster, A., Groffen, D.A.I and Bosma, H. (2017) Perceived classism and its relation with socioeconomic status, health, health behaviours and perceived inferiority: The Dutch Longitudinal Internet Studies for the Social Sciences (LISS) panel, *International Journal of Public Health*, 62 (4): 433–440.

Sinason, V. (2008) How do we help ourselves?, in S. Benamer and K. White (eds.) *Trauma and Attachment*, London: Karnac Books.

Smelser, N.J. (2004a) Psychological trauma and cultural trauma, in J.C. Alexander, R. Eyerman, B. Giesen, N.J. Smelser and P. Sztompka, *Cultural Trauma and Collective Identity*, Berkeley, CA: University of California Press.

Smelser, N.J. (2004b) Epilogue: September 11, 2001, as cultural trauma, in J.C. Alexander, R. Eyerman, B. Giesen, N.J. Smelser and P. Sztompka, *Cultural Trauma and Collective Identity*, Berkeley, CA: University of California Press.

Smothers, B. (2016) Creativity and hospitality: Negotiating whom or what is known in psychoanalytic psychotherapy, in D.M. Goodman and E.R. Severson (eds.) *The Ethical Turn: Otherness and Subjectivity in Contemporary Psychoanalysis*, New York: Routledge.

Snyder, G. (1990) *The Practice of the Wild*, Emeryville, CA: Shoemaker & Hoard.

Soth, M. (2006) How the 'wound' enters the room and the relationship, *Therapy Today*, December. www.academia.edu/3551832/How_the_wound_enters_the_consulting_room_and_the_relationship (accessed 22 April 2021).

Spagnuolo Lobb, M. (2013) *The Now for Next in Psychotherapy: Gestalt Therapy Recounted in Post-Modern Society*, Milan: FrancoAngeli.

Staemmler, F.-M. (2020) Human suffering and the vicissitudes of personal responsibility in the course of psychotherapy, *British Gestalt Journal*, 29 (1): 12–20.

Stawman, S. (2011) Empathy and understanding, *British Gestalt Journal*, 20 (1): 5–13.

Stern, D. (2004) *The Present Moment in Psychotherapy and Everyday Life*, New York: Norton.

Stevens, J.O. (1971) *Awareness: Exploring, Experimenting, Experiencing*, Moab, UT: Real People Press.

Stevenson, H. (2004) *Paradox: A Gestalt theory of change.* www.clevelandconsultinggroup. com/pdfs/paradoxical_theory_of_change_iii.pdf (accessed 5 September 2020).

Stolorow, R.D. (2007) *Trauma and Human Existence: Autobiographical, Psychoanalytic and Philosophical Reflections*, New York: Analytic Press.

Stonewall (undated) *Conversion therapy.* www.stonewall.org.uk/campaign-groups/ conversion-therapy (accessed 11 May 2020).

Straight, J. (2013) Do you know what I know? Examining the therapist's internal experience when a patient dissociates in session, *Doctorate in Social Work (DSW) Dissertations*, 36. https://repository.upenn.edu/cgi/viewcontent.cgi?article=1041&context= edissertations_sp2 (accessed 29 June 2018).

Sztompka, P. (2004) The trauma of social change: A case of postcommunist societies, in J.C. Alexander, R. Eyerman, B. Giesen, N.J. Smelser and P. Sztompka, *Cultural Trauma and Collective Identity*, Berkeley, CA: University of California Press.

Tastan, S.B. (2017) Toxic workplace environment: In search for the toxic behaviours in organizations with a research in healthcare sector, *Postmodern Openings*, 8 (1): 83–109.

Taussig, M. (2004) Terror as usual: Walter Benjamin's theory of history as a state of siege, in N. Sheper-Hughes and P. Bourgois (eds.) *Violence in War and Peace: An Anthology*, Malden, MA: Blackwell.

Taylor, K. (1995) *The Ethics of Caring: Honoring the Web of Life in Our Professional Healing*, Santa Cruz, CA: Hanford Mead.

Taylor, M. (2013) On safe ground: Using sensorimotor approaches in trauma work, *British Gestalt Journal*, 22 (2): 5–13.

Taylor, M. (2014) *Trauma Therapy and Clinical Practice: Neuroscience, Gestalt and the Body*, Maidenhead: Open University Press.

Taylor, M. (2018) Undoing the splits: A relational field perspective on trauma, in M. Spagnuolo Lobb, D. Bloom, J. Roubal, L. Zeleskov Djoric, M. Cannavò, R. La Rosa, S. Tosi and V. Pinna (eds.) *The Aesthetic of Otherness: Meeting at the Boundary in a Desensitised World*, Milan: FrancoAngeli.

Taylor, M. (2019) In the face of trauma: Relationship, ethics, and the possibility of presence, *Gestalt Review*, 23 (3): 261–276.

Taylor, M. (2020) Collective trauma and the relational field, *The Humanistic Psychologist*, 48 (4): 382–388.

Taylor, M. and Duff, V. (2018) Reorganisation in a traumatised relational field: The well-grounded therapist, *British Gestalt Journal*, 27 (2): 18–29.

Thoreau, H.D. ([1854] 1973) *Walden*, London: Dent.

Timberlake, H. (2005) Uncovering unity in diversity, in T. Levine Bar-Yoseph (ed.) *The Bridge: Dialogues Across Cultures*, New Orleans, LA: Gestalt Institute Press.

Todres, L. (2007) *Embodied Enquiry: Phenomenological Touchstones for Research, Psychotherapy and Spirituality*, Basingstoke: Palgrave Macmillan.

Totton, N. (2009) Power in the therapy room, *Therapy Today*, September.

Totton, N. (2011) *Wild Therapy: Undomesticating Inner and Outer Worlds*, Ross on Wye: PCCS Books.

Tronick, E. (1998) Dyadically expanded states of consciousness and the process of therapeutic change, *Infant Mental Health Journal*, 19 (3): 290–299.

Tropianskia, J. (2020) Personal communication, 23 July.

Ullman, D. and Demaris, L. (2020) Nature heals, in M.C. Clemmens (ed.) *Embodied Relational Gestalt: Theories and Applications*, Abingdon: Routledge.

van der Kolk, B. (2014) *The Body Keeps the Score: Mind, Brain and Body in the Transformation of Trauma*, London: Allen Lane.

van der Kolk, B., Weisaeth, L and van der Hart, O. ([1996] 2007) History of trauma in psychiatry, in B. Van der Kolk, A.C. McFarlane and L. Weisaeth (eds.) *Traumatic Stress: The Effects of Overwhelming Experience on Mind, Body, and Society*, New York: Guilford Press.

van der Kolk, B. and, McFarlane A.C. ([1996] 2007) The black hole of trauma, in B. Van der Kolk, A.C. McFarlane and L. Weisaeth (eds.) *Traumatic Stress: The Effects of Overwhelming Experience on Mind, Body, and Society*, New York: Guilford Press.

Van Deurzen, E. (2019) Problems in living: An existential perspective, in J. Watson (ed.) *Drop the Disorder! Challenging the Culture of Psychiatric Diagnosis*, Ross on Wye: PCCS Books.

Vaughan Smith, J. (2019) *Coaching and Trauma: From Surviving to Thriving*, London: Open University Press.

Wall Kimmerer, R. ([2013] 2020) *Braiding Sweetgrass: Indigenous Wisdom, Scientific Knowledge and the Teachings of Plants*, London: Penguin Books.

WaterAid (2018) *The Water Gap – The State of the World's Water 2018*. https://washmatters. wateraid.org/publications/the-water-gap-state-of-the-worlds-water.

Watson, J. (2019) Counselling, psychotherapy and the biomedical model of emotional distress, in J. Watson (ed.) *Drop the Disorder! Challenging the Culture of Psychiatric Diagnosis*, Ross on Wye: PCCS Books.

Weber, A. ([2014] 2017) *Matter and Desire: An Erotic Ecology*, White River Junction, VT: Chelsea Green.

Wenders, W. (dir.) (2014) *The Salt of the Earth* [DVD], Artificial Eye.

Westland, G. (2015) *Verbal and Non-Verbal Communication in Psychotherapy*, New York: Norton.

Wheeler, G. ([1991] 1998) *Gestalt Reconsidered: A New Approach to Contact and Resistance*, Cambridge, MA: GIC Press.

Wheeler, G. (2000) *Beyond Individualism: Toward a New Understanding of Self, Relationship and Experience*, Cambridge, MA: GIC Press.

Wheeler, G. (2004a) Shame and belonging: Homer's *Iliad* and the Western ethical tradition, in R.G. Lee (ed.) *The Values of Connection: A Relational Approach to Ethics*, Cambridge, MA: Gestalt Press.

Wheeler, G. (2004b) The fragility of goodness: How the Jews of Bulgaria survived the Holocaust – A Gestalt field perspective, in R.G. Lee (ed.) *The Values of Connection: A Relational Approach to Ethics*, Cambridge, MA: Gestalt Press.

Wheeler, G. (2005) Culture, self and field, in T. Levine Bar-Yoseph (ed.) *The Bridge: Dialogues Across Cultures*, New Orleans, LA: Gestalt Institute Press.

Widiger, T.A. and Presnall, J.R. (2012) Pathological altruism and personality disorder, in B. Oakley, A. Knafo, G. Madhaven and D. Sloan Wilson (eds.) *Pathological Altruism*, New York: Oxford University Press.

Williamson, I.R. (2000) Internalized homophobia and health issues affecting lesbians and gay men, *Health Education Research*, 15 (1): 97–107.

Wolfort, R. (2000) Self in experience, Gestalt therapy, science and Buddhism, *British Gestalt Journal*, 9 (2): 77–86.

Wollants, G. (2012) *Gestalt Therapy: Therapy of the Situation*, London: Sage.

Woodbury, Z. (2019) Climate trauma: Toward a new taxonomy of trauma, *Ecopsychology*, 11 (1): 1–8.

Woodford, M.R., Han, Y., Craig, S., Lim, C. and Matney, M. (2015) Discrimination and mental health among sexual minority college students: The type and form of discrimination does matter, *Journal of Gay and Lesbian Mental Health*, 18 (2): 142–163.

Wright, S. (ed.) (in press) *The Change Process in Psychotherapy During Troubling Times*, Abingdon: Routledge.

Yontef, G. (2005) Gestalt therapy theory of change, in A.L. Woldt and S.M. Toman (eds.) *Gestalt Therapy: History, Theory, and Practice*, Thousand Oaks, CA: Sage.

Zweifel, T.D. and Raskin, A.L. (2008) *The Rabbi and the CEO: The Commandments for 21st Century Leaders*, New York: Select Books.

Index

This index covers the prologue, all chapters, epilogue and appendices. Page numbers in *italics* refer to figures.

Abjection 29, 84
Aboriginal Australians 28, 41, 182–3
Absence 81–3, 91–2, 149, 186
    see also Dissociated absence
Acceptance 104, 119, *120*
Act of Killing, The (documentary) 37
Adams, Marie 98, 107, 109, 149
Alienation 10, 34, 86
Altruism 100–3
Altruism in the natural world 177
Anti-depressants 61, 63, 68-9
    see also Psychotropic medication
Arousal
    and autonomic nervous system 125
    intersubjective 95, 106, 149
    optimal 194
    stewardship of 9, 117
    see also Hyperarousal; Hypoarousal
Assessing for trauma 8, 66, 127–8, 151
Attachment 126
Auerhahn, Nanette 10, 79–80, 86, 92, 133
Autonomic nervous system 6, 9, 36, 95
    parasympathetic branch 143, 145, 193–4
    sympathetic branch 193–4
Autonomy (over-reach model) 119, *120*

Beginner's mind 72, 137
Bhopal disaster 51
Bias 70, 88–9, 120–1
    see also Difference
Binary oppositions 168–70
    see also Polarities (Gestalt theory)
Bipolar disorder 64
Boarding schools 52–4
Body, lived and unlived 60–1
Body and Earth (Olsen) 151, 154
Body psychotherapies 1, 151
Borderline personality disorder 65–6
Boundaries 12–13, 24, 180–1
Boundary disturbance 23–4, 81, 148, 156, 188–9

Brain 8, 36, 104, 192–3
Brainstem 192–3
Buber, Martin 103, 108, 163, 189

Cameron, D. Ewen 72
Caregiving 102–3
Certainty (over-reach model) 119, 120–1, *120*
Chidiac, Marie-Anne
    fluid responsiveness 24, 132
    mental health services 62, 63, 183
    power 25, 92, 108, 121, 122, 170–2
    presence 92, 140–1, 146, 172
    SOS model 22–3, 90, 131
Child sexual exploitation 35, 54–6
Class, social 28–9, *32*, 39
Classism 29
Clients (terminology) 7
Climate emergency 30, *32*, 156, 172, 174
Collective trauma 21, 36, 184–5, 186
Colonialism 27, *32*, 40–1, 140, 182–3
Communication 94, 124, 126, 140, 176–7
Communication, non-verbal 61, 94, 131, 141, 189
Compartmentalization *see* Splitting
Complexity theory 5, 168–9, 172
Connection 86, 111, 139, 144, 174–6, 178
Consciousness, shifts in 10, 12, 86, 133–4, 181
Contact
    corners of contact model 94–5, *95*
    and dialogue 189
    in Gestalt theory 2, 131, 188–9
    in Gestalt therapy 1, 2, 123–4, 131–2, 165
    over-reach model 119, *120*
    see also Relationality
Contact boundary 6, *24*, 81, 137, 186
Context 13, 21–2, 25, 40, *171*, 172–4
Continuing professional development (CPD)

retreats 17, 160
supervision 108, 119, 123, 124, 126, 165
workshops 148, 160, 163–4
see also Training
Coping strategies 6, 29, 62, 184
Coronavirus 184–7
Corruption 51, 72
Co-transference 17, 112–13, 140
see also Enduring relational themes
Counter-trauma 96, 149
COVID-19 pandemic 184–7
CPD *see* Continuing professional
development
Creative indifference 134, 138, 169
Critical psychiatry 67
Cultural and social conditioning 25, 31–2,
40–1, 61, 73, 102
Cultural trauma 26, 32, 40, 73
Curiosity 15, 104, 136–7, 181
Cycle of experience (Gestalt theory) 136,
188

Decolonization 147, 181–3
Deep ecology 181
Deep listening 180, 182
Dehumanization 36–7, 61, 92, 110
Denham-Vaughan, Sally
fluid responsiveness 24, 132
grace 147
liminal space 13
mental health services 62, 63, 183
power 25, 92, 108, 121, 122, 170–2
presence 92, 140–1, 146, 147, 172
SOS model 22–3, 90, 131
traumatized organizations 50–1
Denial 38–9
Depression 62, 64, 82
Descartes, René *see* Dualism
Developed/less developed countries 185
Diagnosis, psychiatric 64–6, 68
*Diagnostic and Statistical Manual of
Mental Disorders* (DSM) 33, 47, 65
Dialogue 139–40, 155, 189–90
Dialogue (Buber) 150, 163, 189-90
Difference 7, 28, 88–9, 134–6
Differentiation 133–4, 146, 168–9, 172, 189
Disconnection 21, 34, 60, 148–50, 178
see also Dissociation
Disconnection from the natural world 174,
187

see also Natural world
Dissociated absence *24*, 25, 78, 81, 86, 131
Dissociation
attunement to 85, 92
and counter-trauma 149
and mindfulness 142–3
as primary trauma organizer 114–15,
120
and psychiatry 68
Distance 10–11, 82, 126, 143, 186
Drama triangle 43, 114
DSM *see Diagnostic and Statistical
Manual of Mental Disorders*
Dualism
mind-body (Cartesian) 36, 60
self-world 155, 170
Duff, Vienna 17, 148, 157–9

Ecocide 30, *32*
Ecological approaches to therapy 4–6, 93,
167
Eco-psychology, Gestalt 151
Eco-therapy 4–5, 151, 159, 172
ECT *see* Electroconvulsive therapy
Edge states 102
Ego 91
Ego (over-reach model) *120*, 123-4
Electroconvulsive therapy (ECT) 67–8
Embodied social justice 182
Embodiment
cultural aspects 25, 31–2, 61, 89
importance for therapists 119, 124, 131,
135, 138, 149
lived and unlived body 60–1
mind-body (Cartesian) dualism 36, 60
and the natural world 152, 173–5
and phenomenology 189
and presence 141–2
and self 188
Emotionally unstable personality disorder
65–7
Empathy 71, 103, 136
Empowerment 134, 177
see also Power-over and power-with
Enduring relational themes 80, 97, 113,
149
Energy 79, 82–3, 96–7, 115, 124–5, 188–9
Environment *see* Natural world
Environmental psychology 151
Escher, M. C. 12, *13*, 82, *83*

Eshu (mythical character) 20
Ethical presence *22*, 24–5, 86, 92, 172, 178
Ethical turn in psychoanalysis 3–4
Ethics
    Levinasian 77–8, 89–90, 96, 110–11
    and organizations 50–1
    in psychiatry 72–3
    of self-care 107–8, 116, 141, 150
    situated 90, 108
Experiential field 21, 25
Extent (attention restoration theory) 154

Fascination 155
Fear 2, 4, 114–18, *120*
Field
    in Gestalt psychology 190–1
    in Gestalt theory 5
    in Gestalt therapy 5, 170–2, 178, 188–90
    holistic perception 148–50, 155, 167–9
    and SOS model 23–4, *173*
    see also Relational field; Shared
        mindful field; Unitary field
Field theory 5, 23–4, 150, 176, 189–90
Fields of mutual influence 94–6
Figure (Gestalt theory) 40, 82, 150–1, 190
    see also Ground (Gestalt theory)
Figure formation 82, 112, 189–90
Fitness to practice 108
Five stages of acceptance 104, 135–6, 180
Fluid responsiveness 24, 132, 136, 180
Fluidity 1–2, 154, 161–2, 176, 188
Forest bathing 175
Formulation 66, 189
Fractals 5, 42, 170
Fragmentation 12, 36, 148, 189, 191
    see also Splitting
Freud, Sigmund 70

Gender 34, 46, 61, 70
Germer, Christopher 104, 135, 180
Gestalt eco-psychology 151
Gestalt psychology 190
Gestalt theory 5, 131, 139, 168–9, 188–91
Gestalt therapists 2, 5, 146, 152, 170, 188–9
Gestalt therapy
    contact 1, 2, 123–4, 131–2, 165
    co-transference 17, 112–13, 140
    enduring relational themes 80, 97, 113,
        149
    field 5, 170–2, 178, 188–90

figure 40, 82, 150–1, 190
ground 40, 133, 150, 190
inclusion 103, 190
key concepts 188–91
origins 3–4
phenomenology 133–4, 169, 172, 188,
    189
shared mindful field 131–2, 133–4, 146,
    147
theories of change 3, 121, 191
unitary field 156, 158, 164, 170
Grooming 56
    see also Child sexual exploitation
Ground (Gestalt theory) 40, 133, 150, 190
    see also Figure (Gestalt theory)
Ground traumas 26, 32, 45, 63, 93, 185
Groundedness 138–9, 141, 146, 148, 152–3,
    159–63

Habitat loss 130
Habitual responses 2, 3, 181, 188, 192
Habitus 25, 171
Hebb's axiom 192
Helplessness 2, 87, 101, 115–16, *120*
Herman, Judith Lewis 11, 21, 23, 38, 40,
    148, 182
Holocaust 81, 91, 165–6 (note)
Homophobia 45–6, 47–8, 53
Hope 108, 126, 157
Human trafficking 28
Humility 84, 88, 134, 146
Hyperarousal *44*, 50, 56, *105*, 169, 194
Hypoarousal *44*, 51, *105*, 124, 143, 169,
    194

Identification 10, 86, 103, 109, *120*
Identification (over-reach model) 119,
    120, 123
I-It and I-Thou 61, 102, 132, 163, 189
Inclusion 103, 190
Indifference 37–8, 71, 103, 178
Indigenous peoples 27–8, 41, 177, 180,
    182–3
Individualism 5, 23, 25, 57, 102
Inequality 27–30
Infinity (Escher) *13*
Institutional abuse 52–4
Integration 5, 152–3, 165, 169, 189, 194
Interdependence 5, 23–4, 176–8
Intergenerational trauma xiv, 23, 40, 135

Interpersonal neurobiology 9, 140, 192–4
Intersectionality 42–3, 171, 190
Interspecies communication 177
Interspecies dependence 176–7
Intersubjective arousal 95, 106, 149
Intersubjective space 16, 85, 88, 127, 165,
        190
    see also Relational field

Kaplan, Rachel and Stephen 151, 153–6,
        175
Karpman drama triangle 43, 114
Knowing and not-knowing 10, 79–80, 84

Land
    and the author 153–5, 156–7, 180
    colonization 27, 182–3
    destruction 30
    disconnection from 174, 187
    human relationship with 4, 30–1, 151
    and therapists' continuing professional
        development 160–2
    see also Natural world; Place
Land art 151, 159
Laub, Dori 10, 79–80, 86, 92, 133
Legba (mythical character) 76
Levinas, Emmanuel 77–8, 96, 111, 122, 150
    see also Other
Levinasian ethics 77–8, 89–90, 96, 110–11
Lewin, Kurt 23–4, 25, 190
    see also Field theory
Limbic system 161, 192–3
Liminal space 12–13, 181
Limits of capacity (therapists') 10, 92,
        96–7, 108, 127–8, 146
Limits of relationality 34, 81, 126–7
Listening 69–71, 180, 182

Masochism 91, 96–7
Mawu (mythical character) 76
Medication 16, 61, 63–4, 67–9, 71
Meditation practices 142–4
Mental health models 62–3
Mental health services
    attitudes to 59
    discrimination in 47, 57
    and power 59, 69–70
    and psychotherapy 69, 71–2
    and retraumatization 59, 67–8
    and women 69–70

Milgram experiment 37, 86
Mindfulness 142–4
Mobius strip 14, *14*, 167, *167*
Mother-infant communication 140
Mutuality 94, 131, 176

Narcissism 35–6, 37, 72, 109
Narrative 83, 114, 145
Natural world
    and the author 153–5, 156–7, 180
    climate emergency 30, 32, 156, 172, 174
    deep ecology 181
    disconnection from 174, 187
    ecocide 30, *32*
    human connection with 150–2, 174–6
    interspecies communication 177
    interspecies dependence 176–7
    resource scarcity 29
    restorative properties 127, 148, 150,
        155, 165, 167
    trauma event 156–7
    water 29, 154–5, 158, 161–2, 176
    wood-wide web 177
    see also Land; Place
Nature writing 151
Nervous system *see* Autonomic nervous
        system
Neurobiology 9, 21, 62–3, 140, 143, 192–4
Neurochemicals 63, 126, 192–3, 194
Neuroplasticity 177, 192
Neuroscience 7–9, 62–3, 192–4
Non-defensiveness 106, 146
Non-relational caregiving 102
Non-verbal communication 61, 94, 131,
        141, 189
Numbing *see* Dissociation

Obedience to authority (Milgram)
        experiment 37, 86
Olsen, Andrea 151, 153, 154, 162, 176
Oppression 25, 34–6, 61, 171–2
    see also Power; Privilege
Orange, Donna 4, 10, 96, 107, 168
Organismic self-regulation 140, 155, 188
Organizations
    toxic workplaces 48–51
    traumatized 44, 50–1, 57, 149
    unethical practices 51
Other
    and absence 81–3

and altruism 102–3
distancing from 10, 36–7, 86, 87
ethical responsibility to 77, 85, 89–90,
    91, 127
in Gestalt theory 188–9
in Levinasian ethics 77–8, 89, 96, 110
and the shared mindful field 131
in SOS model *22*, 23, *24*, 113, 134, *167*
therapists' obligation to 85, 98, 108, 134
Otherness 78, 86, 155
Over-certainty 72, 88, 120–1, 138
Over-identification 96, 97, 102
Over-reach 118–20, *120*, 123–4
Overwhelm 6, 36–7, 108, 148, 185

Pain
    and altruism 103
    'clean' and 'dirty' 144
    Milgram experiment 37
    and relationality 127
    stuck and fluid 144–5
Paiute people 180
Pandemics 184–6
Parasympathetic responses 143, 145,
    193–4
Parlett, Malcolm 10, 86, 92, 133, 156, 170
Pearlman, Laurie 10, 80–1, 93, 96, 110, 149
Perlman, Stuart 95, 108
Personality disorders 64, 65–7, 68, 69–70
Phenomenology (Gestalt therapy) 133–4,
    169, 172, 188, 189
Pilgrim, David 35, 54, 57
Place xiv, 4, 7, 156, 160
    see also Land; Natural world
Polarities (Gestalt theory) 119, 168–71,
    190–1
Polarization 36, 38, 191
Polyvagal theory 34, 193–4
    see also Vagus nerve
Post-traumatic stress disorder 6, 33, 71,
    156
Poverty 29–30
Power
    abuses of 51, 52–3, 54, 72–3
    gendered aspects 34, 69, 72
    ideological 67
    and mental health services 59, 69–71
    as organizing property 170–2, *171*, *173*
    as situational factor in trauma 34–5,
        72–3

in therapeutic relationships 107, 110,
    121–3
and therapists 71–2, 107, 121–3, 171
Power-over and power-with 121–3, 134,
    171, *173*, 174, 177
Power Threat Meaning Framework 66–7
Presence
    and embodiment 141–2
    ethical *22*, 24–5, 86, 92, 172, 178
    and mindfulness 143
    as reciprocal process 139–40
    and SOS model 24
    therapeutic 106, 131, 141
    and therapists 91–2, 106, 131–2, 139
Primary organizers of trauma 114–18,
    119–20, *120*
    see also Dissociation; Fear;
        Helplessness; Shame
Privilege 35–6, 39, 42–3, 49, 54, 71–2
Process (Gestalt theory) 60–1, 66, 188
Project Implicit (Harvard University) 89
Psychiatric diagnosis 63–6, 71
Psychiatric formulation 66, 189
Psychiatry 59, 62, 67, 68, 69–71, 72–3
Psychotropic medication 16, 67, 68–9
PTMF *see* Power Threat Meaning
    Framework
PTSD *see* Post-traumatic stress disorder
Punch and Judy shows 31–2

Racism 28, *32*, 38, 70
Reciprocity 94, 131, 155, 176, 177, 178
Reductionism 9, 86, 96, 168
Regulation 44, 113, 139–40, 156
    see also Organismic self-regulation
Relational dynamics 3, 10, 43–4, 140
Relational field 40, 93, 94–5, 97, 190–1
Relational ground 22, 82, 96, 104
Relational psychoanalysis 3, 5
Relational therapeutic field 94–5, 110, 149,
    165
    see also Relational field
Relational trauma 22, 37, 98, 148
Relational turn in psychoanalysis 3
Relationality
    and altruism 100–1
    dynamics 3, 10, 43–4, 140
    enduring relational themes 80, 97, 113,
        149
    limits 126–7

and SOS model 22–3
and therapists' self-care 104–6, 125–6, 127–8
Reparation 89
Repetitive trauma processes 190
    see also Retraumatization
Resilience 109–11, 144, 187
Resources
    coping strategies 6, 29, 49, 184
    scarcity 29, *32*
    somatic 107, 119, 127
    therapists' 104, 106–7, 122
Responsibility 85, 89–90, 96–7, 102, 110
Restorative environments 127, 148, 165
    see also Natural world
Retraumatization 8, 17, 67–8, 83
Retreats 17, 160
    see also Continuing professional development
Retroflection 47, 60, 115, 189
    see also Energy
Riddle scale of homophobia 46

Saakvitne, Karen 10, 80–1, 93, 96, 110, 149
Safety 22, 33–4, 119, *120*, 175, 182–3
Scarcity of resources 29, *32*
Schools, abuse in 52–4
Secondary trauma 96
Self
    and altruism 102–3
    in Gestalt theory 23, 188–9
    and shame 123
    in SOS model *22*, 23, *24*, 134, *167*
    of the therapist 15, 131, 149, 165
Self-care
    ethics of 104, 107–8, 134, 141, 150
    importance for therapists 104–6, 107–8, 141, 158
Self-compassion 104, 108, 135
Self-functions 11, 68, 110, 127, 188, 192–3
Self-harm 47, 61, 126
Self-preservation 123, 150
Self-regulation 44, 113, 139–40, 156
Self-regulation, organismic 140, 155, 188
Self-stigma 66
Sensorimotor trauma training 107
Service users 7, 66–7
Sexual orientation 45–6, 47–8
Sexual violence 7, 47, 54, 88
    see also Child sexual exploitation

Shame 33–4, 89, 114–18, *120*, 123–4, 127
Shared mindful field 131–2, 133–4, 146, 147
Siegel, Daniel 8, 139, 172
    see also Window of tolerance
Situated ethics 90, 108
Situated therapeutic relationship 77
Situation 22–3, *22*, *24*, *167*, 172, 190
    see also Context
Situational processes in trauma 16, 33–8, 51, 71, 151, 174
Situational structures in trauma 16, 26–30, 31–2, *32*, 70, 185
Situational vulnerability 171, *173*
Sky and Water (Escher) *83*
Slavery 27–8, *32*
Social and cultural conditioning 25, 31–2, 40–1, 61, 73, 102
Social class 28–9, *32*, 39
Social engagement system 34, 193, 194
Soft fascination 155
Somatic resources 107, 119, 127
Somatic states 9, 111, 144
SOS model 22–5, *22*, *24*, 63, 170–2, *173*, 188
Splitting 36, 38, 191
Stanford prison experiment 37, 50
Stockholm syndrome 56
Stress 30, 47, 188, 193–4
    see also Post-traumatic stress disorder
Structural trauma 26
    see also Systemic trauma
Stubborn Light of Things, The (podcast) 187
Suffering 62–3, 77–80, 89–90, 103
Suicide 67–8, 69, 126
Supervision 108, 119, 123, 124, 126, 150
Survival 8, 33, 110
Survival strategies 35, 65–6
Sympathetic responses (autonomic nervous system) 193–4
Symptom pools 73
Systemic trauma 26, 32, 42–3
Systems thinking 5, 176
    see also Trauma-organized systems

Theories of change 3, 121, 191
Therapeutic animals 175
Therapeutic presence 106, 131, 141
Therapeutic relationship

impact on therapists 148–50
inequality of 59
interdependence 176–8
and the natural world 177
and power 107, 110, 121–3
and shame 123
situated nature 77
Therapeutic space 186
Therapists
  limits of capacity 10, 92, 96–7, 108,
    127–8, 146
  motivations 96, 97–8, 100 *see also*
    Altruism
  obligation to the Other 85, 98, 108, 134
  personal trauma xiv, 15, 97–8, 108–10
  and power 71–2, 107, 121–3, 171
  and presence 91–2, 106, 131–2, 139
  and privilege 49, 72
  resources 104, 106–7, 122
  self-care 104–6, 107–8, 141, 158
  training 10, 107, 109, 127 *see also*
    Continuing professional
    development
  vulnerability 72, 95, 98, 107, 109
  wellbeing 96–7, 141, 158
  working conditions 110
  wounded healers 108–10
  see also Gestalt therapists
Therapy
  body psychotherapies 1, 151
  clients (terminology) 7
  ecological approaches 4–6, 93, *167*
  eco-therapy 4–5, 151, 159, 172
  electroconvulsive 67–8
  medication 64, 67–9, 71
  psychiatry 59, 62, 67, 68, 69–71
  relational therapeutic field 94–5, 110,
    149, 165
  see also Gestalt therapy; Mental health
    services; Therapeutic relationship
Thresholds 12, 154
  see also Boundaries
Toxic workplaces 48–51
Training 10, 107, 109, 127
  see also Continuing professional
    development
Transference 17, 112–13, 140
  see also Enduring relational themes
Trans-species psychology 156
Trauma
  assessing for 8, 66, 127–8, 151

collective 21, 36, 184–5, 186
counter-trauma 96, 149
cultural 26, 32, 40, 73
definitions 6–7
gendered aspects 61, 70
ground traumas 26, 32, 45, 63, 93, 185
intergenerational xiv, 23, 40, 135
misdiagnosis 71
in the natural world 156–7
neurobiological approaches 6, 9, 62–3,
    140, 192–4
primary organizers 114–18, 119–20, *120*
    see also Dissociation; Fear;
    Helplessness; Shame
relational 22, 37, 98, 148
repetitive processes 190
retraumatization 8, 17, 67–8, 83
secondary 96
situational processes 16, 33–8, 51, 71,
    151, 174
situational structures 16, 26–30, 31–2,
    32, 70, 185
structural 26
systemic 26, 32, 42–3
in therapists xiv, 15, 97–8, 108–10
Trickster metaphor 11
vicarious 104–5
Trauma-organized systems 43–4, 48–9, 57,
    169
Traumatized organizations 44, 50–1, 57,
    149
Trickster
  in psychological processes 12–14
  stories 14, 20, 76, 130
  as trauma metaphor 11

Uncertainty 120–1, 137–9, 185
Unitary field 156, 158, 164, 170
Unknowable 81–2, 137–8

Vagal states 145, 193–4
  see also Autonomic nervous system
Vagus nerve 9, 140, 193
  see also Polyvagal theory
Vicarious trauma 104–5
Victimhood 22, 43–4, 88
Victimization 43–4, 47
Victims (terminology) 7
Vulnerability 72, 95, 98, 107, 109,
    171, *173*

War xiv, 23, *32*, 99, 144–6
Water 29, 154–5, 158, 161–2, 176
Wellbeing
   and altruism 100
   and the natural world 155, 167, 175–6
   in therapists 96–7, 141, 158
   see also Self-care
White fragility 28
White privilege 35, 183
Wilderness experience 180
Window of tolerance *44*, 105, *105*, 119,
     120, 169, 194
Women
   diagnostic bias against 65

gender norms 61
and mental health services
   69–70
psychiatric attitudes to 69–70
sexual exploitation 57
Wood-wide web 177
Workplaces, toxic 48–51
Workshops 148, 160, 163–4
   see also Continuing professional
     development
Wounded healer 108–10

Zimbardo experiment (Stanford prison
   experiment) 37, 50